D1635985

THEY SHALL NOT HURT OR DESTROY

Animal Rights and Vegetarianism in the Western Religious Traditions

Vasu Murti

Copyright 2003

Vegetarian Advocates Press, Cleveland, Ohio
0-9716676-1-6

THEY SHALL NOT HURT OR DESTROY. Copyright © 2003 by Vasu Murti. All rights reserved. Printed in the United States of America. No part of this book may be used or reproduced in any manner whatsoever without written permission except in the case of brief quotations embodied in critical articles and reviews. For information, address Vegetarian Advocates Press, P.O. Box 201791, Cleveland, Ohio 44120.

ISBN 0-9716676-1-6

CRITICS PRAISE
THEY SHALL NOT HURT OR DESTROY

"You have a generally deep understanding of Judaism, and the books we hold dear [inspired]."

— Rabbi Jacob Feuerwerker
Marion, Ohio

"For a non-Jew and a non-Christian, you have a remarkable grasp of Biblical interpretation."

— Reverend Frank Hoffman
Athens, New York

"...I want to commend you for the extensive research you have undertaken—especially in your sections on Judaism and Christianity. I do not believe I have read as detailed a study of the rabbinic and Talmudic tradition of concern for animals anywhere... your analysis of the primary sources—especially of the Bible—leaves the reader in no doubt that you have thoroughly absorbed the text and are not just citing material secondhand."

— Martin Rowe
Former Editor, Satya

"The erudition you display is stunning—both in range and depth—and *They Shall Not Hurt or Destroy* will serve me as a treasured sourcebook for years to come.

About three years ago, I came to the conclusion that the animal rights movement will never succeed until we 'convert' the churches and synagogues to our cause...*They Shall Not Hurt or Destroy* is an invaluable contribution to the necessary work of awakening mainstream religion to the spiritual imperative of compassion for all living beings. Every Christian and every animal advocate could benefit from reading it. It is a remarkably clear and comprehensive guide to the animal protection message of the Western spiritual traditions...This is a book that deserves a wide audience."

— Norm Phelps
Spiritual Outreach Director
The Fund for Animals

"This book is the most extensive collection of Vasu Murti's reverence for life philosophy. It is incredibly rich in information about thinkers, ancient and modern, who affirmed a concern for all living things.

Murti's knowledge of writers who affirmed reverence for all living things is amazingly wide. This book includes people from many traditions—Greeks, Romans, Jews, Christians...Mormons, Bahai's, etc."

— *Rose Evans*
Harmony: Voices for a Just Future

"Mr. Murti has unearthed a veritable goldmine of ancient writings from saints, philosophers, preachers and reformers, reaching back to Pythagoras, who have vigorously and in no uncertain terms, roundly condemned not just cruelty to, but the killing of animals for meat, fur, leather or sport...

Mr. Murti has presented this valuable work in a clearly written and organized manner. It is important, and I recommend it to all vegetarians interested in the deep and widespread roots of their movement."

— *James N. Dawson*
Live and Let Live

"In his book, Vasu Murti performs a valuable service indeed: he has made available source materials from within the Christian tradition which are normally in the domain of the academic specialist. His research has been intense, and has extended over a long period. His work deserves recognition, and in promoting it, I hope that his book will move into a wider audience."

— *Brother Aelred*
(Robert Edmunds)
Armidale, Australia

"I am...a devoted Christian who believes that God wants us to have respect for His creation, and that this extends to animals and the environment. I recently read Vasu Murti's *They Shall not Hurt or Destroy* and highly recommend it to other religious vegetarians or anyone who is interested in the relationship between theology and compassionate living."

— *Rachael Price*
SUNY Geneseo

Table of Contents

Preface

"As long as humanity continues to be the ruthless destroyer of other beings, we will never know health or peace. For as long as people massacre animals, they will kill each other. Indeed, he who sows the seed of murder and pain cannot reap joy and love."
— *Pythagoras*

"Compassion, in which all ethics must take root, can only attain its full breadth and depth if it embraces all living creatures and does not limit itself to humankind."
— *Dr. Albert Schweitzer*

I am honored to be writing the preface to Vasu Murti's *They Shall not Hurt or Destroy*, a remarkable work of faith and understanding. Biblical scholars as far back as Augustine and Aquinas have insisted that biblical truth must mirror rational thought. A lack of reconciliation between the two represents not a failure of rational thought or of the Bible, but of the adequacy of the interpretation. Murti's book offers us simultaneously a biblical and a rational view of animals and their rights that is at once cogent, honest, and true.

Using the Bible to advocate vegetarianism and an end to animal slavery is comparable to using the Bible to advocate human rights and the abolition of human slavery. One day, it will be generally recognized that as civil rights activist and feminist novelist Alice Walker stated in her introduction to Marjorie Spiegel's *The Dreaded Comparison* (a book that compares human slavery in the 18th and 19th centuries to animal slavery today): "The animals of the world...were not made for humans any more than black people were made for white, or women were created for men." Prejudice may be prejudice on the basis of many biases, including race, gender, nationality, or species. In each case, a line is drawn placing one group above a line, and everyone else below it. Bias on the basis of species is as unjustified as racism, sexism, or religious intolerance. In fact, Nobel Laureate Isaac Bashevis Singer called speciesism the "most extreme" form of racism.

In his book, Murti discusses biblical and religious reasons for including animals within our realm of moral concern and focuses specifically on vegetarianism. The focus on vegetarianism makes perfect sense since the vast majority of suffering in our world is caused by killing animals for food, and the degree of suffering is almost unimaginable.

Slaughterhouses are perhaps the most violent places on the planet. Animals are routinely sent kicking and screaming through the skinning and dismemberment process, every one bleeding and dying just as they would if they were human beings. Farms today treat animals like so many boxes in a warehouse, chopping off beaks and tails and genitals with no painkillers at all, inflicting third-degree burns (branding) and ripping out teeth and hunks of flesh. Animals transported to slaughter routinely die from the heat or the cold or freeze to the sides of the transport trucks or to the bottom in their own excrement. Dairy cows and egg-laying hens endure the same living nightmare as their brethren who are raised for their flesh, except that their time on the "farm" is longer. They, too, are shipped to the slaughter-house and killed at a fraction of their natural life span.

Every time we sit down to eat, we make a decision about who we are in the world. Do we want to contribute to the level of violence, misery, and bloodshed in the world? Or do we want to be compassionate and merciful? There is much violence, from war-torn regions of Africa and Europe to our own inner cities. Most of this violence is difficult to understand, let alone influence. Vegetarianism is one area where each and every one of us can make a difference—every time we sit down to eat—we can always "pray ceaselessly" (Luke 21:36; I Thessalonians 5:17). I find it empowering that I can promote peace and compassion every time I eat merely by refraining from violence against animals.

Interestingly, the 13th Amendment to the U.S. Constitution (abolition) was passed in 1865; the 19th Amendment (suffrage) was passed in 1920. Labor justice, including the 40 hour work week, is very new. The first child abuse case was tried in this country in 1913. Many good and thoughtful people of the 19th century did not believe that women, children, or Native and African-Americans deserved rights. Women and children were considered (with biblical justification) to be the property of their husbands and fathers. Slavery flourished from the 1520s until the end of the 1800s in this country. The Oxford theologian Reverend Andrew Linzey explains in *Animal Theology*, "[G]o back about two hundred or more years, we will find intelligent, respectable and conscientious Christians supporting *almost without question* the trade in slaves as inseparable from Christian civilization and human progress" (my emphasis, p. 141). I mention these past atrocities to suggest the ability of an entire society (and an overtly religious one, at that) to be engaged in extreme evil but not recognize it, as well as to point out how much society has changed historically.

The animal rights movement is optimistic. We believe with Jeremy Bentham, "The time will come when society will extend its mantle over every[one] [who] breathes." We agree with the Reverend Dr. Martin Luther King Jr. that the arc of history is long, but that it bends toward justice (the fact that King's wife and son, Coretta and Dexter Scott King are vegetarians is evidence). We believe that society will look back on human arrogance and cruelty toward other animals with the same horror and disbelief that we presently feel toward (human) slavery and other atrocities.

Vasu Murti's book is a powerful contribution to an increased understanding of animal rights within the religious community. When societal consciousness finally understands the immorality of speciesism, *They Shall not Hurt or Destroy* will be considered one of the true pieces of philosophical brilliance of the early 21st century, in a class with the abolitionist religious literature of the early 19th century.

Read it prayerfully, and share it with your religious friends.

Bruce G. Friedrich
People for the Ethical Treatment of Animals (PETA)
Norfolk, VA

Foreword

When I first began to read *They Shall Not Hurt or Destroy*, I kept thinking that Vasu Murti could not maintain the quality—or the quantity—of the materials that his research had produced. But he does. From the first chapter to the last, his overview of the ongoing effort to stop the barbarous and ungodly treatment of animals is an unparalleled compilation of the writings of philosophers, saints, theologians, and sacred texts.

In this book, Pythagoras and Plutarch have made common cause with St. Basil and St. Francis of Assisi. John Wesley and Martin Luther have also raised their voices in defense of animals, as have a variety of other religious leaders whose writings the author has researched.

The book also covers the pertinent biblical scholarship of both Jews and Christians, while separate chapters review the statements of Protestant, Islamic, Jewish and Christian spokespersons who, from medieval times to the present, have raised their voices in protest against the victimization of animals. And the author includes the observations of secular spokespersons; of writers, poets, and activists who have called for the compassionate and just treatment of all the creatures with whom we share the earth.

Although Vasu Murti's research is exhaustive, his book is reader-friendly. There is no hint of the ponderous prose that so often obscures, rather than elucidates, the content of a scholarly work. This is a book to be read, and reread. It is a definitive work and destined to become a classic reference for those who understand that the continuing, spiritual development of the human race necessitates the development of a moral and ethical code which recognizes that animals are sentient beings like ourselves; that they too, experience the fear and pain, the joy and happiness that life offers. And that they were given life by the same God who created them for their own sakes—not as commodities to satisfy the whims and the will of human beings.

Reverend J.R. Hyland, IMF
Author of God's Covenant with Animals: A Biblical Basis for the
      Humane Treatment of All Creatures *(Formerly titled:* The
      Slaughter of Terrified Beasts*)*

chapter one
"They Shall Not Hurt or Destroy"

The ethical basis for vegetarianism and animal rights is secular and nonsectarian. The religious basis for vegetarianism in the Western religions, however, has its origin both in the Bible and the Jewish tradition. To this day, the largest number of religious vegetarians outside India can be found in Israel. According to the Bible, God intended the entire human race to follow a vegetarian diet.

> "And God said: 'Behold! I have given you every plant-yielding seed
> which is upon the face of all the earth, and every tree, in which is the
> fruit of a tree-yielding seed; you shall have them for food.'"

> — *Genesis 1:29*

Paradise is vegetarian. Rashi (Rabbi Solomon von Isaac, 1030-1105), the famous Jewish Bible commentator, taught that "God did not permit Adam and his wife to kill a creature and to eat its flesh. Only every green herb shall they all eat together." Ibn Ezra and other Jewish biblical commentators agree.

According to the Talmud (compilations of rabbinical dialogue and commentary on the Bible), "Adam and many generations that followed him were strict flesh-abstainers; flesh-foods were rejected as repulsive for human consumption." Moses Maimonides (1135-1204), Judaism's greatest and most influential theologian thus far, taught that meat was prohibited because living creatures possess a degree of spiritual superiority, resembling the souls of rational beings.

Although man was made in God's image and given dominion over all creation (Genesis 1:26-28), these verses do not justify humans killing animals and then devouring them, because God immediately proclaims He created the plants for human consumption. (Genesis 1:29) Dr. Michael Fox of the Humane Society has argued that the word "dominion" is derived from the original Hebrew word "*rahe*" which refers to compassionate stewardship, instead of power and control. Parents have dominion over their children; they do not have a license to kill, torment or abuse them. The Talmud (Shabbat 119; Sanhedrin 7) interprets "dominion" to mean animals may only be used for labor.

Man was made in God's image (Genesis 1:26) and told to be vegetarian (Genesis 1:29). "And God saw all that He had made and saw that it was very good." (Genesis 1:31) Complete and perfect harmony. Everything in the beginning was the way God wanted it. Vegetarianism was part of God's initial plan for the world.

"It appears that the first intention of the Maker was to have men live on a strictly vegetarian diet," writes Rabbi Simon Glazer, in his 1971 *Guide to Judaism*. "The very earliest periods of Jewish history are marked with humanitarian conduct towards the lower animal kingdom...It is clearly established that the ancient Hebrews knew, and perhaps were the first among men to know, that animals feel and suffer pain."

After humans ate of the forbidden fruit, the earth gradually became "corrupt...and full of violence." (Genesis 6:11) The peace of the garden was destroyed. (Genesis 3:17) Conflict began between humans and animals. (Genesis 3:15) The violence described above quite possibly included the drinking of blood and the tearing of limbs from animals, because both these practices are forbidden in the Bible.

The sacrifice of animals began. (Genesis 4:4) The skins of animals began to be used as clothing. (Genesis 3:21) Human beings began to murder one another. (Genesis 4:8,23) This violence increased to such a degree that God regretted having created humankind. (Genesis 6:13,16) So God decided to

1

destroy the human race; choosing Noah and his family to survive the great Flood.

After the Flood, God revised His commandment against flesh-eating. Human beings, since eating of the forbidden fruit, seemed incapable of obedience on this issue. One Jewish writer comments, "Only after man had proven unfit for the high moral standard set at the beginning, was meat made a part of the humans' diet." Others claim flesh-eating was permitted to prevent cannibalism. We read:

> "The fear of you and the dread of you shall be upon every beast of the earth...Into your hand they are delivered...Only you shall not eat the flesh with its life, that is, its blood."
>
> *— Genesis 9:2-4*

This commandment against consuming blood is repeatedly given throughout both the Old and New Testaments: Genesis 9:3; Leviticus 17:10-12, 19:26; Deuteronomy 12:16,23,25, 15:23; Acts 15:19-20,29. The Bible identifies blood with life itself: "...for the blood is the life..." (Deuteronomy 12:23). The blood of a slain animal, which symbolizes the essence of life, must be returned to the Giver of Life. This commandment against consuming blood was first given to Noah, who was not Jewish; it was intended for all mankind. (Acts 21:25)

Rabbi Samuel Dresner makes this observation: "The removal of blood...is one of the most powerful means of making us constantly aware of the concession and compromise which the whole act of eating meat, in reality, is...it teaches us reverence for life." According to Dresner: "...the eating of meat is itself a sort of compromise....Man ideally should not eat meat, for to eat meat a life must be taken, an animal must be put to death." Rabbi Milgrom regards the commandment against blood as a law that permits man to "indulge in his lust for meat and not be brutalized in the process."

It is important to note that before the Flood, when humans were vegetarian, lifespans were measured in terms of centuries. Adam, for example, lived to be 930 years old. Seth (Adam's son) lived to 912. Enoch (Seth's son) to at least 905. Kenan (Enoch's son) lived to 910, all the way up to Methusalah, who lived for 969 years. After the Flood, when flesh-eating was permitted, human lifespans were reduced to decades. Abraham, for example, lived to be only 175. Genesis 1:29-31 was a blessing; Genesis 9:2-4 a curse.

Thus, the Lord reluctantly allowed His creatures to become innocent victims of human tyranny and brutality. It would be erroneous, however, to assume God became indifferent to the plight of the animals, or that humans have no moral obligation towards them. The Lord is good to all and "His tender mercies are over all His creatures." (Psalm 145:9,16-17) God provides food for the beasts and birds. (Psalm 104:24-28, 147:9) God considered animals as well as humans when admonishing Jonah: "...and should I not have pity on Nineveh, that great city, wherein are more than sixscore thousand persons...and also much cattle?" (Jonah 4:11)

Rebecca was judged to be a good wife for Isaac because of the kindness she showed to animals. Abraham's servant Eleazar asked Rebecca for water. She not only gave him water, but also went to provide water for his camels as well. Rebecca's concern for the camels indicated she had a tender heart and felt compassion for all God's creatures. It convinced Eleazar that Rebecca would make a suitable wife for Isaac. (Genesis 24:11-20)

Jacob also showed concern for animals. After their reconciliation, his brother Esau said to him, "Let us take our journey and let us go, and I will go before thee." But Jacob was concerned about his flocks and his children. He replied: "...the children are tender... the flocks and the herds giving suck are in care to me; and if they overdrive them, one day, all the flocks will die...I will journey on gently, according to the pace of the cattle that are before me, and according to the pace of the children, until I come unto my Lord, unto Seir." (Genesis 33:12-14)

"A righteous man cares for his animals, but even the mercy of the wicked is cruel." (Proverbs 12:10) A Jewish legend says Moses was found righteous by God through his shepherding. While Moses was tending his sheep of Jethro in the Midian wilderness, a young kid ran away from the flock. Moses ran after it until he found the kid drinking by a pool of water. Moses approached the kid and said, "I did not know that you ran away because you were thirsty; now, you must be tired." So Moses placed the animal on his shoulders and carried him back to the flock. God said, "Because thou has shown mercy in leading the flock, thou will surely tend My flock, Israel."

Animals are to be rested on the Sabbath. (Exodus 20:8-10, 23:12; Deuteronomy 5:12-14) One is forbidden to kill a newborn ox, sheep or goat until it has had at least seven days of warmth and nourishment from its mother. (Leviticus 22:27) The Bible also forbids killing a calf or a lamb with an ox or an ewe on the same day. (Leviticus 22:28) It is a biblical commandment to help an animal in pain, even if it belongs to an enemy. (Exodus 23:5) If one sees an injured animal, it is his duty to help. (Deuteronomy 22:4) One is even promised a long life for not disturbing a mother-bird with her children. (Deuteronomy 22:6-7) Moses Maimonides commented that if the Torah teaches that even animals should not be caused grief, "how much more careful must we be that we should not cause grief to our fellow men."

In the Book of Numbers appears the well-known story of Balaam, the pagan soothsayer sent by the Moabites and Midianites to visit and place a curse upon the Israelites. God sends one of His angels to stop Balaam, and the ass upon which he is riding suddenly sees "an angel of the Lord standing in his way." The animal turns away from the path, and crushes Balaam's foot against a wall, finally lying down beneath his rider. Balaam, angry and confused, strikes his ass three times, and finally, "the Lord opened the mouth of the ass and said unto Balaam, 'What have I done unto thee? Am I not thine ass upon which thou hast ridden all thy life long unto this day? Was I ever wont to do this unto thee?' And he said, 'Nay.' Then the Lord opened the eyes of Balaam, and he saw the angel of the Lord standing in the way...and he bowed his head and fell on his face. And the angel of the Lord said unto him, 'Why hast thou struck thine ass three times?'...and Balaam said unto the angel of the Lord, 'I have sinned, for I knew not that thou stoodest in the way against me.'" (Numbers 22:23-35) Maimonides quotes this passage as a basis for the "rule laid down by our sages, that it is directly prohibited in the Torah to cause pain to an animal."

The sages noted animals were created before humans. Fish and birds were created by God on the fourth day (Genesis 1:20-25), while other animals were created on the fifth. The Israelites were commanded to leave fields untilled and unharvested for the poor and the animals every seventh year. (Exodus 23:11) Balaam compared Israel to "a wild bull full of towering might;" its people are like lions. (Numbers 23:22,24) According to the Bible, God provides for animals and their ensoulment. Psalm 104:21-30 praises God for providing animals with food and a life-giving spirit.

The apocryphal *Book of Judith* similarly praises God, saying, "Let every creature serve You, for You spoke and they were made. You sent forth Your spirit and they were created." Throughout the Bible, the Lord is called a Shepherd and Israel His flock. The Lord's protection of His people is compared to that of an eagle towards its young. (Deuteronomy 32:10-12) Isaiah favorably compares the ox and the ass to Israel. (Isaiah 1:2-3) God shields Jerusalem like a bird (Isaiah 31:5) and wild beasts honor the Lord for providing water in deserts and wastelands (Isaiah 43:20).

The prophet Joel says in times of crisis, "even the beasts of the field" cry out to God. (Joel 1:20) Animals, along with men, were even involved in repentance. (Jonah 3:7-8) In Proverbs, the ant is praised for its diligence (6:6-8), while ants, rock-badgers, locusts and lizards are said to be "wise beyond the wisest" (30:24-28).

> "For man is a creature of chance and the beasts are creatures of chance,
> and one mischance awaits them all: death comes to both alike. They all

draw the same breath.

"Men have no advantage over the beasts, for all is emptiness. All go to the same place: all came from the dust, and to dust all return."

— *Ecclesiastes 3:19*

"But now ask the animals to teach you, and the birds of the air to tell you. Or the reptiles on earth to instruct you, and the fish of the sea to inform you.

"Which of all these does not know that the hand of God has done this? In His hand is the soul of every living thing, and the breath of all mankind."

— *Job 12:7-10*

The Bible teaches that Divine Wisdom—the answer to life's most pressing questions—is known only by God. (Job 28:23-28) It is not known to man (Job 28:13) or the animals (Job 28:7,8,21). God speaks to Job and asks him:

"Who puts wisdom in the heart and gives the cock its understanding? Who provides nourishment for the ravens when their young cry out to God and they roam about without food? Do you know about the birth of the mountain goats, watch for the birth pangs of hinds...they deliver their progeny in the desert. Who has given the wild ass his freedom and who has loosed him from bonds? I have made the wilderness his home, and the salt flats his dwelling. Will the wild ox consent to serve you and to pass the nights by your manger? Do you make the steed to quiver while his thunderous snorting spreads terror? Is it by your discernment that the hawk soars, that he spreads his wings toward the south? Does the eagle fly up at your command, to build his nest aloft?"

— *Job 38:36,41; 39:1,3,5-6,19,20,26-27*

According to the Torah (Genesis 6:9), Noah is honored as a "*tzaddik*," or a righteous man. Commentators say this is because he provided charity ("*tzedakah*") for so many animals on the ark. The high level of awareness and concern given to the care and feeding of the animals aboard the ark reflects the traditional Jewish value of not causing harm to animals, or *tsa'ar ba'alei chayim*. This moral principle—officially set down as law in the Bible and elaborated upon in the Talmud (Shabbat 128b), the medieval commentaries and the Responsa literature—permeates the many legends that grew up around the leading figures in the Torah and in Jewish history.

Kindness to animals has always been valued by the Jewish tradition; it has also been considered an important measure of a person's piety, compassion and righteousness. From this value emerged the stories about how shepherds such as Moses and David were elevated to national leadership because of their compassion for their lambs. There are also many "*maysehs*," or moralistic folktales in Judaism about sages who rescued or fed stray cows and hungry chickens, watered thirsty horses and freed caged birds.

The Talmud (Baba Mezia 85a) contains the story of Rabbi Judah. A calf was being taken to be slaughtered. It broke loose, and hid its head under the rabbi's skirt. It cried out in terror. The rabbi said, "Go, for you were created for this purpose." In heaven, the response was, "This man has no pity, let suffering come upon him." The rabbi then began to suffer from disease for the next thirteen years. One day his maidservant was going to sweep away some young weasels. The rabbi said to let them be, quoting Psalm 145:9, "and His tender care rests upon all His creatures." The rabbi's health was then restored.

In the Talmud (Eruvin 100b), Rabbi Yochanon teaches, "Even if we had not been given the Torah, we still would have learned modesty from the cat, honesty from the ant, chastity from the dove, and good manners from the rooster. Thus, the animals should be honored."

According to the Talmud (Shabbat 77b), the entire creation is to be respected: "Thou thinkest that flies, fleas, mosquitos are superfluous, but they have their purpose in creation as a means of a final outcome...Of all that the Holy One, Blessed be He, created in His world, he did not create a single thing without purpose."

The Talmud (Avodah Zorah 18b) also forbids association with hunters. Rabbi Ezekiel Landau (1713-93) was once asked by a man if he could hunt on his large estate. The rabbi replied:

"In the Torah the sport of hunting is imputed only to fierce characters like Nimrod and Esau, never to any of the patriarchs and their descendants...I cannot comprehend how a Jew could even dream of killing animals merely for the pleasure of hunting...When the act of killing is prompted by that of sport, it is downright cruelty."

The Talmud (Gittin 62a) further teaches that one should not own a domestic or wild animal or even a bird if he cannot properly care for it. Although there is no general rule forbidding animal cruelty, so many commandments call for humane treatment, the Talmudic rabbis explicitly declared compassion for animals to be biblical law (Shabbat 128b).

According to the Talmud (Shabbat 151b), "He who has mercy on his fellow creatures obtains mercy for himself." The first century Jewish historian Josephus described *mercy* as the underlying principle of all Jewish laws. These laws, he says, do not ignore the animals: "Ill treatment of a brute beast is with us a capital crime."

The *Tanchuma*, homilies from the 5th century AD, teach:

"If men embark on a sea voyage and take cattle with them, and should a storm arise, they throw the cattle overboard, because people do not love animals as they love human beings.

"Not so is the Lord's love. Just as He is merciful to man, so is He merciful to beasts. You can see this from the story of the Flood. When men sinned, the Lord decided to destroy the Earth. He treated both man and beast alike. But when He was reconciled, He was reconciled to both man and beast alike."

During the Middle Ages Yehudah Ha-Chassid taught, "The greatest sin is ingratitude. It must not be shown even to the brute. That man deserves punishment who overloads his beast, or beats or torments it, who drags a cat by the ears, or uses spurs to his horse..."

The medieval work *Sefer Chasidim*, or *The Book of the Pious*, says, "Be kind and compassionate to all creatures that the Holy One, Blessed be He, created in this world. Never beat nor inflict pain on any animal, beast, bird or insect. Do not throw stones at a dog or a cat, nor should ye kill flies or wasps."

According to *Shulhan Aruch*, the Orthodox Code of Jewish Law, no special blessings are given for meat dishes. "It is not fitting to bless God over something which He created and which man has slain." It is also forbidden to celebrate the acquisition of a leather garment. Similarly, it is a custom never to wear leather shoes on Yom Kippur. "One does not ask for forgiveness of sins while wearing articles made from the skins of slaughtered animals." *Shulhan Aruch* teaches: "It is forbidden, according to the Torah, to hurt any living creature. It is, on the contrary, one's duty to save any living creature, be he ownerless, or if he belongs to a non-Jew."

Rabbi Samson Raphael Hirsch taught, "The boy, who in crude joy, finds delight in the convulsions of an injured beetle or the anxiety of a suffering animal will also be dumb towards human pain." British historian William Lecky noted, "Tenderness towards animals is one of the most beautiful features of the Old Testament."

There is considerable evidence within the Bible suggesting God's plan is to restore His Kingdom on earth and return mankind to vegetarianism. Rabbi Abraham Isaac Kook, the Chief Rabbi of prestate Israel, wrote: "It is inconceivable that the Creator who had planned a world of harmony and a perfect way for man to live should, many thousands of years later, find that this plan was wrong."

Rabbi Kook believed the concession to eat meat (Genesis 9:3) was never intended to be a permanent condition. In his essay, "A Vision of Peace and Vegetarianism," he asked: "...how can it be that such a noble and enlightened moral position (Genesis 1:29) should pass away after it once has been brought into existence?"

The Hebrew words "*nephesh chayah*," or "living soul" are used in reference to animals as well as humans in Genesis 1:21,24, 2:7 and four hundred other places in the Bible. The books of the bible emphasize vegetarian foods. Flesh-foods, however, are mentioned with distaste and associated with bloodshed, lust, slaughter and sacrifice.

Right after Adam and Eve eat of the forbidden fruit, God tells them: "Cursed be the ground because of you. In toil shall ye eat its yield, all the days of your life. Thorns and thistles shall it bring forth to you, as you eat of the plants of the field. By the sweat of your face shall you get bread to eat." (Genesis 3:17-19)

The Bible contrasts the divinely favored Jacob, a man of peace, with his brother Esau, a hunter. (Genesis 25:21-34; Malachi 1:2-3) In Genesis 27:28, the patriarch Isaac blesses his son Jacob, that God may give him the dews of the heavens, the fertility of the earth and an abundance of grain. Jacob prays for bread. (Genesis 28:20-21)

> "Do not mix with winebibbers or with gluttonous eaters of meat."
>
> — *Proverbs 23:20*

In his essay, "The Dietary Prohibitions of the Hebrews," Jean Soler finds in the Bible at least two times when an attempt was made to try the Israelites out on a vegetarian diet. During the period of exodus from Egypt, the Hebrews lived entirely on manna. They had large flocks which they brought with them, but never touched.

The Israelites were told that manna "is the bread which the Lord has given you to eat." (Exodus 16:5) For forty years in the desert, the Israelites lived on manna (Nehemiah 9:15,21). The apocryphal *Wisdom of Solomon* (16:20) calls manna the food of the angels. Manna is described as a vegetable food, like "coriander seed" (Numbers 11:7), tasting like wafers and honey (Exodus 16:31).

On two separate occasions, however, the men rebelled against Moses because they wanted meat. The meat-hungry Hebrews lamented, "Would that we had died by the hand of the Lord in the land of Egypt, when we sat by the flesh pots." God ended this first "experiment in vegetarianism" through the miracle of the quails.

A second "experiment in vegetarianism" is suggested in the Book of Numbers, when the Hebrews lament once again, "O that we had meat to eat." (Numbers 11:4) God repeated the miracle of the quails, but this time with a vengeance: "And while the flesh was between their teeth, before it was even chewed, the wrath of the Lord was kindled against the people, and He struck them down with a great plague." (Numbers 11:33)

The site where the deaths took place was named "The Graves of Lust." (Numbers 11:34;

Deuteronomy 12:20) The quail meat was called "*basar ta'avah*," or "meat of lust." The Talmud (Chulin 84a) comments that: "The Torah teaches a lesson in moral conduct, that man shall not eat meat unless he has a special craving for it, and shall eat it only occasionally and sparingly." Here, according to Soler, as in the story of the Flood, "meat is given a negative connotation. It is a concession God makes to man's imperfection."

Rabbi Kook taught that because humans had an insatiable desire to kill animals and eat their flesh, they could not yet be returned to a moral standard which called for vegetarianism. Kook regarded Deuteronomy 12:15,20 ("Thou mayest slaughter and eat... after all the desire of thy soul,") as poetically misleading. He translated this Torah verse as: "because you lust after eating meat...then you may slaughter and eat."

In his book *Judaism and Vegetarianism*, Dr. Richard H. Schwartz notes that God's blessings to man throughout the Bible are almost entirely vegetarian: products of the soil, seeds, sun and rain.

> "For the Lord thy God bringeth thee into a good land, a land of brooks of water, of fountains and depths that spring out of valleys and hills; a land of wheat and barley, and vines, and fig trees, and pomegranates; a land of olive oil and honey; a land wherein thou shalt eat bread without scarceness, and thou shalt not lack anything in it."
>
> — *Deuteronomy 8:7-9*

In the Bible, Israel is repeatedly called a "land flowing with milk and honey." (Exodus 3:8,17; Leviticus 20:24; Numbers 13:27, 14:8; Deuteronomy 11:9, 26:9,15, 27:3, 31:20; Baruch 1:20; Ezekiel 20:15) God Himself describes Israel as a "garden land," saying He brought His people there to "eat its goodly fruits." (Jeremiah 2:7)

> "The lambs will provide your clothing, and the goats the price of a field. You shall have enough goat's milk for the food of your household, and the nourishment of your maidservants...
>
> "He who tills his land will have plenty of bread, but he who follows frivolity will have poverty enough!"
>
> — *Proverbs 27:26-27, 28:19*

God sent ravens to feed the prophet Elijah. Elijah lived on bread and water; by the grace of God, he provided a widow with flour and oil. (I Kings 17:4-16) When fleeing for his life in the desert, Elijah fell asleep under a tree. An angel later awoke him and gave him a hearth cake and a jug of water. (I Kings 19:3-8) Elijah never died, but was lifted up into heaven. (II Kings 2:11) Elisha raised a child from the dead (II Kings 4:32-37) and multiplied twenty barley loaves to feed one hundred men (II Kings 4:42-44).

God is loving and forgiving: "Come now, let us see things right, says the Lord. Though your sins be as scarlet they may become white as snow; though they be crimson red, they may become white as wool. If you are willing and obey, you shall eat the good things of the land. But if you refuse and resist, the sword shall consume you; for the mouth of the Lord has spoken!" (Isaiah 1:18-20)

God can provide for man's needs: "The Lord will give you the bread you need and the water for which you thirst. He will give you rain for the seed that you sow in the ground and the wheat that the soil produces will be rich and abundant." (Isaiah 30:20,23) The Lord's threat to a disobedient Israel? "No grapes on their vines, no figs on their fig tree." (Jeremiah 8:13) God commanded Ezekiel to live on bread made of wheat, barley, beans, lentils, millet and spelt. (Ezekiel 4:9) God spoke to Jerusalem as His beloved (Ezekiel 16:1-14), saying, "Thus you were adorned with gold and silver; your garments were of fine linen, silk and embroidered cloth. Fine flour, honey and oil were your food."

> "He causes the grass to spring up for the cattle, fruits and vegetables for
> man to cultivate, that he may derive sustenance from the land...and
> bread to improve a man's health."
>
> — *Psalm 104:14-15*

The prophet Joel describes God's blessings as green pastures, grain, oil and fruit-bearing trees. God's "immense good gifts" are described by Ezra as vineyards, olive groves and fruit trees. (Nehemiah 9:25)

The Song of Songs poetically depicts the mutual love between God and Israel as a relationship between the lover and the beloved. The prophets Isaiah (5:1-7, 54:4-8), Jeremiah (2:2,32) and Ezekiel (16:23) also characterized the covenant between God and Israel as a marriage. The divine bounty is mentioned in terms of figs, honey, spices, milk, saffron, cinnamon, fruits, apples and pomegranates.

Philip L. Pick, founder of the International Jewish Vegetarian Society, writes: "The practice of vegetarianism is implicit in the teachings of Judaism and is evident from the oft-repeated phrases in Genesis 'to man and all creatures wherein there is a living soul.' This indicates a common life and a shared destiny and the principle is exemplified throughout biblical writings. Nowhere is it stated that the abundance of flesh shall be the reward for observing the Law; rather, there are promises of fruits of the vine and pomegranates, wheat, barley and oil, and peace when each man shall sit under the shade of his own fig tree, not, let it be noted, under the shadow of his own slaughterhouse."

> "And they shall beat their swords into plowshares
> And their spears into pruning hooks
> Nation shall not lift up sword against nation
> Neither shall they learn war any more
>
> "But they shall sit every man under his vine
> And under his fig tree
> And none shall make them afraid
> For the Lord of hosts has spoken."
>
> — *Isaiah 2:4; Micah 4:3-4*

God's desire is to extend His spirit of divine peace to mankind and the animal kingdom. A reconciliation. To return the world to a vegetarian paradise, so all His creatures may again live together in perfect peace:

> "Then I will make a covenant on behalf of Israel *with the wild beasts, the
> birds of the air, and the things that creep on the earth,* and I will break the
> bow and sword and weapon of war and sweep them off the earth, so that
> *all living creatures* may lie down without fear."
>
> — *Hosea 2:18*

It is important to note that God plans to make His covenant *with the animals themselves.* This is not the first time God deals directly with animals—He made a similar covenant after the Flood:

"I now make My covenant with you and with your descendants after you, and with every living creature that is with you, all birds and cattle, all the wild animals with you on earth, all that have come out of the ark. I will make My covenant with you: never again shall living creatures be destroyed by the waters of the Flood..."

— *Genesis 9:9-11*

The future Kingdom of Peace is described clearly by Isaiah:

"The wolf shall dwell with the lamb
and the leopard shall lie down with the kid
and the calf and the lion and the fatling together
And a little child shall lead them.

"The cow and the bear shall feed
their young shall lie down together
and the lion shall eat straw like the ox.
The suckling child shall play over the hole of the asp
and the weaned child shall put his hand on the adder's den

"They shall not hurt or destroy
in all my holy mountain
For all the earth shall be in full knowledge of the Lord
as the waters cover the sea."

— *Isaiah 11:6-9*

According to the prophet Jeremiah:

"The day is coming, sayeth the Lord, when I will make a new covenant with the house of Israel and the house of Judah. It will not be like the covenant I made with their fathers the day I took them by the hand to lead them forth from the land of Egypt, for they broke My covenant and I had to show Myself their master.

"But this is the covenant which I will make with the house of Israel...I will place My Law within them and write it upon their hearts; I will be their God and they shall be My people."

— *Jeremiah 31:31-33*

The prophet Ezekiel speaks similarly:

"I will make a covenant of peace with them and rid the country of ravenous beasts, that they may dwell securely in the desert and sleep in the forests.

"I will place them about My hill, sending rain in due seasons, rain that shall be a blessing to them. The trees of the field shall bear their fruits, and the land its crops, and they shall dwell securely on their own soil...

"They shall no longer be despoiled by the nations or devoured by beasts
of the earth, but shall dwell secure with no one to frighten them. I will
prepare for them peaceful fields for planting...Thus, they shall know
that I, the Lord, am their God, and they are My people, the house of
Israel, says the Lord God."

— Ezekiel 34:25-30

The Bible thus begins and ends in a Kingdom where slaughter is unknown, and identifies the one annointed by God to bring about this Kingdom as "*Mashiach,*" or the Messiah. Humanity's very beginning in Paradise, and destiny in the age of the Messiah are vividly depicted as vegetarian. "In that future state," taught Rabbi Kook, "people's lives will no longer be supported at the expense of the animals." Isaiah (65:25) repeats his prophecy again. This is God's plan.

"The sacrifices of God are a broken spirit, a broken and contrite heart—
these, O God, You will not despise."

— Psalm 51:17

What, then, are we to make of the ancient practice of sacrificing animals? According to the Christian scholar Erdman, the life, teachings and death of Rabbi Y'shua (Jesus) are "the perfect sacrifice." He regards the entire Book of Leviticus as prophecy.

Y'shua taught that God desires "mercy, and not sacrifice," (Matthew 9:13, 12:7) and he opposed the buying and selling of animals for sacrifice (Matthew 21:12-14; Mark 11:15; John 2:14-15). Christian doctrine implicitly teaches that Y'shua came to do away with animal sacrifice. (Hebrews 10:5-10) Clement of Alexandria, an early Christian theologian, wrote: "...I believe that sacrifices were invented by men to be a pretext for eating flesh."

Rav Yoseph Albo (c. 1500 AD), the great Jewish mystic, taught that God acknowledged sheer human weakness, and therefore, decided to permit humans to eat meat. Albo cites the story of Cain and Abel, arguing that when Cain saw Abel kill an animal as a sacrifice—and receive a reward—Cain misunderstood, and assumed that killing was permissible. Albo states that Cain, "conveniently interpreted" the whole situation. Albo warns us not to do the likewise.

Some scholars believe the sacrifices were of Egyptian origin. The medieval Jewish philosopher Abarbanel cites a Midrash (a teaching based on Jewish values and tradition) that indicates that the Hebrews had become accustomed to animal sacrifices while in Egypt. To wean them from their idolatrous practices, God tolerated the sacrifices, but commanded that they be offered to Him in one central sanctuary. Abarbanel writes: "Thereupon the Holy One, blessed be He, said, 'Let them at all times offer their sacrifices before Me in the Tabernacle, and they will be weaned from idolatry, and thus be saved.'"

Moses Maimonides writes that by redefining the sacrifices, "idolatry was eradicated, and the vital principle of our faith, the existence and unity of God, was firmly established—without confusing the minds of the people by the abolition of sacrificial worship to which they were accustomed." Maimonides further teaches that animal sacrifice served as a substitute for child sacrifice, a practice which was widespread among ancient peoples.

The story of Abraham and Isaac implies animal sacrifice was replacing human sacrifice. The ram caught in the thicket suggested to Abraham that he could substitute an animal as an offering to God. God never commanded Abraham to sacrifice the ram. Abraham saw the ram caught in the thicket, and concluded that it could serve as a substitute for his son.

Rabbi Joseph Hertz writes that human sacrifice was a religious practice, "rife among the Semitic peoples, as well as their Egyptian and Aryan neighbors." Among these ancient peoples, the sacrifice of animals was a well-established mode of religious worship, much like the reciting of prayers or the singing of hymns is today.

According to Rabbi Hertz, the sacrificial cult was necessary to ancient religious practice, and unless the laws of Moses included this "universal expression of religious homage," Moses' mission "would assuredly have failed, and his work would have disappeared."

Animal sacrifice was an acceptable form of worship in biblical times. At no place in Leviticus, or any of the other books of the Bible, is the ritual of animal sacrifice formally explained. Like prayer and praise, animal sacrifice was regarded as a "universally current expression of religious homage." The rabbis say animal sacrifices were too prevalent in the ancient world to be abolished. Thus, they had to be reformed, replacing pagan values with those of Judaism.

Other scholars are of the opinion that animal sacrifices were never divinely ordained. In his 1961 book, *Moses and the Original Torah*, Abba Hillel Silver cites biblical texts such as Jeremiah 7:21-22 and Amos 5:25, and notes differences in the style and content of passages referring to animal sacrifice when compared with other parts of Torah, to prove his thesis that the original Mosaic Law contained no instructions concerning sacrifice. The sacrificial cult, Silver insists, was a pagan practice which became absorbed into Torah. Few rabbis, of course, would agree with Silver's analysis. They would voice the traditional view, that the Hebraic sacrificial system differed considerably from those in the pagan world.

In his book, *Moses: The Revelation and the Covenant*, Jewish theologian Martin Buber explains that most historians believe the tale about the Exodus and the Passover was a legend used to make an ancient pagan festival appear to have been ordained by Moses. "Moses reintroduces the holy and ancient shepherd's meal," Buber observes, "renewed in meaning and form." Ancient shepherds annually slaughtered the first-born of their flock.

During the night of the full moon, shepherds would smear the blood of the animal to keep demons from hurting their own first-born. The original meaning of the word "*pessah*" (Passover) has been lost. Buber asserts that Moses took already existing practices in the pagan world and merely centered them around God. "Moses did not change the custom of the ages into a cult," writes Buber, "he did not add any specific sacrificial rite to it, and did not make it dependent on any sanctuary; but he consecrated it to YHVH."

In his excellent *A Guide to the Misled*, Rabbi Shmuel Golding explains the orthodox Jewish position concerning animal sacrifices: "When G-d gave our ancestors permission to make sacrifices to Him, it was a concession, just as when he allowed us to have a king (I Samuel 8), but He gave us a whole set of rules and regulations concerning sacrifice that, when followed, would be superior to and distinct from the sacrificial system of the heathens."

The Hebraic sacrificial cult followed certain basic rules of conduct:

1. Human sacrifice was completely forbidden. Leviticus 20:2 declares, "Whosoever of the children of Israel...that giveth his seed (children) unto Moloch, he shall surely be put to death." And in Psalm 106, human sacrifice is described as one of the sins of past generations: the worship of the golden calf, the worship of Baal, and the offering of "the blood of sons and daughters...to the gods of Canaan."

2. Blood rituals were limited to only "clean" animals; grazing animals—the herbivores. The meat of carnivorous creatures is forbidden, since their predatory habits might become a part of man's

already too aggressive nature. This may be seen as a step towards vegetarianism.

3. No eating of fat or drinking of blood—blood symbolizes the essence of life, and must be returned to the Giver of Life.

4. Animal sacrifices were first supplemented by vegetarian offerings— first fruits and fine cakes of flour.

Thus, the Book of Leviticus radically transformed the pagan ritual of animal sacrifice, and used this ritual to confront man with the glaring contradiction between his desire for animal flesh and God's designation of life as something holy. Animal sacrifice was once an occasion for indulging in magical, sadistic and gluttonous impulses. It was subsequently redefined as a rite of atonement performed by Temple priests.

Animals were supposedly sacrificed primarily to celebrate the glory of God, and only secondarily to satisfy the cravings of the worshippers. Select portions of the carcass, and sometimes entire carcasses, were offered before God on a flaming altar. Blood, believed to contain the essence of life, was ceremonially separated from the flesh. The blood was returned to the Giver of Life. With wine, bread, and music, the corpse of the animal became part of a banquet of thanksgiving. In this reshaped and reformed sacrificial cult, the pagan values were replaced with those of Judaism: monotheism, holiness, cleanliness, thanksgiving, etc.

Significantly, one could not slaughter an animal whimsically, outside of religious sacrifice. To do so was to commit a very sinful act: "Bloodguilt shall be imputed to that man; he has shed blood, and shall be cut off from among his people." (Leviticus 17:3-4) Indeed, throughout the Bible, the spilling of innocent blood is condemned. The exact Hebrew in Exodus 20:13 ("Thou shalt not kill,") is "*lo tirtzach.*" One of the greatest modern Hebrew scholars, Dr. Reuben Alcalay, writes that "*tirtzach*" refers to any form of killing whatsoever.

A Midrash states: "In the Messianic era, all offerings will cease, except the thanksgiving offering, which will continue forever." God makes it known throughout the Bible that He values acts of love, justice and mercy more than bloody rituals:

"Doth the Lord desire holocausts and victims, and not rather that the voice of the Lord should be obeyed? For obedience is better than sacrifice: and to hearken rather than to offer the fat of rams."

— *I Kings 15:22*

"To what purpose is the multitude of your sacrifices unto Me? Saith the Lord: I am full of the burnt offerings of rams, and the fat of fed beasts, and *I delight not* in the blood of bullocks, or of lambs, or of he-goats.

"When ye spread forth your hands, I will hide Mine eyes from you; yea, when ye make many prayers, *I will not hear,* for your hands are full of blood."

— *Isaiah 1:11,15*

"Add whole-offerings to sacrifices and eat the flesh if you will. *But when I brought your forefathers out of Egypt, I gave them no commands about sacrifices. I said not a word about them.*

"The children of Judah have done evil in My sight...they have set abominations in the House which is called by My name, to pollute it."

— *Jeremiah 7:21-22,30*

"Loyalty is My desire, not sacrifice. Not burnt offerings, but the knowledge of God."

— *Hosea 6:6*

"As for sacrificial gifts, they sacrifice flesh and eat it. But in these the Lord has no delight."

— *Hosea 8:13*

"I *hate*, I spurn your pilgrim feasts, I do not delight in your sacred ceremonies. When you present your sacrifices and offerings, I will not accept them, nor look on the buffaloes of your shared offerings...

"But let justice roll down as waters and righteousness as a mighty stream. *O house of Israel, did you offer Me victims and sacrifices for forty years in the wilderness?*"

— *Amos 5:21-25*

"With what shall I come before the Lord and bow before Him? Shall I come to Him with burnt offerings, with baby calves? Will the Lord be pleased with thousands of rams or ten thousand rivers of oil?

"Shall I give Him my firstborn for my transgression? The fruit of my body for the sin of my soul? He has shown you, o man, what is good. And what does the Lord require you to do, but justice, love, kindness, and to walk humbly with thy God?"

— *Micah 6:6-8*

"God, the Lord God, has spoken and summoned the world from the rising to the setting sun...'Shall I not find fault with your sacrifices, though your burnt offerings are before Me always?

'I will not take a calf from your house, nor a he-goat from your folds. For all the animals of the forest are Mine, and the cattle in thousands on My hills.

'If I were hungry, I would not tell you, for the earth and its fullness are Mine. Shall I eat the flesh of bullocks or drink the blood of goats?

'Offer the sacrifice of praise to God, and pay your vows to the Most High.'"

— *Psalm 50:1-14*

"Sacrifice and offering Thou hast not desired...Let my prayer be prepared as an incense offering before Thee, the lifting of my hands as the evening sacrifice."

— Psalm 40:6, 141:2

"To practice righteousness and justice is more acceptable to the Lord than sacrifice."

— Proverbs 21:3

"Guard your steps when you go to the House of God: to draw near to listen is better than to offer the sacrifice of fools, for they do not know they are doing *evil*."

— Ecclesiastes 5:1

Rabbi Zalman Schachter makes no apologies for past injustices inflicted upon animals in the name of religion. Much of the Bible was spoken to primitive tribes, wandering through the desert. "Our forefathers were a pastoral people," he writes. "Raising animals for food was their way of life. Not only did they eat meat, they drank water and wine from leather flasks, they lived in tents and wore clothes made from skins and sewed together with bones and sinews. They read from a Torah written on parchment, used a ram's horn as a *shofar*, and said their morning prayers with leather *tefellin*." He adds, "Are we ashamed to recall that Abraham had two wives because in today's Western world he would be called a bigamist? Vegetarianism is a response to *today's* world...Meat-eating, like polygamy, fit into an earlier stage of human history."

The Bible calls for compassion towards animals and exalts vegetarianism as a moral and spiritual ideal. The healing powers of a vegetarian diet are not ignored. We have the example of Daniel, who lived as a vegetarian, and refused to eat the meat (or drink the wine) that King Nebuchadnezzar ordered his servant to give him while he was imprisoned in Babylon. We read in Daniel 1:8-15: "he would not defile himself with...the King's meat... but (lived on) beans, lentils and pulse." After ten days, Daniel and his companions looked healthier and stronger than those who ate the king's food.

But it is Isaiah, who consistently denounces the slaughter and bloodshed of humans and animals. He declares that God does not hear the prayers of animal-killers (1:15), repeating this again: "But your iniquities have separated you and your God. And your sins have hid His face from you, so that He does not hear. For your hands are stained with blood...their feet run to evil and they hasten to shed innocent blood...they know not the ways of peace."

Elsewhere, we read, *"You have not honored Me with your sacrifices...rather you have burdened Me with your sins, you have wearied Me with your iniquities."* (43:23-24) Isaiah laments that in a time of repentance he saw "joy and merrymaking, slaughtering of cattle and killing of sheep, eating of meat and drinking of wine, as you thought, 'let us eat and drink, for tomorrow we die.'" (22:13) Isaiah equates the killing of animals with murder: "He that killeth an ox is as if he slew a man. He that sacrificeth a lamb is as if he cut off a dog's neck..." (66:3) On two separate occasions (11:6-9, 65:25), he speaks of a future world, where "the lion shall eat straw like the ox," and the whole earth is returned to a vegetarian paradise.

With the destruction of the Temple at Jerusalem by the Romans in 70 AD, the sacrificial system of the Hebrews came to an end. Since the killing of animals outside of sacrifice was forbidden (Leviticus 17:3-4), many Jews gave up meat-eating altogether. Meat consumption virtually died out at the time. In the Talmud (Tracte Babba Bathra 60b), Rabbi Yishmael is quoted as saying, "From the day that the holy Temple was destroyed, it would have been right to have imposed upon ourselves the law prohibiting the eating of flesh."

A complicated set of dietary laws and ritual slaughter evolved to replace the sacrificial system as a means of atonement for killing God's innocent creatures. The process of slaughter is strictly regulated. The procedures are described in the Talmud. The slaughterers must be specially-trained, God-fearing, observant Jews. The knife used in killing the animals must be sharper than a razor, with no indentation.

The killing involves cutting the esophagus and the trachea, severing the jugular vein and carotid arteries. This is intended to cause virtually instantaneous unconsciousness. The only pain the animal is intended to experience is the cutting of its skin—a pain minimized by the sharpness of the knife. "Humane slaughter," an oxymoron, is the intention behind such ritual killing.

In "*Kashruth* and Civil Kosher Law Enforcement," Sol Friedman explains the meaning behind ritual slaughter: "In Judaism, the act of animal slaying is not viewed as a step in the business of meat-preparation. It is a deed charged with religious import. It is felt that the flame of animal life partakes of the sacred, and may be extinguished only by the sanction of religion, and only at the hands of one of its sensitive and reverential servants."

Rabbi Zalman Schachter writes: "When our grandmother brought a live chicken to the *schochet* (slaughterer), she witnessed a sacred and skillful act intended to minimize the distress that is felt by both the victim and the meat-eater when an animal is killed for food. By direct observation, she was thus qualified to transmit to her family the sentiment that, unlike everything else on the table, animal food comes to a Jewish table as a special dispensation and through the hands of a person dedicated to the service of God."

Rabbi Schachter further states: "The ranks of the vegetarians might be swelled considerably if one had to watch a creature being killed before one could eat of its flesh."

Dietary laws replaced the sacrificial system. Leviticus 17:10 states, "And whosoever...that eateth any manner of blood, I will even set My face against the soul that eateth blood." The Talmudic literature even declares that the soul or life-force can be found in the blood. This concept is also found in early Hinduism, in which it is taught that as the heart pumps the blood throughout the body, it also pumps the symptom of the life-force—consciousness. Therefore, the blood of living creatures is considered sacred. To free the meat from blood, it is salted and soaked in water several times. This process is defective, however, in that all the blood is never completely drained out.

"Thou shalt not boil a kid in his mother's milk." (Exodus 23:19; Deuteronomy 14:11) According to Rabbi Kook, this practice is forbidden because it reflects both the moral wrong of denying a calf the natural enjoyment of its mother's breast as well as the "hard and cruel" practice of eating animal flesh. The very same concern for the relationship between the mother and the offspring is expressed in Leviticus 22:28; a cow and its calves or an ewe and its lambs cannot be killed on the same day.

These concerns have led to dietary restrictions separating the consumption of meat and dairy products. Meat cannot be touched by any utensil or cooked in any pot used in the preparation of dairy foods. This also applies to serving vessels and utensils. No butter, milk, or cream can be on the table, and dairy products can only be eaten no less than three hours after a meal has been served.

Implicit in the separation of meat from dairy products in the Jewish dietary laws is the moral question of consuming the milk of animals while eating their flesh. In the Hindu traditions which also call for vegetarianism, the cow is especially revered as the mother of humanity, because she provides humans with her milk.

> "Thy righteousness is like the mountains of God; Thy judgements are a
> great deep; Lord, Thou dost preserve man and beast."
>
> — *Psalm 36:6*

Expressing concern for cruelty to animals, the Jewish dietary laws also forbid the consumption of animals that have been killed by hunters, even if they are "clean" or "kosher" animals. Similarly, Jewish law mandates that when catching fish, the fish be netted and not hooked, because hooks cause injury and pain to the fish. The word "hook" is mentioned in the Bible only as a symbol of cruelty or as an instrument of torture used by foreigners.

On the one hand, it would seem that Talmudic law *discourages* killing animals and eating their flesh, by surrounding the practice with all sorts of prohibitions and taboos. Conversely, one could also argue that the dietary laws *facilitate* flesh-eating by ritually undoing a moral wrong—the killing of a living creature—with acts of atonement to make eating the corpses of animals fitting for a holy people; a people worshipping a God who has mercy on everything that lives.

The inconsistency in Judaism's sanctioning the slaughter of animals while worshipping a God who has mercy on all His creatures is dealt with in Rabbi Jacob Cohen's *The Royal Table*, an outline of the Jewish dietary laws. His book begins: "In the perfect world originally designed by God, man was meant to be a vegetarian." The same page also quotes from *Sifre*: "Insomuch as all animals possess a certain degree of intelligence and consciousness, it is a waste of this divine gift, and an irreparable damage to destroy them."

In her 1975 book, *The Vegetable Passion*, writer Janet Barkas observes: "The first law in the Bible is a dietary one—do not eat the forbidden fruit. It is a '*hukim*,' or an unexplained edict with the purpose of inspiring man's obedience and building his character. There is no reason to avoid that infamous fruit except that it is the 'will of God.'

"Significantly, it is only *after* Eve defies God and eats the apple that killing animals for food is recorded in the Old Testament. Then, until the time of Noah, he who killed an animal was as guilty as he who killed a man. Abel killed an animal; Cain slew Abel; and the chain of retribution for both crimes is, allegorically, responsible for all the evils that follow.

"The rabbis explain that meat-eating is a punishment to a Jew, not a reward," concludes Barkas. "All the rules of kosher are attempts to make the punishment more palatable to the animals as well as man. It is as a consequence of original sin that man eats meat; it is not supposed to be a pleasure, and throughout history, Jews have rarely been hunters."

During the 1970s, Rabbi Everett Gendler and his wife studied Talmudic attitudes towards animals, and came to "the conclusion that vegetarianism was the logical next step after *kashrut*—the proper extension of the laws against cruelty to animals." After becoming a vegetarian, a rabbinical student in the Midwest said, "Now I feel I have achieved the ultimate state of *kashrut*."

In their book, *The Nine Questions People Ask about Judaism*, Dennis Prager and Rabbi Telushkin explain: "Keeping kosher is Judaism's compromise with its ideal vegetarianism. Ideally, according to Judaism, man would confine his eating to fruits and vegetables and not kill animals for food."

Along with the concession to eat meat, many laws and restrictions were given. Rabbi Kook taught that the reprimand implied by these regulations is an elaborate apparatus designed to keep alive a sense of reverence for life, with the aim of eventually leading people away from their meat-eating habit. This idea is echoed by Jewish Bible commentator Solomon Efraim Lunchitz, author of *K'lee Yakar*:

"What was the necessity for the entire procedure of ritual slaughter? For the sake of self-discipline. It is far more appropriate for man not to eat meat; only if he has a strong desire for meat does the Torah permit it, and even this only after the trouble and inconvenience necessary to satisfy his desire. Perhaps because of the bother and annoyance of the whole procedure, he will be restrained from such a strong and uncontrollable desire for meat."

A similar statement was made by a modern rabbi, Pinchas Peli:

> "Accordingly, the laws of *kashrut* come to teach us that a Jew's first
> preference should be a vegetarian meal. If however, one cannot control

a craving for meat, it should be kosher meat which would serve as a
reminder that the animal being eaten is a creature of God, that the
death of such a creature cannot be taken lightly, that hunting for sport is
forbidden, that we cannot treat any living thing callously, and that we
are responsible for what happens to other beings (human or animal)
even if we did not personally come into contact with them."

In the face of cultural assimilation, Rabbi Robert Gordis does not believe the dietary laws will be maintained by Jews today in their present form. He suggests that vegetarianism, a logical conclusion of Jewish teaching, would effectively protect the kosher tradition: "Vegetarianism offers an ideal mode for preserving the religious and ethical values which *kashrut* was designed to concretize in human life."

In his 1987 book, *Food for the Spirit: Vegetarianism and the World Religions*, writer Steven Rosen makes a well-reasoned case for Jewish vegetarianism, concluding:

"...even if one considers the process of koshering to be legitimate, it is an
obvious burden placed upon the Jewish people, perhaps in the hope that
they will give up flesh-foods altogether. If eating meat is such a detailed,
long, and drawn-out process, why not give it up entirely?"

Stanley Rubens of the Jewish Vegetarian Society says: "I believe man's downfall is paralleled by his cruelty to animals. In creating slaughterhouses for them, he has created slaughterhouses for himself...What is the future for mankind? When the Day of Judgement comes, we will be given that same justice that we gave the less fortunate fellow creatures who have been in our power." According to Rubens, "it is essential for an orthodox Jew to be vegetarian."

Rabbi Chaim Zundel Maccoby settled in London around 1890. He was a great and saintly preacher and a dedicated vegetarian, who wore shoes of cloth to indicate his revulsion towards leather. He brought happiness into the lives of London's East End Jews by teaching them compassion for all living creatures. A deeply religious man, he had an enormous following. The crowds were so large that traffic was held up whenever he preached in the streets.

Isaac Bashevis Singer, who won the Nobel Prize in Literature, became a vegetarian in 1962. He asked, "How can we pray to God for mercy if we ourselves have no mercy? How can we speak of rights and justice if we take an innocent creature and shed its blood?" Singer has compared humanity's mass slaughter of 45 billion animals every year to the Nazi Holocaust. In 1987 he wrote, "This is my protest against the conduct of the world. To be a vegetarian is to disagree—to disagree with the course of things today. Nuclear power, starvation, cruelty—we must make a statement against these things. Vegetarianism is my statement. And I think it's a strong one."

Singer has also expressed the view that unnecessary violence against animals by human beings will only lead to violence in human society: "I personally believe that as long as human beings will go on shedding the blood of animals, there will never be any peace. There is only one little step from killing animals to creating gas chambers a la Hitler and concentration camps a la Stalin—all such deeds are done in the name of 'social justice.' There will be no justice as long as man will stand with a knife or with a gun and destroy those who are weaker than he is."

Shlomo Goren, the former Chief Rabbi of Israel is vegetarian. Rabbi David Rosen, former Chief Rabbi of Ireland, and Shear Yashuv Cohen, the Chief Rabbi of Haifa, endorse the vegetarian way of life. One of the greatest modern Jewish thinkers, Martin Buber, advocated vegetarianism, as did Albert Einstein. Austrian writer and poet Franz Kafka (1883-1924) was vegetarian. The late Rabbi M.

Kossowsky, who was not a vegetarian, called vegetarianism, "The very pinnacle of ethical achievement."

The Pythagoreans, Neoplatonists, Hindus, Buddhists and Jains have all forbidden animal slaughter at various times in human history because of a belief in transmigration of souls and, consequently, the equality of all living beings. The doctrine of reincarnation is held by the Kabbalists, and was used to justify vegetarianism in *Sedeh Hermed,* a huge Talmudic encyclopedia authored by Rabbi Hayyim Hezekiah Medini (1837-1904).

In *Wheels of a Soul*, Rabbi Phillip S. Berg, a renowned contemporary Kabbalist, explains: "...the concept of reincarnation is by no means exclusive to Judaism. The idea was prevalent among Indians on the American continent; and in the Orient, the teaching of reincarnation is widespread and influential. It is the basis of most of the philosophical systems of India where hundreds of millions accept the truth of reincarnation the way we accept the truth of gravity—as a great natural and inevitable law that only a fool would question."

According to Rabbi Jacob Shimmel, "We are reborn until we reach perfection in following the Torah...In Hebrew, reincarnation is called *gilgul*, and there is a whole section of the *Kabbala* entitled *Sefer HaGilgulim*. This deals with details in regard to reincarnation."

One remarkable figure from this mystical school of Jewish thought is Rabbi Isaac Luria (1534-72). Born in Jerusalem, he became a brilliant student, noted for his intelligence, logic and reasoning abilities. By the age of 15, Luria had surpassed all the sages in Egypt in his understanding of Talmudic law.

With a thirst for higher knowledge, he studied the *Zohar* and the *Kabbala*. For seven years, he lived as an ascetic on the banks of the Nile River; fasting often, seeing his wife only on the Sabbath, and merely for brief conversation, if necessary. During this time, he experienced many strange voices and ecstatic visions. At times, the prophet Elijah appeared to teach him the secrets of the Torah. Luria later went to Safed (in Palestine) and became the spiritual master of the community of mystics there. He taught that the good souls in heaven could be brought down to inhabit human bodies.

Luria saw spirits everywhere. He heard them whispering in the rushing water of rivers, in the movement of trees, in the wind and in the songs of birds. He could see the soul of a man leave the body at the time of death. Intimate conversations were often held with the souls of past figures in the Bible, the Talmudic sages and numerous respected rabbis.

His disciples said he could perform exorcisms and miracles and speak the language of animals. They wrote: "Luria could read faces, look into the souls of men, recognize that souls migrated from body to body. He could tell you what commandments a man had fulfilled and what sins he had committed since youth."

Many of Rabbi Luria's contemporaries were convinced he was "*Mashiach*," the Messiah or the one anointed by God to establish His Kingdom on earth. It is said Luria's respect for life was so great that he would avoid stepping on insects, or treading on grass. Rabbi Y'shua also taught that only the meek and gentle would inherit God's Kingdom (Matthew 5:5), and this is consistent with Genesis 1:29-31, Psalm 37:11 and the prophecies of Isaiah 11:6-9, 62:25.

The late Rabbi Isaac ha-Levi Herzog once predicted that "Jews will move increasingly to vegetarianism out of their own deepening knowledge of what their tradition commands...Man's carnivorous nature is not taken for granted or praised in the fundamental teachings of Judaism...A whole galaxy of central rabbinic and spiritual leaders...has been affirming vegetarianism as the ultimate meaning of Jewish moral teaching."

> "...I am the Lord, who practices kindness, justice and righteousness in
> the earth...in these things I delight, sayeth the Lord."
>
> — *Jeremiah 9:23*

According to Rabbi Arthur Hertzberg: "'Whoever is merciful to all creatures is a descendant of our ancestor Abraham.' (Bezoh 32b) In the sacred writings of Judaism, Jews are described over and over again as 'merciful people, the children of merciful people' (Yebamot 79a, Shabbat 133b)."

Man is said to have been made in the image of God. (Genesis 1:26) Humans are to be holy, because God is holy. (Leviticus 19:2) Humans are commanded to walk in God's ways. (Deuteronomy 10:12) "After the Lord your God ye shall walk." (Deuteronomy 13:5) The Talmud (Sota 14a) asks, "How can man walk after God? Is He not a consuming fire? What is meant is that man ought to walk after (imitate) the attributes of God. Just as the Lord clothes the naked, so you shall clothe the naked. Just as He visits the sick, so you shall visit the sick. Just as the Lord comforted the bereaved, so you shall also comfort the bereaved; just as He buried the dead, so you shall bury the dead." Rabbi Y'shua also taught his disciples:

> "...for I was hungry and you gave me food; I was thirsty and you gave me
> drink...naked and you clothed me; in prison, and you visited me...insofar
> as you do it to the least of these brothers of mine, you did it to me."
>
> — *Matthew 25:35-36,40*

In Judaism, this spirit of compassion extends to animals. A New York monthly, *The Jewish Spectator*, stated in June 1969:

> "Cruelty to animals is forbidden by Jewish law...Cruelty to animals is
> known...as *tza'ar ba'aley hayim*—pain inflicted upon living creatures.
> This is a grave sin according to Jewish law."

Dr. Richard H. Schwartz reported in *The Jewish Spectator* in 1980 that legislation outlawing meat-eating had been unsuccessfully introduced in the Israeli Knesset (Parliament) by Mordecai Ben Porat. In secular, political language, Porat argued that Israel's fragile economy was impaired by rising health care costs—the increasing expenditures went primarily to combating diseases caused by eating animal flesh.

Dr. Schwartz makes a very rational case for Jewish vegetarianism on moral, economic, and physiological grounds, as well as religious grounds, in his own book, *Judaism and Vegetarianism.*

Unfortunately, Judaism does not yet condemn meat-eating as a sin, nor are animals unequivocally given the right to life. However, a strong case can be made that Judaism does revere vegetarianism as a moral ideal. It may be argued that whereas Christianity desperately needs more personalities like St. Basil, St. Filippo Neri, John Wesley, and Dr. Albert Schweitzer, to awaken believers' God-given compassion for animals, Judaism has never excluded animals from moral concern.

Many Jewish teachings on *tsa'ar ba'alei chayim,* or concern for animals, are consistent with the animal rights ethic. The Talmudic rabbis interpreted the permission to eat meat given in Genesis 9:3 as a concession to human lust and brutality. Man's earliest beginnings in Paradise, as well as his destiny in the coming Kingdom of Peace are vividly depicted in the Bible as vegetarian.

Commandments and teachings that clearly define compassion towards animals, including dietary laws to determine what kind of animals humans may eat and how to slaughter and prepare them, were deemed necessary to guide the human race through this dark period of time that will eventually give way to an era of peace among men, and peace among all creatures.

chapter two
"Mercy and Not Sacrifice"

It is said that Lord Jesus Christ was born not among kings or the wealthy, but in a manger, among the animals, while shepherds and their flocks heard the good news from an angelic choir. (Luke 2:1-20) "O great mystery and wonderous sacrament, that animals should see the Lord born and lying in a manger," is the Response to the Second Nocturne' before Midnight Mass on Christmas Eve in the Roman liturgy. The title "Lord" was used in biblical times, as it is now, to denote respected personalities. The patriarch Jacob addressed his brother Esau as "my Lord" after their reconciliation. (Genesis 33:12-14) The name "Jesus" is the Greek translation of "Y'shua," or "Joshua," which means "YHVH saves" in Hebrew. (YHVH, the most sacred name of God in Judaism, has often been mistranslated as "Yahweh" or "Jehovah.") Christ, or "*Christos*," is the Greek translation of the Hebrew title "*Mashiach*," or Messiah, which means "anointed one."

The title "Messiah" was used in ancient Israel to identify the ruling king. Saul, the first king, was called "Messiah." (I Samuel 26:9) The subsequent rulers form the house of David who ruled in Jerusalem were also called "Messiah." Proof of this can be found in some of the Psalms, which may have been used in conjunction with the coronation and enthronement of the Davidic kings. (Psalm 2:2, 89:51)

The kings were called "Messiah," because they had been anointed with oil. (I Samuel 10:1; I Kings 1:39) There was also the implication of a spiritual anointing with God's presence for special service. Messiah was a title, therefore, which could be used as a designation not just for kings, but for priests and prophets.

The prophet Isaiah considered Cyrus the Persian ruler a Messiah, because he had been chosen by God to liberate the Jewish captives. (Isaiah 45:1) Isaiah and Micah expressed hope for an ideal Davidic ruler who would perform God's will. Jeremiah and Ezekiel hoped for the restoration of the Jewish nation under the leadership of a just and righteous Davidic ruler. "Messiah" thus represented a future king of the house of David. According to the Gospel of Matthew, Jesus was descended from David (1:1-17) and was frequently addressed as "son of David" (9:27, 12:23, 15:22, 20:30-31, 21:9,15, 22:42). His father Joseph was also called "son of David." (Matthew 1:20)

Jesus has been called the "Son of God." God adopted Israel as His son; Israel is called the son of God in the Bible. (Exodus 4:22-23; Hosea 11:1) With the establishment of monarchy, the king was also identified as a son of God. His coronation was the occasion on which he became the adopted son of God. (Psalm 2:7; II Samuel 7:14) In the Book of Job (1:6, 2:1, 38:7), the angels are called sons of God. In Hebrews 1:5 and 5:5, God proclaims, "Thou art My beloved son, this day I have begotten thee." Hebrews 2:10-13, John 1:12 and Romans 8:16-19 all describe God bringing many sons to glory.

Jesus called himself the "Son of Man." The prophet Ezekiel was addressed by God as "Son of Man." (Ezekiel 2:1) In Hebrew, "son of man" ("*ben adam*") was a synonym for "man." Psalm 8:4 uses it in plural. Daniel refers to "one like a son of man," (Daniel 7:13), representing a coming Messiah and "the saints of the Most High" receiving the kingdom from God at the closing of the age.

Both Jesus and John the Baptist were considered prophets by the people. (Matthew 11:9, 21:11, 21:26, 21:46; Mark 6:15, 11:32; Luke 7:16, 7:26, 9:19, 24:19; John 4:19, 6:14, 7:40, 9:17) Jesus placed himself in the tradition of the prophets before him. (Matthew 13:57; Mark 6:4; Luke 4:24, 13:33; John 4:44) He frequently compared his ministry to the ministries of Noah, Lot and Jonah. (Matthew 10:15, 11:24, 12:39-40, 16:4, 24:37-39; Luke 10:12, 11:29,32, 17:26-29,32)

Jesus was called "Rabbi," meaning "Master" or "Teacher," 42 times in the gospels. The ministry of Jesus was a rabbinic one. Jesus related Scripture and God's laws to everyday life, teaching by personal example. He engaged in healing and acts of mercy. He told stories or parables—a rabbinic method of teaching. He went to the synagogue (Matthew 12:9), taught in the synagogues (Matthew 4:23, 13:54; Mark 1:39), expressed concern for Jairus, "one of the rulers of the synagogue" (Mark 5:36) and it "was his custom" to go to the synagogue on the Sabbath (Luke 4:16). John the Baptist, like Jesus, was also addressed as "Rabbi," or Teacher of Scripture. (Luke 3:12)

"Both Mark and Matthew describe the Baptist as eating 'locusts and wild honey' (Matthew 3:4; Mark 1:6)," writes Joseph A. Grassi in his 1975 book, *Underground Christians in the Earliest Church.* "This is the typical diet of a vegetarian who took seriously the injunction in Genesis that God had originally created the plants of the earth as man's food, and had only reluctantly permitted him later to kill animals for meat. (Genesis 1:29, 9:3) Jesus' first disciples came from John the Baptist (John 1:35-51; Acts 1:21-22). Jesus was influenced enough by John to be baptized by him."

John the Baptist appeared in Judea, calling upon people to repent, preaching that the kingdom of heaven was at hand, and to prepare the path of the Lord. (Matthew 3:1-10; Luke 3:2-9) The multitudes went to John to confess their sins and be baptized. Jesus was among those baptized by John. During Jesus' baptism, the heavens parted, the Spirit of God descended upon him in the form of a dove, and the voice of God proclaimed Jesus to be His beloved Son. (Matthew 3:16-17; Mark 1:10-11; Luke 3:21-22; John 1:32; Hebrews 1:5, 5:5) The Spirit then took Jesus into the wilderness, where he fasted for forty days and forty nights. (Matthew 4:2) He resisted every kind of temptation (Luke 4:13), living amongst the animals (Mark 1:12-13). During Jesus' preparation in the wilderness, John the Baptist was imprisoned. Jesus returned from the wilderness preaching an almost identical message. (Matthew 4:17; Mark 1:15) "The kingdom of God is at hand. Repent and believe in the gospel (good news)." Jesus began his ministry around age thirty. (Luke 3:23)

"Blessed are the meek," taught Jesus, repeating Psalm 37:11, "for they shall inherit the earth." (Matthew 5:5) Here Jesus refers to Isaiah's vision (11:6-9) of the future Kingdom of Peace, where the earth is restored to a vegetarian paradise. (Genesis 1:29-31) Jesus taught his followers to pray for the coming of God's kingdom and to do God's will "on earth as it is in heaven." (Matthew 6:9-10) John the Baptist taught his disciples the very same prayer. (Luke 11:1-2)

The kingdom of God belongs to the gentle and kind. "Blessed are the merciful, for they shall obtain mercy. Blessed are the pure in heart, for they shall see God. Blessed are the peacemakers, for they shall be called sons of God." (Matthew 5:7-9) "Be merciful, just as your Father is also merciful." (Luke 6:36) Jesus called the peacemakers or pacifists sons of God, because they emulate God's universal and unconditional love. "He makes His sun rise on the evil and on the good, and sends rain on the just and on the unjust. For if you love those who love you, what reward have you? And if you greet your brethren only, what do you do more than others? Therefore, be perfect, just as your Father in heaven is perfect." (Matthew 5:45-48; Luke 6:32-35)

Although the Ten Commandments teach "thou shalt not kill," Jesus extended this morality to the point where one must never even get angry without cause. (Matthew 5:21-22) And although the Ten Commandments teach "thou shalt not commit adultery," Jesus taught that "whoever looks upon a woman with lust has already committed adultery with her in his heart." (Matthew 5:27-28)

The Bible limits compensation to "an eye for an eye and a tooth for a tooth," but Jesus taught his followers not to defend themselves against attack or aggression. "All who take up the sword must perish by the sword," Jesus warned. (Matthew 26:52) The Bible teaches men to love their neighbors and hate their enemies, but Jesus taught them to love their enemies and bless and pray for their persecutors. (Matthew 5:38-44; Luke 6:27-29)

Jesus forbade divorce, except for unfaithfulness. When asked why Moses permitted divorce, Jesus replied that it was a concession to human weakness. He insisted upon the moral standards given by God at the beginning. (Matthew 5:31-32, 19:3-9; Mark 10:2-12; Luke 16:18)

Jesus told his followers there is no need to pray to God for material blessings or even necessities. (Matthew 6:8,31-33; Luke 12:29-30) God's compassion extends to all creation and He will easily provide for all of man's needs:

"Look at the birds of the air, for they neither sow nor reap nor gather into barns; yet your heavenly Father feeds them...Consider the lilies of the field, how they grow, they neither toil nor spin. And yet I say to you that even Solomon in all his glory was not arrayed like one of these. Now if God so clothes the grass of the field...will He not much more clothe you, O you of little faith? (Matthew 6:26-30; Luke 12:24-28)

"Do not suppose I have come to abolish the Law and the Prophets," insisted Jesus. "I did not come to destroy but to fulfill...till heaven and earth pass away, not one jot or tittle pass from the Law till all is fulfilled. Whoever, therefore, breaks one of the least of these commandments and teaches men so shall be called least in the kingdom of heaven; but whoever does and teaches them, he shall be called great in the kingdom of heaven... unless your righteousness exceeds the righteousness of the scribes and Pharisees, you will by no means enter the kingdom of heaven." (Matthew 5:17-20) Jesus also upheld the Torah in Luke 16:17: "And it is easier for heaven and earth to pass than for the smallest portion of the Law to become invalid."

"If you love me, keep my commandments." (John 14:15) Jesus repeated this instruction in John 14:21-23 and John 15:10. "For this is love of God," wrote his disciple, "that we keep His commandments; and His commandments are not irksome." (I John 5:3) Nor do these texts refer merely to the Ten Commandments: Jesus meant the entire Torah –613 Commandments. When a man asked Jesus what he must do to inherit eternal life, Jesus replied, "You know the commandments." He then quoted not just the Ten Commandments, but a commandment from Leviticus 19:13 as well: "Do not defraud." (Mark 10:17-22)

"Not everyone that says to me, 'Lord, Lord' shall enter the kingdom of heaven," Jesus warned, "but he who does the will of my Father in heaven." (Matthew 7:21; Luke 6:46) When Jesus was accused of violating the Sabbath with his disciples, he tried to illustrate how his actions were consistent with Torah. (Matthew 12:1-8; Mark 2:23-28; Luke 6:1-5) Jesus further stated that the Sabbath was made for man; not man for the Sabbath. (Mark 2:23-28) This is also taught in the Hebrew Scriptures. (Exodus 31:14)

Jesus' disciples were once accused by the scribes and Pharisees of violating rabbinical tradition (Matthew 15:1-2; Mark 7:5), but never biblical law. At no place in the entire New Testament does Jesus ever proclaim Torah or the Law of Moses to be invalid or annulled; this was the theology of Paul, a former Pharisee who never knew Jesus, but who used to persecute Jesus' followers.

When a scribe asked Jesus what is the greatest commandment in Torah, Jesus began with "Hear O Israel, the Lord, thy God, is One Lord." This is the *Shema*, which is still heard in every synagogue service to this day. "And you shall love the Lord with all your soul, with all your mind, and with all your strength...And you shall love your neighbor as yourself," Jesus concluded.

When the scribe agreed that God is one and that to love Him completely and also love one's neighbor as oneself is "more important than all the whole burnt offerings and sacrifices," Jesus replied, "You are not far from the kingdom of God." (Matthew 22:36-40; Mark 12:29-34; Luke 10:25-28)

Jesus' words in Matthew 7:12, "Accordingly, whatever you would have people do for you, do the same for them; for this covers the Law and the Prophets," are sometimes taken to mean the Torah has been annulled—one need only "do unto others." However, Jesus' response to the scribe proves otherwise. To believe in one God and love Him with all one's heart, soul and mind is not "covered" by "do unto others," which is merely a secular humanist moral philosophy. Nor is it a new teaching. Jesus was merely repeating in the positive what Rabbi Hillel had stated a generation earlier. Hillel had been asked, "What is Judaism?" He replied, "What is hateful to you, do not do unto others. That is Judaism. Everything else is commentary." Hillel's statement has never been taken to mean the Law has been abolished. There is no reason why Jesus' words should be interpreted as such, either.

It is said that Jesus went about all the cities and villages, teaching in the synagogues, preaching the gospel of the kingdom of God, and healing sickness and disease among the people. He felt compassion for the multitudes; they were sheep without a shepherd. (Matthew 9:36; Mark 6:34) So he began to teach them many things.

Jesus began by teaching the multitudes not to "give what is sacred to the dogs, nor cast your pearls before swine." (Matthew 7:6) Dogs, like swine, were considered foul and unclean by the Hebrew people. (Deuteronomy 23:18; I Samuel 24:14; II Kings 8:13; Psalm 22:16,20; Matthew 7:6; Luke 16:21; Revelations 22:15) These words were used by the children of Israel to describe the neighboring heathen populations. When sending his disciples out to preach, Jesus instructed them not to go to the gentiles, but to "go rather to the lost sheep of the house of Israel." (Matthew 10:5-6) When a Canaanite woman asked Jesus to heal her daughter, he replied, "I was sent only to the lost sheep of the house of Israel...It is not fair to take the children's bread and throw it to the dogs." (Matthew 15:22-28) Jesus regarded the gentiles as "dogs." His gospel was intended for the Jewish people.

Jesus gave his disciples the authority to cast out demons and unclean spirits from people's bodies, to heal all kinds of sicknesses and diseases and to preach the good news of God's kingdom. They were to travel as wandering monks or mendicants, with no possessions. He told his disciples to bless the homes of people deemed "worthy," or receptive to God's word. Such people would be called "sons of peace." Jesus knew his disciples would encounter hostility. "Behold, I send you out as lambs among wolves. Therefore, be as wise as serpents and as harmless as doves." (Matthew 10:7-13,16; Mark 6:7-12; Luke 10:3-11)

Jesus spoke of God's tender concern for all creatures while reminding his disciples of the importance of their preaching. "Are not five sparrows sold for two copper coins? And not one of them is forgotten before God. Do not fear...you are of more value than many sparrows." (Matthew 10:29-31; Luke 12:6-7)

While teaching in one of the synagogues on the Sabbath, Jesus healed a woman who had been ill for eighteen years. He justified his healing work on the Sabbath by referring to biblical passages calling for the humane treatment of animals as well as their rest on the Sabbath. "So ought not this woman, being a daughter of Abraham...be loosed from this bond on the Sabbath?" Jesus asked. (Luke 13:10-16)

Jesus compared the kingdom of God to a mustard seed which grows into a huge tree, with the birds of the air nested in its branches. (Matthew 13:31-32; Mark 4:30-32; Luke 13:18-19) On yet another occasion, Jesus again referred to Torah teaching on "*tsa'ar ba'alei chayim*" or compassion for animals to justify healing on the Sabbath. "Which of you, having a donkey or an ox that has fallen into a pit, will not immediately pull him out on the Sabbath day?" (Luke 14:1-5)

Jesus compared saving sinners who had gone astray from God's kingdom to rescuing lost sheep. He recalled a Jewish legend about Moses' compassion as a shepherd for his flock:

"For the Son of Man has come to save that which was lost. What do you think? Who among you, having a hundred sheep, if he loses one of them, does not leave the ninety-nine in the wilderness, and go after the one which is lost until he finds it? And when he has found it," Jesus continued, "he lays it on his shoulders, rejoicing. And when he comes home, he calls together his friends and neighbors saying to them, 'Rejoice with me, for I have found my sheep which was lost!'

"I say to you, likewise there will be more joy in heaven over one sinner who repents than over ninety-nine just persons who need no repentance...there is joy in the presence of the angels of God over one sinner who repents." (Matthew 18:11-13; Luke 15:3-7,10)

Jesus and his disciples lived lives of voluntary poverty and preached God's word among "the poor." When asked why he ate with sinners, he replied, "Those who are well have no need of a physician, but those who are sick. But go and learn what this means, 'I desire mercy and not sacrifice.' For I did not come to call the righteous, but sinners, to repentance." (Matthew 9:10-13; Mark 2:15-17; Luke 5:29-32)

"Mercy and not sacrifice," is the phrase best describing Jesus' ministry. (Matthew 12:6-7) The prophets before Jesus had indicated that God is more pleased by acts of mercy and righteousness than with burnt offerings of slaughtered animals. There are also many verses throughout the Bible indicating that animal sacrifices and bloodshed are offensive to a God whose compassion extends to all living creatures. When Jesus entered Jerusalem with his disciples, he went directly into the Temple and drove out all those who bought and sold in the Temple. Here he attacked the institution of animal sacrifice. The merchants were selling animals for slaughter, sacrifice and consumption. Jesus overturned the tables of the money-changers and the seats of those who sold doves, sheep and oxen. He did not allow anyone to carry goods through the Temple. He justified his actions by telling them: "It is written, 'My house shall be called a house of prayer,' but you have made it a 'den of thieves,'" and "Do not make my Father's house a house of merchandise!" Jesus healed the blind and the lame in Temple—acts of "mercy and not sacrifice." (Matthew 21:12-14; Mark 11:15-17; Luke 19:45-46; John 2:14-17)

In the 1986 edition of *A Vegetarian Sourcebook*, Keith Akers notes that there was a link in Judaism between meat-eating and animal sacrifices, that the prophetic tradition to which Jesus belonged attacked animal sacrifices, and that Jesus attacked the practice of animal sacrifice by driving the money-changers and their animals out of the Temple. He concludes, "The evidence indicates that for those who first heard the message of Jesus... the rejection of animal sacrifices had directly vegetarian implications."

Otto Pfleiderer, in his 1906 work, *Christian Origins*, observed: "When he (Jesus) saw the busy activity of the dealers in sacrificial animals and Jewish coins overrunning the outer court he drove them out with their wares. This business was connected with the sacrifice service and therefore Jesus' reformatory action seemed to be an attack on the sacrificial service itself and indirectly on the hierarchs who derived their income from and based their social position of power on the sacrificial service."

The scribes and the Pharisees were the religious authorities in Jesus' day. Jesus acknowledged their righteousness. (Matthew 5:20) The multitudes followed Jesus because "he taught them as one having authority, and not as the scribes." (Matthew 7:29; Mark 1:22; Luke 4:32) There were scribes that followed Jesus. (Matthew 8:19) Jesus often dined with Pharisees. (Luke 7:6, 11:37, 14:1) Pharisees were concerned enough about Jesus to warn him when his life was in danger. (Luke 13:31) Pharisees even accompanied Jesus en route to Jerusalem, while his disciples sang in praise of God. (Luke 19:37-40)

The Pharisees had mixed opinions concerning Jesus. (John 9:16) One ruler, Nicodemus, accepted Jesus as a teacher from God. (John 3:1-2) Many Pharisees eventually came to follow Jesus. (Acts 15:5)

Jesus told the multitudes, "The scribes and the Pharisees sit in Moses' seat. Therefore whatever they tell you to observe, that observe and do..." (Matthew 23:1-3) Yet, as a religious reformer, Jesus disagreed with many doctrines and practices of the Pharisees. He held them accountable for the religious hypocrisy of his day.

"Do not do according to their works," Jesus warned. "For they say and do not do. For they bind heavy burdens, hard to bear, and lay them on men's shoulders; but they themselves will not move them with one of their fingers...all their works they do to be seen by men...They love the best places at feasts, the best seats in the synagogues, greetings in the market places, and to be called by men, 'Rabbi, Rabbi.' But you must not be called 'Rabbi,' for one is your Teacher, the Messiah. And you are all brethren...do not call anyone on earth your father, for One is your Father, He who is in heaven. And do not be called teachers; for one is your Teacher, the Messiah." (Matthew 23:3-10; Mark 12:38-41; Luke 11:43)

The scribes and Pharisees, Jesus claimed, "devour widows' houses, and for a pretense make long prayers...have neglected the weightier matters of the Law; justice and mercy and faith." Jesus accused the Pharisees of valuing the gold of the Temple more than the Temple itself and the sacred gifts upon the altar more than the altar itself. (Matthew 23:14,16-23; Luke 11:42, 20:45-47)

Jesus taught humility and servitude. "You know that the rulers of the gentiles lord it over them, and those who are great exercise authority over them. Yet it shall not be so among you, but whoever desires to become great among you, let him be your servant. And whoever desires to be first among you, let him be your slave." (Matthew 20:25-27; Mark 10:42-44; Luke 22:25-27) When his disciples argued amongst themselves who would be the greatest, Jesus told them, "If anyone desires to be first, he shall be last of all and servant of all." (Matthew 23:11; Mark 9:33-35) On another occasion he explained, "For he who is least among you all will be great." (Luke 9:48) According to Jesus, "Whoever exalts himself will be humbled, and he who humbles himself will be exalted." (Matthew 23:12; Luke 14:11)

Jesus told his disciples they were to think of themselves as unprofitable servants who simply do their duty. (Luke 17:7-10) Jesus even washed the feet of his disciples after the Last Supper, to set an example to his disciples about humility and equality before God. (John 13:1-16)

Jesus taught that before God, no one can be called good. (Matthew 19:17; Mark 10:18; Luke 18:19) He saw the righteous and the wicked with equal vision. When Jesus was informed about Galileans who suffered at the hands of Pontius Pilate, the Roman governor, he responded: "Do you suppose that these Galileans were worse sinners than all other Galileans, because they suffered such things? I tell you no; but unless you repent you will all likewise perish.

"Or those eighteen on whom the tower in Siloam fell and killed them," Jesus continued. "Do you think that they were worse sinners than all other men who dwelt in Jerusalem? I tell you, no; but unless you repent you will all likewise perish." (Luke 13:1-5)

The Pharisees apparently claimed religious leadership without such humility before God. "If you were (spiritually) blind," Jesus told them on one occasion, "you would have no sin; but now you say, 'We see.' Therefore, your sin remains." (John 9:41)

According to Luke, the Pharisees trusted in their own righteousness and therefore looked down upon others. Jesus told a parable of two men—a Pharisee and a tax collector—praying at Temple. The Pharisee prayed, "God, I thank You that I am not like the other men—extortioners, unjust, adulterers, or even as this tax collector. I fast twice a week; I give tithes of all I possess."

Meanwhile, the tax collector stood off in the distance. He would not even raise his eyes towards heaven, but merely prayed, "God, be merciful to me a sinner!" Jesus said it was the tax collector who went home justified, not the Pharisee, for "everyone who exalts himself shall be humbled and he who humbles himself will be exalted." (Luke 18:9-14)

Jesus instructed his followers to perform their charity, prayer and fasting in private. Religious devotion must never become a means to adulation, fame and social recognition. (Matthew 6:1-6,16-18) Jesus' disciples did not fast in the same manner as the disciples of John the Baptist or the Pharisees (Matthew 9:14-17; Mark 2:18-22; Luke 5:33-39), but they did fast. (Matthew 6:16-18) Jesus even taught that certain kinds of demons could only be exorcised through prayer and fasting. (Matthew 17:14-21; Mark 9:17-29) Jesus taught constant prayer. (Luke 21:36) He often withdrew into the wilderness to pray. (Luke 5:16) At least once, Jesus went to the mountains and spent the night in prayer. (Matthew 14:23; Mark 6:46; Luke 6:12)

Jesus explained that celibacy is not something everyone can practice; it is meant only for those whom God has ordained it. He used the euphemism "eunuchs for the sake of the kingdom of heaven," recalling his euphemism about denying or dismembering bodily urges rather than having the entire body destroyed by sin. (Matthew 5:29-30, 18:8-9, 19:10-12) The apparent celibacy of Jesus is unusual by ancient Hebrew standards. The Bible does call for temporary abstinences, under certain circumstances. According to the Talmud, Moses voluntarily chose to give up sexual relations with his wife after he received his call from God. He reasoned that if the Israelites, to whom the Lord spoke only once and briefly, were ordered to abstain from sexual relations temporarily (Exodus 19:10,15), then he—being in continual dialogue with

God—should remain celibate.

Philo of Alexandria tells us that to sanctify himself, Moses cleansed himself of "all the mortal calls of nature, food and drink and intercourse with women. This last he had disdained for many a day, almost from the time when, possessed by the Spirit, he entered on his work as a prophet, since he held it fitting to hold himself always in readiness to receive the oracular messages." Given this information, Jesus' apparent voluntary embrace of celibacy, from the time of his baptism and reception of the Spirit of God, becomes meaningful to Jews and Christians alike.

Jesus' response to rabbinical law and the excesses of the Pharisaic tradition is often misunderstood. "There is nothing that enters a man from outside which can defile him;" taught Jesus, "but the things which come out of him, those are the things that defile a man." His disciples could not understand this. "What comes out of a man," Jesus explained, "that defiles a man. For from within out of the heart of men proceed evil thoughts, adulteries, fornications, murders. Thefts, covetousness, wickedness, deceit, lewdness...blasphemy, pride, foolishness. All these evil things defile a man, but to eat with unwashed hands does not defile a man." (Matthew 15:11-20; Mark 7:14-23)

Jesus was more concerned with one's internal nature that he was with one's external behavior. Jesus attacked not just killing and adultery, but the inner mentality and desires which cause such actions. (Matthew 5:21-22,27-28) Jesus went to the root cause of sin, looking past social factors and one's surrounding environment to the individual conscience before God. Proof of this can be seen in Jesus' opposition to the Pharisaic method of saving sinners. "For you cleanse the outside of the cup and dish, but inside they are full of extortion and self-indulgence. Blind Pharisee, first cleanse the inside of the cup and dish, that the outside of them may be clean also. Did He who made the outside make the inside also?" (Matthew 23:25-26; Luke 11:37-40)

A person's heart or conscience can be known by his words and his deeds. Jesus warned his followers to "Beware of false prophets, who come to you in sheep's clothing, but inwardly they are ravenous wolves. You will know them by their fruits. Do men gather grapes from thornbushes or figs from thistles? Therefore, by their fruits you will know them...Out of the abundance of the heart the mouth speaks. A good man out of the good treasure of his heart brings forth good things, and an evil man out of the evil treasure brings forth evil things." (Matthew 7:15-20, 12:34-35; Luke 6:43-45)

According to Mark, Jesus' conclusion that nothing from the outside can defile a man indirectly made all foods permissible. If this were true, however, Simon (Peter) would not have resisted a divine command to kill and eat both "clean" and "unclean" animals. (Acts 10:9-16)

Nor would James, the brother of Jesus (Matthew 13:55; Mark 6:3; Galatians 1:19), who held a leading position at the church in Jerusalem (Acts 12:17, 15:13, 21:13), have required all gentile converts to Christianity to abstain from blood, strangled meat, fornication, and foods offered to pagan gods. (Acts 15) Jesus himself demanded that his followers refrain from eating food offered to other gods (Revelations 2:14).

It is significant that the idea that all foods are permissible is not recorded in Matthew, only in Mark. Even if true, would it justify unnecessarily harming or killing animals to begin with? Jesus' teachings on nonviolence, the kingdom of God, the moral standards given by God at the beginning of creation, and God's compassion for all living creatures suggest otherwise.

John the Baptist told the people to share half of their food and clothing with the needy. (Luke 3:11) Jesus was pleased when Zacchaeus, a wealthy tax collector, promised to give half his goods to the poor. "Today salvation has come to this house, because he is also a son of Abraham. For the Son of Man has come to seek and save that which was lost." (Luke 19:2-10)

However, Jesus went even further, and called for renunciation of worldly goods. He did not regard the accumulation of material possessions as a meaningful goal in life. "Do not lay up for yourselves treasures on earth, where moth and rust destroy...But lay up for yourselves treasures in heaven...for where your treasure is, there will your heart be also." (Matthew 6:19-20; Luke 12:33-34)

Jesus told the multitudes that followed him, "...whoever of you does not forsake all that he has cannot be my disciple." (Luke 14:25,33) "No one can serve two masters," Jesus explained. "...he will be loyal to one and despise the other. You cannot serve God and Mammon." (Matthew 6:24; Luke 16:13)

Jesus had little interest in worldly disputes over money and property. (Luke 12:13-14) "Take heed and beware of covetousness, for one's life does not consist in the abundance of the things he possesses." Jesus condemned those who lay up treasures for themselves, but are not rich towards God. (Luke 12:15-21)

In his parable of the Rich Man and Lazarus (Luke 16:19-31), Jesus expressed concern for materialistic persons. When a rich, young ruler came to Jesus and said he had kept God's commandments since youth, Jesus prized him dearly and replied, "You still lack one thing. Sell all that you have and distribute to the poor, and you will have treasure in heaven; and come follow me." The man went away, saddened. Jesus observed that it is difficult for those attached to earthly riches to enter the kingdom of God. (Matthew 19:16-24; Mark 10:17-23; Luke 18:18-25)

Jesus even demanded the renunciation of family ties. (Luke 14:26) It appears Jesus had little contact even with his own family; he regarded only those who do God's will as his brethren. (Matthew 12:46-50; Mark 3:31-35; Luke 8:19-21) When a woman said to Jesus, "Blessed is the womb that bore you and the breasts which nursed you," Jesus replied, "More blessed still are those who hear and keep the word of God." (Luke 11:27-28)

Perhaps the most famous narrative depicting Jesus as a Jewish religious reformer is John 8:1-11. Jesus was teaching people at Temple early in the morning. The scribes and Pharisees brought to him a woman caught in the act of adultery. "Now Moses, in the Law, commanded us that such should be stoned. But what do you say?"

"Let he among you who is without sin," Jesus responded, "cast the first stone." The woman's accusers all found themselves convicted by their own conscience. They released her and went away. No one was left to condemn her. "Neither do I condemn you;" Jesus told her, "go and sin no more."

Aside from the Pharisees, the gospels and Book of Acts mention the Sadducees as the only other major school of Judaic thought. The Sadducees tended to be rich, nationalist and secularist.

The Jewish historian Josephus, who lived during the time of Jesus, wrote that the "Pharisees have delivered to the people a great many observances...which are not written into the laws of Moses and" which "the Sadducees reject," but they "are able to persuade none but the rich," whereas "the Pharisees have the multitude on their side." Thus Jesus never rejected Mosaic Law (Matthew 5:17-19; Luke 16:17); only its Pharisaic excesses.

chapter three
"Prepare the Way of the Lord"

Obviously, Jesus was neither Pharisee nor Sadducee. No analysis of the history of Christianity and the teachings of Jesus can ignore the Essenes. The Jewish historian Josephus, who lived during the time of Jesus, wrote that there were but three Jewish sects in his day: the Pharisees, the Sadducees and the Essenes. Josephus actually spent time in an Essene monastery and compiled a detailed account of their doctrines and way of life—all of which were quite similar to primitive Christianity.

New Testament scholars such as Bahrdt (1784-1792), Venturini (1800), Gfoerer (1831-38), Hennel (1840) and von der Alm (1863), have all suggested that Jesus may have been an Essene. The Pharisees and Sadducees appear in the gospels and book of Acts as parties inimical to the new church, but no mention is made of the Essenes. It is quite possible Christianity grew out of Essenism. Essenism began around 180 BC as a reaction to Hellenistic influence among the Jewish people. They called themselves the Zadokites or the Hasidim (pious). In addition to the canonical books of the Old Testament, they composed and studied their own scriptures, commentaries and prophecies, written between 170 and 60 BC. These scriptures were uncovered by modern archaeology in the Essene monastery at Khirbet-Qumran, west of the Dead Sea. The Essenes flourished until 69 AD, when they were killed by the Romans.

The Essene community called itself by the same name ("*Edah*") used by the early Christians to denote the church. The same term used to designate its legislative assembly was also used to denote the council of the early Christian church. There were twelve "men of holiness" serving as general guides for the community—strikingly similar to the twelve apostles. These men had three superiors, designated as pillars of the community—exactly the positions held by John, Peter and James in the early Christian church. (Galatians 2:9)

Both the Essenes and the earliest Christians referred to themselves as "the poor in the world," "the sons of light" and "the chosen of God who shall judge the nations at the end of time." The earliest Christians called themselves "the saints," "the brethren," "the elect," "the believers," "those in Messiah," "those of the Lord," "the sons of peace," "the disciples" and "the poor." The word most used to refer to Christians in the New Testament is "brethren." The *Manual of Discipline* and other Essene texts, found in the Dead Sea Scrolls, indicate that they spoke of each other as "brethren."

During the Last Supper, Peter motioned to one of the disciples "to ask who it was of whom he (Jesus) spoke." (John 13:24) This was consistent with the practice of the Essenes when they met together in sessions: "Nor shall a man speak in the midst of the words of his neighbor, before his brother finishes speaking. Neither shall he speak before his proper order." It appears the disciple next to Jesus held a higher rank in the group than Peter, and was the one posing the question to Jesus.

The Essene monastery communal meal resembles the Last Supper of the New Testament. In both meals, only men participated in a large upper room. (Mark 14:15) In both groups the recognized leader presided over the meal. Lastly, the leader blessed both the bread and the drink. Because of these close parallels, the depiction of the Last Supper more closely resembles the communal meals of the Essenes than it does the Passover meal, which is traditionally a patriarchal family rite in which the father of a family presides.

The epistle of James is regarded as one of the earliest epistles in the New Testament. It is addressed to the twelve Jewish tribes of the Dispersion. Its writer, James the Just, the brother of Jesus (Matthew 13:55; Mark 6:3; Galatians 1:19), held a leading position at the church in Jerusalem. (Acts 12:17, 15:13, 21:13) James (4:5) appears to quote directly from Essene scripture.

He asks, "Do you think that Scripture says in vain, 'The spirit which God made to dwell in us lusteth to envy?'" The scripture he refers to are not the canonical books of the Old Testament, because such a statement cannot be found in them. However, a similar statement can be found in the *Manual of Discipline*: "God has made two spirits to dwell in us, each rivaling the other; the evil one lusteth and envies the good." Jesus' instructions in Matthew 18:15-17 concern disputes among the brethren. He mentions evidence, witnesses and an already existing church hierarchy. Jesus was quoting a set of Essene rules which can also be found in the *Manual of Discipline.*

John the Baptist is said to have been raised in the desert from childhood. The Essene monastery was not far from where John supposedly lived. The Essenes were the only Jewish sect with a celibate priesthood, practicing baptism. The *Manual of Discipline* says they followed Isaiah 40:3, "go to the wilderness to prepare there the way...make level in the desert a path for the Lord."

This was John's description of himself, as found in the canonical gospels (John 1:23). "Repent," he preached, "for the kingdom of heaven is at hand." (Matthew 3:2) The Essenes believed they belonged to a "covenant of repentance." (*Zadokite Document*) John the Baptist said that one greater than he would baptize with fire and the Holy Spirit. The *Manual of Discipline* declares that the time would come when God would cleanse man through the Holy Spirit and through His Messiah, God would make His chosen know the Holy Spirit.

Josephus writes that the Essenes adopted children and brought them up in God's service. According to the gospels, John the Baptist was in the desert from boyhood until the day of his showing in Israel. The gospels are also silent about Jesus' life from the age of twelve to thirty. Both Jesus and his relative John were about the same age. According to Jewish tradition, a student must reach his thirtieth birthday before he can qualify as a priest or rabbi. Both Jesus and John met this requirement. John, a few months older than Jesus, was the first to preach. Jesus followed shortly thereafter.

The title of "Rabbi" was conferred by the priests of the synagogue or temple. Neither Jesus nor John received this honor from either the Pharisees or the Sadducees. Joesphus mentions only three sects: the Pharisees, Sadducees and the Essenes. (*Antiquities* G.13,1,2; *Antiquities* B.13,5,9; *Wars of the Jews* B.2,8,2)

"Both Mark and Matthew describe the Baptist as eating 'locusts and wild honey' (Matthew 3:4; Mark 1:6)," writes Joseph A. Grassi in his 1975 book, *Underground Christians in the Earliest Church.* "This is the typical diet of a vegetarian who took seriously the injunction in Genesis that God had originally created the plants of the earth as man's food, and had only reluctantly permitted him later to kill animals for meat. (Genesis 1:29, 9:3) Jesus' first disciples came from John the Baptist (John 1:35-51; Acts 1:21-22). Jesus was influenced enough by John to be baptized by him."

The Essenes were vegetarian. One of their earliest scriptural texts, the *Zadokite Document* proclaims: "Let not a man make himself abominable with any living creature or creeping thing by eating them."

> "Thou hast created plants for the service of man and all things that spring
> from the earth that he may be fed in abundance and to them that acknowl-
> edge Thy truth Thou has also given insight to divine Thy wondrous works."
>
> — *Hymns of the Initiates*
> *X,14 - XI,2*

These verses appear to be based on Genesis 1:26-31 and Daniel 1:9-21. Epiphanius, a Christian bishop during the fourth century, wrote that "the Essenes eschewed the flesh of animals." According to Josephus, "they all sit down together to one sort of food...live the same kind of life as those whom the Greeks call Pythagoreans."

The French philosopher Voltaire observed, "It is well known that Pythagoras embraced the humane doctrine of anti-flesh-eating. There was a rivalry as to who could be the most virtuous—the Essenes or the Pythagoreans." Philo of Alexandria wrote, "They live the longest lives...about a hundred years, owing to the simplicity of their diet." The Roman teacher Porphyry, a vegetarian, also spoke of the Essene meals as a "single simple dish of pure, clean food." St. Jerome admired the Essenes: "those men who perpetually abstained from meat and wine and had acquired the habit of everyday fasting."

According to Philo, "Not a single slave is to be found among them, but all are free, exchanging services with each other, and they denounce the owners of slaves...they have shown themselves especially devout in the service to God, not by offering sacrifices of animals, but by resolving to sanctify their minds." Josephus writes, "they do not offer sacrifices because they have more pure lustrations of their own; on which account they are excluded from the common court of the temple."

The Essenes were pacifists. "As for darts, javelins, daggers, or the helmet, breastplate or shield," Philo explained, "you could not find a single manufacturer of them nor, in general, any person making weapons or engines or plying any industry concerned with war; nor, indeed, any of the peaceful kind which easily lapse into vice." These descriptions parallel Jesus' teachings (Matthew 5:9,39,43-44, 26:52) where he blesses the peacemakers, tells his followers to "turn the other cheek" if attacked, to bless and pray for their enemies and to refrain from taking up arms.

"They do not hoard gold and silver," continues Philo, "but provide what is needed for the necessary requirements of life...they have become moneyless and landless by deliberate action..." Jesus also told his followers to seek the treasures in heaven, calling for the renunciation of earthly possessions and family ties. (Matthew 6:19-21, 6:25-34, 10:34-39, 19:20-21,29; Luke 9:57-62, 14:25-26,33)

The Essenes observed the Sabbath in synagogues and shared their homes and possessions. These were the practices of the apostles and the earliest Christian communities. (Acts 1:13, 2:44,46, 4:32-37) According to Philo, "They are trained in piety, holiness, justice, domestic and civil conduct, knowledge of what is good through the love of God, love of virtue, and love of men. Their love of God they show by a multitude of proofs: by religious purity constant and unbroken throughout their lives, by abstinence from oaths, by veracity...by their freedom from the love of either money or reputation or pleasure; by self-mastery and endurance; again by frugality, simple living, contentment, humility, respect for the law; steadiness and all similar qualities."

Like the Essenes, Jesus taught his followers not to use oaths (Matthew 5:33-37), to serve God rather than Mammon (Matthew 6:24; Luke 16:13), and to respect both civil and religious authorities. (Matthew 22:21, 23:1-3) Jesus also emphasized humility and servitude over glory, honor and exaltation. (Matthew 20:24-28; Mark 10:41-45; Luke 9:46-48, 14:7-11, 17:7-10; John 13:3-17)

Josephus wrote that the Essenes faced death calmly and joyfully at the hands of the Romans, knowing "their bodies shall decay and become dust...the souls are immortal, and shall live eternally." The Essenes, said Josephus, taught that in worldly existence, the soul is chained to the body like a prisoner to his cell, but when set free from the flesh, then "already tasting heavenly bliss, it soars up to the bright kingdom of joy and peace." (Compare Matthew 13:43)

Around 1830, Thomas de Quincey wrote an essay claiming the Essenes never existed; that Josephus merely mistook early Christians for these godly people. It would be sacreligious, he argued, to accept the existence of such large communities of worshippers, with doctrines and practices identical to those found in Christianity, prior to Jesus' life and ministry!

No historical evidence proving a relationship between the Essenes and early Christianity has ever been found. The striking similarities between the two faiths, however, strongly suggest that the earliest Christians were influenced by the Essenes. No serious student of Christian thought can ignore the direct influence of Judaism and the possible influence of the Essenes (and the Dead Sea Scrolls) upon the theological development of early Christianity.

chapter four
"The Good Shepherd"

"The compassionate, sensitive heart for animals is inseparable from the proclamation of the Christian gospel," writes the Reverend Andrew Linzey in *Love the Animals*. "We have lived so long with the gospel stories of Jesus that we frequently fail to see how his life and ministry identified with animals at almost every point.

"His birth, if tradition is to be believed, takes place in the home of sheep and oxen. His ministry begins, according to St. Mark, in the wilderness 'with the wild beasts' (1:13). His triumphal entry into Jerusalem involves riding on a 'humble' ass (Matthew 21). According to Jesus, it is lawful to 'do good' on the Sabbath, which includes the rescuing of an animal fallen into a pit (Matthew 12). Even the sparrows, literally sold for a few pennies in his day, are not 'forgotten before God.' God's providence extends to the entire created order, and the glory of Solomon and all his works cannot be compared to that of the lilies of the field (Luke 12:27).

"God so cares for His creation that even 'foxes have holes, and birds of the air have nests; but the Son of Man has nowhere to lay his head.' (Luke 9:58) It is 'the merciful' who are 'blessed' in God's sight and what we do to 'the least' of all we do to him. (Matthew 5:7, 25:45-46) Jesus literally overturns the already questionable practice of animal sacrifice. Those who sell pigeons have their tables overturned and are put out of the Temple (Mark 11:15-16). It is the scribe who sees the spiritual bankruptcy of animal sacrifice and the supremacy of sacrificial love that Jesus commends as being 'not far from the Kingdom of God'. (Mark 12:32-34)

"It is a loving heart which is required by God, and not the needless bloodletting of God's creatures," concludes Reverend Linzey. "We can see the same prophetic and radical challenge to tradition in Jesus' remarks about the '*good* shepherd' who, unlike many in his day, '*lays down his life for the sheep*.' (John 10:11)"

Jesus' miracle of multiplying loaves and fishes is often cited as evidence that he did not favor the vegetarian way of life. His first disciples Simon, Andrew, James and John were all fishermen by the Sea of Galilee. Jesus called them away from their livelihood. "Follow me," he commanded, "and I will make you fishers of men." (Matthew 4:18-22; Mark 1:16-20)

Jesus then performed a miracle illustrating that God can easily provide for human sustenance. He wanted people to seek first the kingdom of God and His righteousness. (Matthew 6:8,26-33; Luke 12:24-31) On the Lake of Gennesaret, Jesus told Simon to drop his nets. Huge numbers of fish were caught to the point where the nets began to break and the boat began to sink. The fish presumably went back into the lake. Simon knelt before Jesus and called himself a sinner. "Do not be afraid," Jesus replied. "From now on you will be catching men." They forsook all and followed him. (Luke 5:1-11)

After John the Baptist's execution, Jesus withdrew into solitude. The multitudes followed him on foot from the cities. Jesus healed many. When evening came, his disciples said, "This is a deserted place, and the hour is already late. Send the multitudes away, that they may go into the villages and buy themselves food." And Jesus replied, "They do not need to go away. You give them something to eat."

"Shall we go and buy them two hundred denarii worth of bread and give them something to eat?" they asked. "We have here only five barley loaves and two fish," which had been given to the disciples by a boy in the crowd. Jesus took the loaves and the fish, "and looking up to heaven, he blessed and broke and gave the loaves to the disciples; and the disciples gave to the multitudes." Over five thousand ate and were satisfied. (Matthew 14:13-21; Mark 6:31-44; Luke 9:11-17; John 6:9)

On another occasion, Jesus multiplied seven loaves and a few fish for over four thousand people. Jesus explained: "I have compassion on the multitude, because they have now continued with me three days and have nothing to eat. And I do not want to send them away hungry, lest they faint on the way." (Matthew 15:32-38; Mark 8:1-9) Jesus raised no objection to the eating of already dead fish when there was no other food available. This is consistent with the vegetarian way of life. The prophet Elisha raised people from the dead. (II Kings 4:32-37) Elisha also multiplied twenty barley loaves to feed one hundred men. (II Kings 4:42-44) Jesus appears to have repeated the same miracle on a larger scale, using what little resources were available to him.

Matthew 14:19 reads as follows: "he took the five loaves and the two fish, and looking up to heaven, he blessed and broke and gave the loaves to the disciples; and the disciples gave to the multitudes." This text implies only loaves, and not fishes, were multiplied to give the crowds something to eat.

Jesus' own recollection of the events suggests only loaves were multiplied. Jesus warned his disciples about "the yeast (teachings) of the Pharisees and Sadducees." The disciples, having forgotten to bring bread, misunderstood. "O you of little faith," exclaimed Jesus. "Do you not...remember the five loaves of the five thousand...the seven loaves of the four thousand and how many large baskets you took up?" (Matthew 16:5-12; Mark 8:14-21)

The Fourth Gospel describes the event in almost mystical terms. Jesus multiplied five barley loaves and two fish for over five thousand. Yet he later told the crowds, "I say to you, you seek me not because you saw the signs, but because you at of the loaves and were filled. Do not labor for the food which perishes, but for the food which endures to everlasting life, which the Son of Man will give you...I am the bread of life. He who comes to me shall never hunger, and he who believes in me shall never thirst." These verses suggest Jesus really satisfied the multitudes spiritually, giving them "the food which endures to everlasting life." (John 6:1-35)

According to contemporary Christian teacher Abbot George Burke, "...there is a very interesting distinction made between the bread and the fish in the Gospels of Saints Matthew (14:19), Mark (6:41) and John (6:11). When writing of the feeding of the five thousand, all three Evangelists are careful to note that Jesus first took the bread, blessed it, divided it and gave it for distribution. *But the fish He simply gave for distribution!* He gave no blessing to the eating of fish because it was not given by God to man for food. Moreover, since it was already dead He did not kill anything—He just made more of it."

The New Testament mentions the feeding of the multitudes on four separate occasions, and fish is listed as one of the items present. However, the church father Irenaeus, in his great thesis *Against Heresies* (180-188 AD), wrote: "He there, seeing a great crowd had followed Him, fed all that multitude with five loaves of bread and twelve baskets of fragments remained over and above." Irenaeus makes no mention of fish. In a later text, Irenaeus again says, "Our Lord after blessing the five loaves, fed with them 5,000 men." How do we explain this discrepancy? Our oldest existing Greek manuscript of the New Testament, the *Codex Sinaiticus*, can be found in the British Museum. It was written in 331 AD. We have no New Testaments from before this time. It is possible that early copies of the gospels made no mention of fish being fed to the multitudes, while later copyists added this symbol in order to enhance the miracle.

Students of the Bible are familiar with the use of bread as a mystical symbol of Jesus' body, or divine substance. In the early Christian church, the fish was also a divine symbol. The symbol of the fish was a secret sign, used in times of persecution. It can be found in the catacombs of ancient Rome and it remains in popular use today. The Greek word for fish is "*ichtus*." This word was used in the early church as an acronym for the Greek phrase, "*Iesus Christos Theou Uious Soter*," or "Jesus Christ, Son of God, Savior."

The early church father Origen wrote, "while every passage of Scripture has a spiritual meaning, many passages have no other meaning, but that there is often a spiritual meaning under the literal fiction."

Gospel references to fish may be symbolic. The earliest depictions of the Eucharist in the catacombs were inspired by the story of the multiplication of the loaves and fishes; believed to symbolize the Eucharist. A bishop in the early church wrote, "Faith hath provided as my food a fish of exceeding great size, and perfect, which a holy virgin drew with her hands from a fountain." In the 2nd century, the church father Tertullian wrote, "We little fish, after the image of our Ichtus (Fish) Jesus Christ, are born in the water."

Some of Jesus' parables do refer to slaughter and violence. In the Gospel of Matthew, Jesus teaches his disciples: "The kingdom of heaven is like a certain king who arranged a marriage for his son, and sent out his servants to call those who were invited to the wedding; and they were not willing to come.

"Again, he sent out other servants, saying, 'Tell those who are invited, 'See, I have prepared my dinner; my oxen and fatted cattle are killed, and all things are ready. Come to the wedding.' But they made light of it and went their ways, one to his own farm, another to his business. And the rest seized his servants, treated them spitefully, and killed them. But when the king heard about it, he was furious. And he sent out his armies, destroyed those murderers, and burned up their city. Then he said to his servants, 'The wedding is ready, but those who were invited were not worthy. Therefore, go into the highways, and as many as you find, invite to the wedding.'

"So those servants went out into the highways and gathered together all whom they found, both bad and good. And the wedding hall was filled with guests. But when the king came in to see the guests, he saw a man there who did not have on a wedding garment. So he said to him, 'Friend, how did you come in here without a garment?' And he was speechless. Then the king said to the servants, 'Bind him hand and foot, take him away, and cast him into outer darkness; there will be weeping and gnashing of teeth.' For many are called, but few are chosen." (Matthew 22:1-14)

However, Jesus tells a similar parable in Luke's Gospel: A certain man gave a great supper and invited many. He sent his servant at suppertime to welcome everyone. All the guests began making excuses. The servant reported this to his master. The master told his servant to go out into the streets and bring in the poor, the maimed, the lame and the blind. The guests he originally invited were to be excluded. This parable in Luke makes no reference to bloodshed or violence of any kind. It may very well be the original narrative.

Jesus' own morality precedes this parable. He is dining with the Pharisees. He tells his hosts:

"When you give a dinner or a supper, do not ask your friends, your brothers, your relatives, nor rich neighbors, lest they also invite you back, and you be repaid. But when you give a feast, invite the poor, the maimed, the lame, the blind. And you will be blessed, because they cannot repay you; for you shall be repaid at the resurrection of the just." (Luke 14:12-24)

The true, gentle nature of Jesus can be found in his life, his teachings and the Jewish tradition to which he belonged. On the way to Jerusalem, a Samaritan village would not receive him. When James and John saw this, they asked him, "Lord, do you want us to command fire to come down from heaven and consume them, just as Elijah did?" Jesus rebuked them. "You do not know your attitude. The Son of Man did not come to destroy human lives, but to save." (Luke 9:51-56)

Passover remains one of the most important holy days in the Jewish calendar. Passover is an annual spring festival, serving as a memorial of the exodus of the Jews from Egypt under Moses. In first century Judea, Passover was centered around two events. On the 14th day of the month of Nisan, innocent lambs were ritually slain in the Temple at Jerusalem. This was the day of Preparation. On the 15th day of Nisan, the Passover feast would take place. The Passover meal would be eaten by congregations and by families, in selected places throughout Jerusalem.

The Passover meal consisted of slaughtered lamb, unleavened bread, bitter herbs and wine, which was sipped periodically. The prayers at the table invoked the remembrance of God's deliverance of His people from past bondage; asking for His continued blessings upon the children of Israel. The first three gospels imply Jesus' Last Supper was a Passover meal (Matthew 26:17-19; Mark 14:12-14; Luke 22:7-15), and that his crucifixion occurred the very same day.

If Jesus' Last Supper with his disciples was a Passover meal, then Jesus may have eaten the Passover lamb. This would mean it was unlikely that he was a vegetarian. The account of the Last Supper given in the Fourth Gospel clearly indicates it was not a Passover meal, but a meal shared on the day of Preparation:

"Before the Passover feast Jesus, aware that his hour had come that he should depart from this world to the Father, having loved his own who were in the world, he loved them to the end. And supper being ended..." (John 13:1-2)

This text explicitly states that Jesus' Last Supper with his disciples took place before the feast known as Passover.

John 18:28 states that the Jewish religious authorities would not enter the Roman Praetorium where Jesus was being tried, "so that they might not be defiled, but that they might eat the Passover." Pontius Pilate told the Jews, "This is your king," as he ordered Jesus crucified. This occurred on the twelfth hour of the day of Preparation. (John 19:14) After crucifixion, the Jews asked Pontius Pilate that Jesus' body be taken from the cross and given a decent burial before the Sabbath which was Passover. (John 19:31)

Friday was the day of Preparation for the Sabbath, which began at sundown. According to the Jewish calendar, a new day begins at six p.m., while the week concludes with the Sabbath, or Saturday. The first three gospels (Matthew, Mark and Luke) state that Jesus celebrated Passover with his disciples and suffered arrest, trial and crucifixion on Friday evening, the 15th of Nisan. Only the Fourth Gospel explicitly places the Last Supper on Thursday evening, the 14th of Nisan. Jesus' final meal with his disciples, his arrest, trial and crucifixion all take place on Nisan 14 in this gospel.

To some extent, the accounts given by Matthew, Mark and Luke conform to the Fourth Gospel. In Matthew 26:5, the authorities decided not to apprehend Jesus during the Passover feast, "lest there be an uproar amongst the people." All four gospel writers record Jesus' burial on the day of Preparation. (Matthew 27:57-62; Mark 15:42; Luke 23:54; John 20:42)

Passover was a holy day, regarded as a Sabbath by the Jews. Its holiness was protected by traditional Sabbath restrictions. The gospels describe incidents connected with Jesus' crucifixion which would not have occurred on a holy day.

To begin with, it is unlikely crowds would carry weapons once Passover had begun. (Matthew 26:47,55; Mark 14:43,48-49; Luke 22:52; John 18:3) There would have been no Jewish involvement in the Roman legal proceedings against Jesus. (Matthew 27:12; Mark 15:3; Luke 23:5) Nor would the trial and crucifixion of Jesus have occurred. (Matthew 27:27-50; Mark 15:16-37; Luke 23:26-46; John 19:17-30)

Simon the Cyrenian would not have journeyed from the country (Matthew 27:32; Mark 15:21; Luke 23:26) Nor would Joseph of Arimathea have been able to purchase a linen shroud and see to the burial of Jesus' body. The fact that Jesus was quickly taken down from the cross and buried in his tomb is consistent with the Jews' desire that he not be left on the cross once the feast had begun. (Matthew 27:57-60; Mark 15:43-47; Luke 23:50-57; John 19:38-57)

The accounts of the Last Supper all center on the meal itself. As the meal proceeded, Jesus took the bread and gave thanks before God. Because his position in relation to God was like that of a high priest (Hebrews 4:14-16, 5:5-10, 7:17, 8:1), Jesus more than likely presented the bread before God as an offering. He then broke the bread and gave it to his disciples, saying, "Take it, eat. This is my body...broken for your sakes; given up on your behalf. Do this in remembrance of me."

Jesus also took the cup, gave thanks before God, and gave it to his disciples, saying, "All of you drink of it; for this is my blood of the new covenant, poured out for many for the forgiveness of sins. Do this as often as you drink it, in remembrance of me. I tell you, from now on I shall not drink of the fruit of the vine at all until that day when I shall drink it new with you in my Father's kingdom." They sang hymns, and went out to the Mount of Olives. (Matthew 26:26-30; Mark 14:22-26; Luke 22:17-20; I Corinthians 12:23-26)

Passover is traditionally a patriarchal family rite in which the father of a family presides. This meal does not resemble a traditional Passover Seder. During the meal, Jesus identified his body and blood (soul, or life-force in the Jewish tradition) with food and drink offered to God through word and prayer. There is no mention of the Passover lamb; the foods described are vegetarian.

Paul, who called himself an apostle to the gentiles, provides the earliest written account of the Last Supper in I Corinthians 11:20-32. He writes of the "Lord's Supper," but does not refer to a Passover meal. However, in I Corinthians 5:7, he proclaims: "Christ, our passover, has been sacrificed for us." Early Christians observed the day of Jesus' crucifixion on Nisan 14th. Claudius Appollinaris, Clement of Alexandria and Hippolytus attest to this. Jesus Christ, "the Lamb of God who takes away the sin of the world," (John 1:29) died at the same time as countless other innocent lambs of God.

A tradition soon arose, however, that Jesus was crucified on Friday. The church father Irenaeus (120-200 AD) wrote that Jesus died in obedience to God's will on the same day (Friday) Adam ate the forbidden fruit. For centuries, one of the most bitter disputes in the Christian Church was over the date of the crucifixion. Next to the Trinitarian dispute, this was the most serious issue facing the First Ecumenical Council at Nicaea in 325.

The Eastern Church had celebrated the resurrection on Nisan 16, in April, which was also the Jewish Passover. The early Christian father Lactanius wrote that Jesus was crucified on March 23, with his resurrection on the 25th. Curiously, these are the dates on which the passion, death, and resurrection of Attis, a pagan savior, had been celebrated for nearly two thousand years. The rites performed in honor of Attis closely resembled the Christians' Easter liturgy.

Jesus was arrested, tried and crucified on Thursday, Nisan 14. He died at the same time the Passover lambs were being slain in the Temple at Jerusalem. Jesus promised his disciples he would be resurrected on the third day (Sunday) from his execution. (Matthew 16:21; Mark 10:34; Luke 18:33) A trial and execution on Thursday, the day of Preparation for Passover, is therefore, more consistent with Scripture.

The Reverend Charles Gore, Bishop of Oxford, writes in *A New Commentary on Holy Scripture*: "We will assume John is right when he corrects Mark as to the nature of the Last Supper. It was not the Paschal meal proper, but a supper observed as a farewell supper with his disciples. Nor do the accounts of the supper suggest the ceremonial of the Passover meal."

In his commentary on Luke in the *Cambridge Bible for Schools*, Dean Farrar suggests the Last Supper "was not the actual Jewish Paschal meal, but one which was intended to supersede it by a Passover of far more divine significance."

Finally, many of the verses in the New Testament which refer to "meat" were mistranslated from the original Greek. The Reverend V.A. Holmes-Gore published his research on this subject in the autumn 1947 issue of *World Forum* in an article entitled "Was the Master a Vegetarian?" The following texts are examples of incorrect translations:

Matthew 3:4

"And the same John (the Baptist) had his raiment of camel's hair, and a leathern girdle about his loins, and his meat was locusts and wild honey."

The original Greek word used for "meat" here is "*broma*," which means "food." Also, the word "locusts" refers to locust beans, or carob, also known as St. John's bread.

Luke 8:55

"And her spirit came again (referring to a woman Jesus raised from the dead), and she arose straightaway: and he (Jesus) commanded to give her meat."

The word used here for "meat" is "*phago,*" meaning "to eat." Jesus commanded that she be given something to eat.

Luke 11:37

"And as he (Jesus) spake, a certain Pharisee besought him to dine with him: and he went in, and sat down to meat."

The word used here for "meat" is "*anepesen,*" or "reclined." This verse says Jesus went in and sat down.

Luke 24:41-43

"And while they yet believed not for joy, and wondered, he (Jesus) said unto them, 'Have ye here any meat?' And they gave him a piece of a broiled fish, and of a honeycomb. And he took *it,* and did eat before them."

The word used here is "*brosimos,*" or "eatable." Note the use of the word "it," which is in the last sentence and is in the singular. Jesus was offered a fish and a honeycomb, but chose only one of them.

John 4:8

"For his disciples were gone away unto the city to buy meat."

The word used here is "*trophe,*" or "nourishment."

Acts 9:19

"And when he had received meat, he was strengthened."

The word used here is "*trophe,*" or "nourishment."

Acts 16:34

"...he set meat before them, and rejoiced, believing in God with all his house."

The word used here is "*trapeza,*" or "table."

Acts 27:33-36

"And while the day was coming on, Paul besought them all to take meat, saying, 'This is the fourteenth day ye have tarried and continued fasting, taking nothing. Wherefore, I pray you to take some meat; for this is your health; for there shall not an hair fall from the head of any of you.'

"And when he had thus spoken, he took bread, and gave thanks to
God in the presence of them all: and when he had broken it, he began
to eat. Then were they all of good cheer, and they also took some
meat."

All three words used here are "*trophe,*" or "nourishment." Note that even though they have been
mistranslated to read "meat," the text shows clearly that what Paul was referring to was bread.

Romans 14:15

"But if thy brother be grieved with thy meat, now walkest thou not
charitably. Destroy him not with thy meat, for whom Christ died."

Both words used here are "*broma,*" or "food."

Romans 14:17

"For the kingdom of God is not meat and drink, but righteousness, and
peace and joy in the Holy Ghost."

The word used here is "*brosis,*" or the act of eating.

Romans 14:20-21

"For meat destroy not the work of God. All things indeed are pure, but it
is evil for that man who eateth with offense. It is good neither to eat
flesh, nor to drink wine..."

The word for "meat" used here is "*broma,*" which means "food." On the other hand, the word "flesh"
used in this text comes from the Greek "*kreas,*" which translates literally as "flesh," or "meat."

I Corinthians 6:13

"Meats for the belly, and the belly for meats, but the Lord shall destroy
both it and them. Now the body is not for fornication, but for the Lord,
and the Lord for the body."

The words used here are "*broma,*" or "food." Also, the word "*porneia,*" or fornication, is used, rather
than "*moicheia,*" adultery.

I Corinthians 8:8

"But meat commendeth us not to God, for neither, if we eat, are we the
better, neither, if we eat not, are we the worse."

The word used here is "*broma,*" or "food." This verse teaches eating itself has nothing to do with our
relationship with God.

I Corinthians 8:13

"Wherefore, if meat makes my brother to offend, I will eat no flesh while
the world standeth, lest I make my brother to offend."

The word for "meat" used here is "*broma*," or "food," while the word for "flesh" used here is "*kreas*,"
which means "flesh."

I Corinthians 10:3

"And (they) did all eat the same spiritual meat."

The word used here is "*broma*," or "food."

I Timothy 4:1-3

"Now the Spirit speaketh expressly, that in the latter times some shall
depart from the faith, giving heed to seducing spirits and doctrines of
devils; speaking lies in hypocrisy; having their conscience seared with a
hot iron; forbidding to marry, and commanding to abstain from meats,
which God hath created to be received with thanksgiving of them which
believe and know the truth."

The word used for "meat" here is "*broma*," or "food." Which food has God "created to be received with
thanksgiving"? The verse that follows:

"For everything God created is good, and nothing is to be rejected when
it is gratefully received, for it is consecrated through the word of God and
prayer."

...refers to Genesis 1:29-31: "...And God saw all that He had made and saw that it was very good."

Bible scholar Kenneth Rose says, "To use this passage to discredit Christian vegetarianism...is really a
misapplication of these verses, since the issue here is not food but Christian freedom."

The phrase "forbidding to marry" is especially significant. Paul was warning against forced asceticism; *not* vegetarianism based upon compassion for animals.

Paul's statement in I Corinthians 9:9-10, "Doth God take care for oxen, or saith He it altogether for
our sakes? For our sakes, no doubt..." is often misunderstood to mean God is indifferent towards the
animal creation. Paul was referring to Deuteronomy 25:4, a verse, like many others from the Bible,
which calls for humane treatment of animals.

Frances Arnetta, founder of Christians Helping Animals and People, explains:

"...because of the way the King James version has been translated, there is some misunderstanding as
to the meaning of Paul's words. Referring to the verse in Deuteronomy, Paul asks in I Corinthians 9,
verse 9, 'Doth God take care for oxen?' But in the original Greek, the word 'only' is implied, so that verse
9 means: 'Doth God take care *only* for oxen?' Verse 10: 'Or saith He it altogether for our sakes?' That
actually means: 'Or does He say it for the sake of us and the oxen *all together*?' Then Paul answers: 'For
our sakes (the oxen *and* us), no doubt this is written...'

"Of course God cares for oxen," insists Arnetta, "or He wouldn't have given the command to Moses in the first place." Arnetta cites Jonah 4:11, Psalm 50:10, Job 38 and 39, as well as Matthew 6:26 and Luke 12:6 as proof that God cares not only for oxen, but for His entire creation. This is consistent with I Timothy 5:17-18, where Paul again quotes Deuteronomy 25:4 in a favorable context.

chapter five
"A Perpetual Obligation"

Christianity remained a part of Judaism even after the death and resurrection of Jesus. From the Acts of the Apostles (2:22), we learn that Jesus' followers believed him to be "a man certified by God..." It was God who made Jesus Lord and Messiah (2:36), and they hoped Jesus would soon "restore the kingdom of Israel" (1:6). The first Jewish Christians went to Temple daily (2:46), celebrated the festival of Weeks (2:1), observed the Sabbath (1:12), and continued to worship the "God of Abraham, Isaac, and Jacob..." (3:13)

These Jewish Christians carried their belief in Jesus as Lord and Messiah from Jerusalem to Judea, Samaria and Galilee (1:4,8, 8:1, 9:31). Their numbers began to gradually increase. The initial 120 members of the Pentecostal assembly in Jerusalem grew to three thousand (2:41), then five thousand (4:4). Their numbers continued to grow; a great number of priests embraced the faith (6:7).

The church enjoyed peace as it was being built up. (9:31) There was a strong community spirit; they broke bread and said prayers together (2:42). They shared property (2:44,46) and lived without personal possessions (4:32). Many Pharisees came to believe in Jesus (15:5) and this Jewish messianic movement was on friendly terms with Gamaliel, a powerful and highly respected Pharisee, who intervened on their behalf (5:33).

The *Didache* or the *Teachings of the Twelve Apostles*, was a manual used by the earliest Christians. Most of the ethics of Jesus' Sermon on the Mount (Matthew 5-7) are repeated in the *Didache*.

This book teaches one to love God with all one's heart, love one's neighbor as oneself, pray for one's enemies, "turn the other cheek" if attacked or abused, and share one's possessions with one's brethren. The *Didache* admits that the gospel ethics may be too hard to observe, because it says, "If thou canst bear the whole yoke of the Lord, thou wilt be perfect; but if not, do what thou canst."

Simon (Peter) exercised authority in the early church (1:15, 2:14, 15:7). Peter's vision of a divine command to kill and eat animals (Acts 10:9-29) is often misunderstood. Frances Arnetta, a Christian vegetarian and founder of Christians helping Animals and People, explains:

"...Peter had a vision while he was very hungry. In it, he saw a huge sheet lowered from heaven containing many kinds of animals which it was not lawful for a Jew to eat. A voice said to him, 'Rise, Peter, kill and eat.' But Peter said, 'No, Lord. I have never eaten anything common or unclean.' Then the voice said, 'What God hath cleansed, call not common.' After this exchange had taken place three times, the sheet was drawn back up to heaven with the animals safe on it.

"Some mistakenly believe that Peter was literally being commanded to slay and eat the animals. But if that were the case, they would not have been taken back to heaven alive. The correct interpretation of the Scripture is this. Like the other followers of Jesus, Peter was a Jew, and he thought the Gospel of Jesus Christ was meant *only* for the nation of Israel.

"But God was showing him, through the analogy of food, which Peter, being hungry, could relate to, that Jesus died for *all* humankind, and that the Gospel was also meant to be taken to the gentiles, whom Peter considered unclean.

"The proof of this is that after reflecting on the vision, Peter was led by the Spirit of God to go to the house of Cornelius, a gentile, and he preached the Messianship of Jesus to him, saying, 'God hath shewed me that I should not call any man common or unclean.' So one cannot find a command to eat meat in this passage or in any other in the New Testament."

Chapter 15 of the Book of Acts gives an account of a dispute which had divided the early church: to what extent were the gentile converts to observe the Law of Moses? The final verdict came from James, the brother of Jesus (Matthew 13:55; Mark 6:3; Galatians 1:19). He said the gentile converts were to abstain from food offered to pagan idols, from blood, from anything that had been strangled, and from fornication. (Acts 15:29, 21:25)

These commands were not whimsically concocted; they were originally given by God Himself concerning any strangers dwelling amongst the Israelites (Leviticus 17:1-18,30). The prohibition against consuming animal blood was given by God to Noah, who was not a Jew. (Genesis 9:3) This prohibition was intended for the entire human race.

Author Joseph Benson noted, "It ought to be observed that the prohibition of eating blood, given to Noah and all his posterity, and repeated to the Israelites...has never been revoked, but, on the contrary, has been confirmed under the New Testament, Acts XV; it is, thereby, a perpetual obligation."

Christian theologian Etienne de Courcelles (1586-1659) believed the apostles had discouraged at least the eating of blood, if not meat altogether: "Although some of our brothers would reckon it a crime to shed human blood, they did not think the same against eating animal (blood). The apostles, by their decree, wished to remedy the ignorance of these persons."

Church history relates that when the early Christians were accused of eating children, a woman named Biblias (AD 177) bravely protested against such charges, even under torture: "How would such men eat children, when they are not allowed to even eat the blood of irrational animals?"

Centuries later, during the Trullan council held at Constantinople in AD 692, the following rule was established: "The eating of the blood of animals is forbidden in Holy Scripture. A cleric who partakes of blood is to be punished by deposition, a layman with excommunication."

William Bancroft Hill explains the Apostles' decree in his book, *The Apostolic Age*: "A pious Jew shrank from contact with the gentile world, because it seemed to him everywhere foul with pollution of idols, disgusting foods and licentiousness. Food offered to idols was held to be a communion with demons (Deuteronomy 32:17; I Corinthians 10:20), blood was the life element and therefore sacred to God; things strangled retained blood."

According to Hill, the rule against fornication referred not only to sex outside of marriage (I Thessalonians 4:3-5), but also to incest, which was prevalent amongst the gentiles (I Corinthians 5:1). Many temples in the gentile world also functioned as religious brothels. The apostle Paul had to warn his followers of all this. (I Corinthians 6:15,18)

Contemporary Bible scholar William Barclay describes the impact of Christianity upon gentile converts: "...Christianity would disrupt their *social* life. In the ancient world, most feasts were held in the temple of some god...part of the meat went to the priests as their prerequisite; and part of this meat was returned to the worshipper. With his share he made a feast for his friends and relations.

"One of the gods most commonly worshipped was Serapis. And when the invitations to the feast went out, they would read: 'I invite you to dine with me at the table of our Lord Serapis.' Could a Christian share in a feast held in the temple of a heathen god? Even an ordinary meal in an ordinary house began with a libation, a cup of wine, poured out in honor of the gods. It was like a grace before meat.

"Could a Christian become a sharer in a heathen act of worship like that? Again, the Christian answer was clear. The Christian must cut himself off from his fellows rather than by his presence give approval to such a thing. A man had to be prepared to be lonely in order to be a Christian."

James held a respected position in the church at Jerusalem (Acts 12:17, 15:13, 21:18). According to Albert Henry Newman in *A Manual of Church History*, "Peter had compromised himself in the eyes of the Jewish Christians by eating with gentiles. (Acts 11:1-3) James thus came to be the leader of the church at Jerusalem. It seems he never abandoned the view that it was vital for Christian Jews to observe the Law. He supported missionary work among the gentiles, and agreed to recognize gentile converts without circumcision, but as a Jew he felt obliged to practice the whole Law and require Jewish converts to do the same."

Later Christian writers (Clement of Alexandria, Eusebius, etc.) called James the Bishop of Jerusalem. However, this term was not used in the early days of Christianity. James' authority came about because of the strength of his character, his relationship to Jesus, and his staunch adherence to Judaism. He had a reputation of purity among the Jews, and was known as "James the Just." The church historian Eusebius, in his *Church History*, Book II, Chapter 23, quotes from the early church father Hegisuppus' 5th book of "Memoirs" (AD 160). James, the brother of Jesus, was holy from birth. He never drank wine, nor ate the flesh of animals, nor had a razor touch his head.

"Both Hegisuppus and Augustine, 'orthodox' sources, testify that James was not only a vegetarian, but was *raised* a vegetarian," writes Keith Akers in the 1986 edition of *A Vegetarian Sourcebook*. "If Jesus' parents raised James as a vegetarian, why would they not also be vegetarians themselves, and raise Jesus as a vegetarian?"

James wrote an epistle refuting Paul's interpretation of salvation by faith. James stressed obedience to Jewish Law (James 2:8-13), and concluded that "faith without works is dead." (2:26) When Paul, who used to persecute Jesus' followers, visited the church at Jerusalem, James and the elders told him all its members were "zealous for the Law." They reminded Paul that the gentile converts were to abstain from idols, blood, strangled meat, and fornication. (Acts 21:20,25)

From both history and the epistles of Paul, we learn there was an extreme Judaizing faction within the early church that insisted all new converts to the faith be circumcised and observe Mosaic Law. This must have been the original (Jewish) faction of Christianity. These Jewish Christians eventually became known as "Ebionites," or "the poor." Jesus' teachings focus on poverty and nonviolence. Jesus preached both the renunciation of worldly possessions in favor of a life of simplicity and voluntary poverty, as well as acts of mercy towards the less fortunate. In his epistles, Paul referred to the poor among the saints at Jerusalem (Romans 15:26; Galatians 2:10).

Jesus blessed the poor, the meek, the humble and the persecuted. His brother James wrote: "Listen, my dear brothers. Has not God chosen the poor in the world to be rich in faith and to be heirs of the kingdom He has promised to those who love Him?" (James 2:5) The Ebionites took note of biblical passages in which the people of Israel are called "the poor." For them, this was a designation of the true Israel; the pious amongst the people. The Ebionites connected the Beatitudes (Luke 6:20) with themselves.

They read from a Hebrew version of the Gospel of Matthew, perhaps the earliest written gospel; now lost to us, except in fragments. They believed Jesus to have been a man gifted with Messianship by the grace of God; at the time of his baptism, the Holy Spirit descended upon him like a dove. The voice of God then proclaimed, "Thou art My beloved son, this day I have begotten thee." (Hebrews 1:5, 5:5) Jesus was no longer a mere mortal, but the "elect of God," greater than all the angels. (Hebrews 1:4-5)

The Ebionites were strict vegetarians. Their Gospel describes the food of John the Baptist as wild honey and cakes made from oil and honey. The Greek word for oil cake is "*enkris*," while the Greek word for locust is "*akris*" (Mark 1:6). This suggests an error in translation from the original Hebrew into the Greek. In the Gospel of the Ebionites, when the disciples ask Jesus where they should prepare the Passover, Jesus replies, "Have I desired with desire to eat this flesh of the Passover with you?" According to the Ebionites, Jesus was a vegetarian.

The Ebionites taught that Jesus did not come to abolish the Law and the Prophets (Matthew 5:17-19; Luke 16:17), but only the institution of animal sacrifice (Matthew 9:13, 12:7; Hebrews 10:5-10). The Ebionite Gospel of Matthew quotes Jesus as saying, "I came to destroy the sacrifices, and if ye cease not from sacrificing, the wrath of God will not cease from you."

According to the Ebionites, animal sacrifice was a pagan custom which became incorporated into

Mosaic Law. In Jeremiah 7:21-22, God says: "Add whole-offerings to sacrifices and eat the flesh if you will. But when I brought your forefathers out of Egypt, I gave them no commands about whole-offerings and sacrifice; I said not a word about them." Abba Hillel Silver, in his 1961 book, *Moses and the Original Torah*, documents that God never commanded the Israelites to sacrifice animals. There is an echo of this in the New Testament in the speech of Stephen, the first Christian martyr. Stephen quotes Amos 5:25-27 (at Acts 7:42-43), which implies that no sacrifices were ever made by the Israelites in the desert. Most Christians today would naturally deny that sacrifices were necessary, but Stephen is the only person in the entire New Testament to imply that Mosaic Law never condoned animal sacrifice in the first place.

Ernest Renan's controversial 19th century book, *The Life of Jesus*, was one of the first secular studies of Jesus and the history of Christianity. Renan described Jesus as the very human child of Joseph and Mary. According to Renan, "Pure Ebionism" was the original doctrine of Jesus. Renan depicted Jesus as seeking "the abolition of the sacrifices which had caused him so much disgust...", and wrote, "The worship which he had conceived for his Father had nothing in common with scenes of butchery."

Reverend Norman Moorhouse, of the Church of England, admits: "There is an ancient tradition that Jesus was a vegetarian. Whether this is actually true I do not know. But I would go as far as to say that St. John the Baptist was a vegetarian, and those who belonged to the same sect as he. And, of course, in the Old Testament we have the example of Daniel, who lived as a vegetarian...So the Christians are many times bidden to be vegetarian. Adam and Eve, before they fell, lived a simple life by eating those things that God provided for them. They didn't kill animals for food. We should all try to get back to that way of life..."

According to Christian scholar Dr. Edgar J. Goodspeed, "Symmachus, the first Christian translator of the Old Testament into Greek, in the days of Marcus Aurelius (AD 161-80) was an Ebionite; in fact he made his translation for the Greek-speaking Jewish Christians of that sect."

We learn from the early church fathers that the Ebionites followed Torah, or Jewish Law, practiced chastity, circumcision and baptism. To them, baptism was vital, because it was through baptism that Jesus became adopted as God's son. They observed a Saturday Sabbath and celebrated the Eucharist with unleavened bread and water. The devil and temptation rule this world (compare II Corinthians 4:4), but Jesus would rule in the world to come; as such, they instructed their followers to abandon all worldly possessions.

The early church fathers tell us the Ebionites revered James and rejected Paul as both a false prophet and an apostate from Judaism. As an apostle to the gentiles, Paul acknowledged that the gospel was first intended for the Jews (Romans 1:16), and that the Jews have advantage over the gentiles in every respect, because they were entrusted with the utterances of God (3:1-2). Paul admitted that the gentiles "have no knowledge of God." (I Thessalonians 4:3-5)

According to Paul, "Circumcision has no value...but the observance of God's commandments does count." (I Corinthians 7:19) Paul taught his followers to bless their persecutors and not curse them (Romans 12:14), to care for their enemies by providing them with food and drink (12:20), and to pay their taxes and obey all earthly governments (13:1-7). He mentioned giving all his belongings to feed the hungry (I Corinthians 13:3), and taught giving to the person in need (Ephesians 4:28). He told his followers it was wrong to take their conflicts before non-Christian courts rather than before the saints. (I Corinthians 6:1)

Paul taught that it is best to be celibate, but because of prevailing immoralities, marriage is an acceptable alternative. Divorce, however, is not permissible, except in the case of an unbeliever demanding separation. (I Corinthians 7) Paul repeatedly attacked sexual immorality (I Corinthians 6:15,18; I Thessalonians 4:3-5). He told his followers not to associate with sexually immoral people (I

Corinthians 5:9-12). He condemned homosexuality (Romans 1:24-27) and incest (I Corinthians 5:1). He taught that profligates, idolaters, adulterers and robbers will not inherit the kingdom of God. (I Corinthians 6:9-10)

Paul taught that the entire creation exists not for man's exploitation, but for the glory of God through Jesus. "For through him all things were created in heaven and on earth, the visible and the invisible, whether thrones or lordships or rulers or authorities; they are all created through him and for him, and he is himself before all, and in him all things hold together."

Paul condemned wickedness, immorality, depravity, greed, envy, murder, quarreling, deceit, malignity, gossip, slander, insolence, pride (Romans 1:29-30), drunkenness, carousing, debauchery, jealousy (Romans 13:13), sensuality, magic arts, animosities, bad temper, selfishness, dissensions, envy (Galatians 5:19-21); greediness (Ephesians 4:19; Colossians 3:5), foul speech, anger, clamor, abusive language, malice (Ephesians 4:29-32), dishonesty (Colossians 3:13), materialism (I Timothy 6:6-11), conceit, avarice, boasting and treachery. (II Timothy 3:2-4)

Paul told the gentiles to train themselves for godliness, to practice self-control and lead upright, godly lives (Galatians 5:23; I Timothy 4:7; II Timothy 1:7; Titus 2:11-12). He instructed them to pray constantly. (I Thessalonians 5:17)

Paul praised love, joy, peace, kindness, generosity, fidelity and gentleness (Galatians 5:22-23). He told his followers to conduct themselves with humility and gentleness (Ephesians 4:2), to speak to one another in psalms and hymns; to sing heartily and make music to the Lord (Ephesians 5:19; Colossians 3:16).

Paul wrote further that women should cover their heads while worshipping, and that long hair on males is dishonorable. (I Corinthians 11:5-14) According to Paul, Christian women are to dress modestly and prudently, and are not to be adorned with braided hair, gold or pearls or expensive clothes. (I Timothy 2:9)

Paul repeatedly attacked idolatry. (Romans 1:23; I Corinthians 6:9-10; II Corinthians 6:16; Galatians 5:19-21) He recognized the immorality of accepting food offered to idols and pagan gods: "...that which they sacrifice they are offering to demons and not to God, and I do not want you to have fellowship with demons." (I Corinthians 10:20) Yet Paul then proceeded to give his followers permission to eat food offered to pagan idols! "You may eat anything sold in the meat market without raising questions of conscience; for the earth is the Lord's and everything in it." (I Corinthians 10:14-33)

Paul told his followers they need only abstain from such foods if it offends their "weaker" brethren: "For if someone sees you...sitting at the table in an idol temple, will not his conscience, weak as it is, encourage him to eat food offered to idols?...If my eating causes my brother to stumble, I shall eat no meat for ever, so that my brother will not be made to fall into sin." (I Corinthians 8:1-13)

Not only does this contradict the Apostles' decree concerning gentile converts (Acts 15), it contradicts the teachings of Jesus himself. In Revelations 2:14-16,20, the resurrected Jesus specifically instructs John to write to two churches that they not eat food offered to idols. Secular historian Dr. Martin A. Larson writes in *The Story of Christian Origins* that the seven Asian churches Jesus wrote to (Revelation 1:4) were Jewish Christian churches that had repudiated Paul. (II Timothy 1:15)

Paul, who once persecuted the brethren, openly identified himself a Roman (Acts 22:25-26) and an apostate from Judaism (Philippians 3:4-8). Jesus, on the other hand, insisted that even seemingly insignificant demands from the Law of Moses could not be set aside. (Matthew 5:17-19; Luke 16:17) It is difficult to tell at times if Paul rejected the entire Law or only its Pharisaic excesses, since he quoted the Law as spiritual authority (e.g., I Corinthians 14:21,34). On at least one occasion, he acknowledged the Law to be spiritual, but admitted his own inability to observe it. (Romans 7:12,14-25)

On another occasion, Paul stated that laws are laid down for the lawless: morality is meant for those who would otherwise lack morals. (I Timothy 1:8-11) Many of Paul's statements are not against the Law itself, but against the hypocrisy with which it was being enforced or observed (Galatians 2:1-14), and the fact that the gentiles were not obliged to follow all of Mosaic Law. (Acts 15)

According to writer Holger Kersten:

"What we refer to as Christianity today is largely an artificial doctrine of rules and precepts, created by Paul and more worthy of the designation 'Paulinism.'

"The church historian Wilhelm Nestle expressed the issue in the following manner, 'Christianity is the religion founded by Paul; it replaced Christ's gospel with a gospel about Christ.'

"Paulinism in this sense means a misinterpretation and indeed counterfeiting of Christ's actual teachings, as arranged and initiated by Paul.

"It has long been a truism for modern theologians as well as researchers on ecclesiastical history that the Christianity of the organized Church, with its central tenet of salvation through the death and suffering of Jesus, has been based on a misinterpretation. 'All the good in Christianity can be traced to Jesus, all the bad to Paul,' wrote the theologian Overbeck.

"By building on the belief of salvation through the expiatory death of God's first-born in a bloody sacrifice, Paul regressed to the primitive Semitic religions of earlier times, in which parents were commanded to give up their first-born in a bloody sacrifice.

"Paul also prepared the path for the later ecclesiastical teachings on original sin and the trinity. As long ago as the 18th century, the English philosopher Lord Bolingbroke (1678-1751) could make out two completely different religions in the New Testament, that of Jesus and that of Paul. Kant, Lessing, Fichte and Schelling also sharply distinguish the teachings of Jesus from those of the 'disciples.' A great number of reputable modern theologians support and defend these observations."

The Reverend J. Todd Ferrier, founder of the Order of the Cross, wrote in 1903:

"But Paul, great and noble man as he was, never was one of the recognized heads at Jerusalem. He had been a Pharisee of the Pharisees...He strove to be all things to all men that he might gain some. And we admire him for his strenuous endeavors to win the world for Christ. But no one could be all things to all men without running the great risks of most disastrous results...

"But here as a further thought in connection with the teaching of the great Apostle an important question is forced upon our attention, which one of these days must receive the due consideration from biblical scholars that it deserves. It is this:

> "How is it that the gospel of Paul is more to many people than the gospel of
> those privileged souls who sat at the feet of Jesus and heard His secrets in
> the Upper Room?"

Christian theologian Dr. Upton Clary Ewing also says, "With all due respect for the integrity of Paul, he was not one of the Twelve Apostles...Paul never knew Jesus in life. He never walked and prayed with Him as He went from place to place, teaching the word of God."

Paul's writings indicate that vegetarianism was a tenet of early Christianity and debate about foods were widespread in a church that Paul sought to make more open to gentiles (Romans 14; Colossians 2:16). Paul thus characterized his vegetarian brethren as "weak." Paul told his gentile followers that it is best to abstain from meat or from food offered to idols so as not to offend the "weaker" brethren. (I Corinthians 8:1-13)

Paul's use of the word "weak" has been debated. Dr. Upton Clary Ewing believes Paul used the word "weak" with a positive connotation. According to Paul, "God has chosen the weak things in the world to shame the strong." (I Corinthians 1:27)

Describing his tribulations for the cause of Christ, being caught up in the heavenly spheres, and a revelation from Jesus, Paul wrote:

"If I must boast, I shall boast of matters that show my weakness...I will boast, but not about myself—unless it be about my weakness...the Lord...he told me, '...my strength comes to perfection where there is weakness.' Therefore," Paul concluded, "I am happy to boast in my weaknesses...I delight, then, in weaknesses...for when I am weak, then I am strong." (II Corinthians 11:30, 12:1-10)

Paul wrote further that Jesus "was crucified out of weakness, yet he lives through divine power, and we, too, are weak in him; but we shall live with him for your benefit through the power of God...We are happy to be weak when you are strong." (II Corinthians 13:4,9)

Taken in this context, the word "weak" suggests complete dependence upon God.

Frances Arnetta, herself a Christian vegetarian, explains the traditional Christian interpretation of Romans 14 and I Corinthians 8 as follows:

"Paul deals at length with the subject of meat-eating versus vegetarianism in Romans, chapter 14 (happily, indicating a widespread interest in the subject at the time). Basically, his message is that one should not be judgemental towards another in respect to diet, because it is our free choice whether or not to eat meat.

"Paul was always careful not to put conditions on those coming into the faith, since God's Grace (forgiveness and salvation) is a free gift for the asking, not to be earned by good works. He makes it clear that it is wrong to eat meat only if it violates one's own conscience or causes another to violate his or her conscience...

"Paul admonishes believers that if their meat-eating offends someone, they should refrain from eating meat. While we should never try to force another into a particular lifestyle, we can certainly educate and encourage others into vegetarianism..."

Gentile followers of Jesus address him as "Christ," which means "Messiah." The Bible teaches that with the coming of God's annointed one will be the establishment of the Kingdom of Peace on earth. The prophecies of Isaiah 11:6-9 indicate this new world will in many ways resemble the Garden of Eden (Genesis 1:29-31), where everyone was vegetarian.

Christ's return, Judgement Day, and the creation of a new heaven and a new earth were believed to be imminent. The earliest generations of Christians lived with this expectation. (Matthew 24:29-25:46; Mark 13:24-37; Luke 21:25-36; I Thessalonians 4:13-18; James 5:7-9; I Peter 5:7; II Peter 3:3-12; I John 2:18; Jude 17-18; Revelations 22:20) Vegetarianism was practiced in expectation of Christ's coming kingdom. Among the various early Christian sects, the Montanists practiced vegetarianism with the belief that Christ would soon return.

From history, we learn that the earliest Christians were vegetarian. For example, Clemens Prudentius, the first Christian hymn writer, in one of his hymns exhorts his fellow Christians not to pollute their hands and hearts by the slaughter of innocent cows and sheep, and points to the variety of nourishing and pleasant foods obtainable without blood-shedding.

Seneca (5 BC - 65 AD), a leading Stoic philosopher and a tutor of Nero, was an ardent vegetarian. He started a vegetarian movement during one of Rome's most decadent periods. Yet he had to abandon his cause. The early Christians were vegetarian. The Emperor became suspicious that Seneca might also be a Christian, so Seneca went back to eating animal flesh. He wrote:

> "Certain foreign religions (Christianity) became the object of the
> imperial suspicion and amongst the proofs of adherence to the foreign
> culture or superstition was that of abstinence from the flesh of animals.

At the earnest entreaty of my father, I was induced to return to my former habits."

Pliny, who was Governor of Bithynia, where Peter had preached, wrote a letter to Trajan, the Roman Emperor, describing the early Christian practices:

"...they met on a day before it was light (before sunrise) and addressed a form of prayer to Christ as to a god, binding themselves by a solemn oath never to commit any sin or evil and never to falsify their word, nor deny a trust, after which it was their custom to meet together again to take food, but ordinary and innocent food."

The church father Irenaeus preserved a fragment of a quote by Papias, disciple of John the Evangelist:

"Papias related how the elders and John and heard the Lord teach that creation renewed and liberated shall yield an abundance of all kinds of food, seeds, grass, fruits, grains, and flour in corresponding proportion, and that all animals will use these foods and become in turn peaceful and in harmony with another and with man."

This teaching of Jesus corresponds to the visions of peace and vegetarianism given in Isaiah (11:6-9, 65:25). Clement I, Bishop of Rome, in an epistle to the Corinthians (AD 88-97) wrote: "Perrenial springs, created for enjoyment...offer their life giving breasts to man and even the smallest of animals that they get together in peace. All things the Creator ordered to be in peace and harmony...take refuge through our Lord Jesus Christ."

The *Clementine Homilies*, Jewish Christian teachings written during the 2nd century, give us a picture of the life of Clement I, Bishop of Rome. Clement is portrayed as a spiritual seeker, going to various schools of thought, looking for solutions to his doubts about the origin of the world, the immortality of the soul, etc... Eventually, he hears about how Jesus appeared in Judea. He undertakes a long journey through Egypt to Palestine, where he meets the apostle Peter in Caesarea. Clement becomes a Christian and is invited by (Simon) Peter to accompany him on his missionary journeys.

The text includes debates between Peter and Simon Magus. Peter refers to Jesus as "Teacher" and "Master," teaches Clement to love his enemies and persecutors, insists upon the renunciation of worldly goods, and connects flesh-eating to idolatry. In the *Clementine Homilies*, we read:

"The unnatural eating of flesh-meats is as polluting as the heathen worship of devils, with its sacrifices and impure feasts, through participation in which a man becomes a fellow-eater with devils."

Genesis 6 describes the "sons of the gods" (angels) having sexual intercourse with the daughters of men, and giving rise to a race of giants. The *Clementine Homilies* explain that the eating of animal flesh began with this perversion:

"...from their unhallowed intercourse spurious men sprang, much greater in stature than ordinary men, whom they afterwards called

> giants...wild in manners, and greater than men in size, insamuch as they were sprung of angels; yet less than angels, as they were born of men.

> "Therefore God, knowing that they were barbarized to brutality, and that the world was not sufficient to satisfy them (for it was created according to the proportion of men and human use), that they might not through want of food turn, *contrary to nature, to the eating of animals*, and yet seem to be blameless, as having ventured upon this through necessity, the Almighty God rained manna upon them, suited to their variant tastes; and they enjoyed all that they would.

> "But they, on account of their bastard nature, not being pleased with purity of food, longed only after the taste of blood. Wherefore they first tasted flesh."

The apocryphal *Acts of Thomas* was used by many of the early Christian sects. Dr. Edgar J. Goodspeed, in his book *History of Early Christian Literature*, writes that this scripture depicts the disciple of Jesus as an ascetic: "He continually fasts and prays, wears the same garment in all weather; accepts nothing from anyone; gives what he has to others, and abstains from meat and wine." Abstinence from animal flesh thus came to be regarded in gentile Christianity as abstinence from luxury and sensuality; asceticism. The apocryphal *Shepherd of Hermas*, written in the 1st century, says:

> "...it is an evil desire to covet another's wife; as also to desire the dainties of riches; and a multitude of superfluous meats and drunkenness... Whosoever therefore shall depart from all evil desires, shall live unto God; but they that are subject unto them shall die forever. For this evil lusting is deadly."

> — *2 Hermas 12:4-6*

The early church father Origen (AD 185-254), a vegetarian, explained: "when we do abstain (from eating meat), we do so because 'we keep under our body and bring it into subjection' (I Corinthians 9:27), and desire 'to mortify our members that are upon the earth, fornication, uncleanness, inordinate affection, evil concupiscence' (Colossians 3:5); and we use every effort to 'mortify the deeds of the flesh.' (Romans 8:13)"

One of the greatest theologians in the early Christian church, Tertullian, or Quintus Septimius Florens Tertullianus, was born in Carthage about AD 155-160. Cyprian, the Bishop of Carthage, called him the "Master." Tertullian was one of four early church fathers who wrote extensively on the subject of vegetarianism. According to Tertullian, flesh-eating is not conducive to the highest life, it violates moral law, and it debases man in intellect and emotion.

Responding to the apparent permissiveness of Paul, Tertullian argued: "and even if he handed over to you the keys of the slaughter house...in permitting you to eat all things...at least he has not made the kingdom of Heaven to consist in *butchery*: for, says he, eating and drinking is not the Kingdom of God."

Tertullian similarly scorned those who would use the gospel to justify gratifying the cravings of the flesh:

"How unworthily, too, do you press the example of Christ as having come 'eating and drinking' into the service of your lusts: He who pronounced not the full but the hungry and thirsty 'blessed,' who professed His work to be the completion of His Father's will, *was wont to abstain*—instructing them to labor for that 'meat' which lasts to eternal life, and enjoining in their common prayers petition not for gross food but for bread only."

Tertullian made his case for moderate eating by referring to the history of the Israelites (Numbers 11:4-34):

"And if there be 'One' who prefers the works of justice, not however, without sacrifice—that is to say, a spirit exercised by abstinence—it is surely that God to whom neither a gluttonous people nor priest was acceptable—monuments of whose concupiscence remain to this day, where lies buried a people greedy and clamorous for flesh-meats, gorging quails even to the point of inducing jaundice.

"It was divinely proclaimed," insisted Tertullian, "'Wine and strong liquor shall you not drink, you and your sons after you.' Now this prohibition of drink is essentially connected with the vegetable diet. Thus, where abstinence from wine is required by the Deity, or is vowed by man, there, too, may be understood suppression of gross feeding, *for as is the eating, so is the drinking.*

"It is not consistent with truth that a man should sacrifice half of his stomach only to God—that he should be sober in drinking, but intemperate in eating. Your belly is your God, your liver is your temple, your paunch is your altar, the cook is your priest, and the fat steam is your Holy Spirit; the seasonings and the sauces are your chrisms, and your belchings are your prophesizing..."

Tertullian sarcastically compared gluttons to Esau, who sold his birthright in exchange for a meal:

"I ever recognize Esau, the hunter, as a man of taste and as his were, so are your whole skill and interest given to hunting and trapping...It is in the cooking pots that your love is inflamed—it is in the kitchen that your faith grows fervid—it is in the flesh dishes that all your hopes lie hid...Consistently do you men of the flesh reject the things of the Spirit. But if your prophets are complacent towards such persons, they are not my prophets...

"Let us openly and boldly vindicate our teaching. We are sure that they who are in the flesh cannot please God...a grossly-feeding Christian is akin to lions and wolves rather than God. Our Lord Jesus called Himself Truth and not habit."

In general, Tertullian railed against gluttony, and taught that spiritual life consists of simple living. He explained, "if man could not follow even a simple taboo against eating one fruit, how could he be expected to restrain himself from more demanding restrictions? Instead, after the Flood, man was given the regulation against blood; further details were length to his own strength of will."

According to Tertullian, the entire creation prays to God:

"Cattle and wild beasts pray, and bend their knees, and in coming forth from their stalls and lairs look up to heaven. Moreover the birds taking flight lift themselves up to heaven and instead of hands, spread out the cross of their wings, while saying something which may be supposed to be a prayer."

In his commentary on the Book of Daniel, Hippolytus (AD 200) depicted the Biblical hero and his three companions as pious ascetics. Referring to the passage in Scripture which states that these four men did not wish to defile themselves with the king's meat, Hippolytus equated the purity of their vegetarian diet with the purity of their thoughts: "These, though captives in a strange land, were not seduced by delicate meats, nor were they slaves to the pleasures of wine, nor were they caught by the bait of princely glory. But they kept their mouth holy and pure, that pure speech might proceed from pure mouths, and praise with such (mouths) the Heavenly Father."

Clement of Alexandria (AD 150-220), or Titus Flavius Clemens, founded the Alexandrian school of Christian Theology and succeeded Pantaenus in AD 190. In his writings, he referred to vegetarian philosophers Pythagoras, Plato, and even Socrates as divinely inspired. But the true teachings, he insisted, are to be found in the Hebrew prophets and in the person of Jesus Christ.

Clement taught that a life of virtue is one of simplicity, and that the apostle Matthew was a vegetarian. According to Clement, eating flesh and drinking wine "is rather characteristic to a beast and the fumes rising from them, being dense, darken the soul...Destroy not the work of God for the sake of food. Whether ye eat or drink, do all to the glory of God, aiming after true frugality. For it is lawful for me to partake of all things, yet all things are not expedient...neither is the regimen of a Christian formed by indulgence...man is not by nature a gravy eater, but a bread eater.

"Those who use the most frugal fare are the strongest, the healthiest and the noblest...We must guard against those sorts of food which persuade us to eat when we are not hungry," warned Clement, "bewitching the appetite...is there not within a temperate simplicity, a wholesome variety of eatables— vegetables, roots, olives, herbs, milk, cheese, fruits...?

"But those who bend around inflammatory tables, nourishing their own diseases, are ruled by a most licentious disease which I shall venture to call the demon of the belly: the worst and most vile of demons. It is far better to be happy than to have a devil dwelling in us, for happiness is found only in the practice of virtue. Accordingly the apostle Matthew lived upon seeds, fruits, grains and nuts and vegetables, without the use of flesh."

Clement acknowledged the moral and spiritual advantages of the vegetarian way of life: "If any righteous man does not burden his soul by the eating of flesh, he has the advantage of a rational motive...The very ancient altar of Delos was celebrated for its purity, to which alone, as being undefiled by slaughter and death, they say that Pythagoras would permit approach. "And they will not believe us when we say that the *righteous soul* is the truly sacred altar? But I believe that sacrifices were invented by men to be a pretext for eating flesh."

St. Basil (AD 320-79) taught, "The steam of meat darkens the light of the spirit. One can hardly have virtue if one enjoys meat meals and feasts...In the earthly paradise, there was no wine, no one sacrificed animals, and no one ate meat. Wine was only invented after the Deluge...

"With simple living, well being increases in the household, animals are in safety, there is no shedding of blood, nor putting animals to death. The knife of the cook is needless, for the table is spread only with the fruits that nature gives, and with them they are content."

St. Basil prayed for universal brotherhood, and an end to human brutality against animals:

> "The earth is the Lord's and the fullness
> Thereof. Oh, God, enlarge within us the
> Sense of fellowship with all living
> Things, our brothers the animals to
> Whom Thou gavest the earth as
> Their home in common with us
>
> "We remember with shame that
> In the past we have exercised the
> High dominion of man and ruthless
> Cruelty so that the voice of the earth
> Which should have gone up to Thee in
> Song, has been a groan of travail.
>
> May we realize that they live not
> For us alone but for themselves and
> For Thee and that they love the sweetness
> Of life."

According to St. Gregory Nazianzen (AD 330-89):

> "The great Son is the glory of the Father and shone out from Him like light...He assumed a body *to bring help to suffering creatures...*

> "He was sacrifice and celebrant sacrificial priest and God Himself. He offered blood to God to cleanse the entire world."

"Holy people are most loving and gentle in their dealings with their fellows, and even with the lower animals: for this reason it was said that 'A righteous man is merciful to the life of his beast,'" explained St. John Chrysostom (AD 347-407). "Surely we ought to show kindness and gentleness to animals for many reasons and chiefly because they are of the same origin as ourselves."

Writing about the Christian saints and ascetics, Chrysostom observed: "No streams of blood are among them; no butchering and cutting of flesh...With their repast of fruits and vegetables even angels from heaven, as they behold it, are delighted and pleased."

Chrysostom considered flesh-eating a cruel and unnatural habit for Christians: "We imitate the ways of wolves, the ways of leopards, or rather we are worse than these. For nature has assigned that they should be thus fed, but us God hath honored with speech and a sense of equity, yet we are worse than the wild beasts."

In a homily on Matthew 22:1-4, Chrysostom taught: "We the Christian leaders practice abstinence from the flesh of animals to subdue our bodies...the unnatural eating of flesh-meat is of demonical origin...the eating of flesh is polluting." He added that "flesh-meats and wine serve as materials for sensuality, and are a source of danger, sorrow, and disease."

In a homily on II Corinthians 9, Chrysostom distinguished between nourishment and gluttony:

"No one debars thee from these, nor forbids thee thy daily food. I say 'food,' not 'feasting'; 'raiment' not 'ornament,'...For consider, who should we say more truly feasted—he whose diet is herbs, and who is in sound health and suffered no uneasiness, or he who has the table of a Sybarite and is full of a thousand disorders?

"Certainly the former. Therefore, let us seek nothing more than these, if we would at once live luxuriously and healthfully. And let him who can be satisfied with pulse, and can keep in good health, seek for nothing more. But let him who is weaker, and needs to be dieted with other vegetable fruits, not be debarred from them."

In a homily on the Epistle to Timothy, Chrysostom described the ill effects of becoming a slave to one's bodily appetites:

"A man who lives in selfish luxury is dead while he lives, for he lives only to his stomach. In other senses he lives not. He sees not what he ought to see; he hears not what he ought to hear; he speaks not what he ought to speak. Nor does he perform the actions of living.

"But as he who is stretched upon a bed with his eyes closed and his eyelids fast, perceives nothing that is passing; so is it with this man, or rather not so, but worse. For the one is equally insensible to things good and evil, while the other is sensible to things evil only, but as insensible as the former to things good.

"Thus he is dead. For nothing relating to the life to come moves or affects him. For intemperance, taking him into her own bosom as into some dark and dismal cavern full of all uncleanliness, causes him to dwell altogether in darkness, like the dead. For, when all his time is spent between feasting and drunkenness, is he not dead, and buried in darkness?

"Who can describe the storm that comes of luxury, that assails the soul and body? For, as a sky continually clouded admits not the sunbeams to shine through, so the fumes of luxury...envelop his brain...and casting over it a thick mist, suffers not reason to exert itself.

"If it were possible to bring the soul into view and to behold it with our bodily eyes—it would seem depressed, mournful, miserable, and wasted with leanness; for the more the body grows sleek and gross, the more lean and weakly is the soul. The more one is pampered, the more the other is hampered."

The orthodox, 4th century Christian Hieronymus connected vegetarianism with both the original diet given by God and the teachings of Jesus:

"The eating of animal meat was unknown up to the big Flood, but since the Flood they have pushed the strings and stinking juices of animal meat into our mouths, just as they threw quails in front of the grumbling sensual people in the desert. Jesus Christ, who appeared when the time had been fulfilled, has again joined the end with the beginning, so that it is no longer allowed for us to eat animal meat."

St. Jerome (AD 340-420) wrote to a monk in Milan who had abandoned vegetarianism:
"As to the argument that in God's second blessing (Genesis 9:3) permission was given to eat flesh—a permission not given in the first blessing (Genesis 1:29)—let him know that just as permission to put away a wife was, according to the words of the Saviour, not given from the beginning, but was granted to the human race by Moses because of the hardness of our hearts (Matthew 19:1-12), so also in like manner the eating of flesh was unknown until the Flood, but after the Flood, just as quails were given to the people when they murmured in the desert, so have sinews and the offensiveness been given to our teeth.

"The Apostle, writing to the Ephesians, teaches us that God had purposed that in the fullness of time he would restore all things, and would draw to their beginning, even to Christ Jesus, all things that are in heaven or that are on earth. Whence also, the Saviour Himself in the Apocalypse of John says, 'I am the Alpha and Omega, the beginning and the end.' From the beginning of human nature, we neither fed upon flesh nor did we put away our wives, nor were our foreskins taken away from us for a sign. We kept on this course until we arrived at the Flood.

"But after the Flood, together with the giving of the Law, which no man could fulfill, the eating of flesh was brought in, and the putting away of wives was conceded to hardness of heart...But now that Christ has come in the end of time, and has turned back Omega to Alpha...neither is it permitted to us to put away our wives, nor are we circumcised, nor do we eat flesh."

St. Jerome was responsible for the Vulgate, or Latin version of the Bible, still in use today. He felt a vegetarian diet was best for those devoted to the pursuit of wisdom. He once wrote that he was not a follower of Pythagoras or Empodocles "who do not eat any living creature," but concluded, "And so I too say to you: if you wish to be perfect, it is good not to drink wine and eat flesh."

The 4th century St. Blaise is said to have established an animal hospital in the wilderness. The wildlife, in turn, protected him. St. Patrick (389?-481?) is said to have saved a mother deer and her baby from hunters. Commentators say it was this act of compassion which led to the conversion of the pagan.

"By saving the fawn they were about to kill," writes Richard Power in *The Ark*, St. Patrick made the Christian religion meaningful to the hardened Ulster warriors. Before that act of compassion, his preaching had failed to convince them." (*The Ark* is a bulletin published by the Catholic Study Circle for Animal Welfare.)

St. Ciaran of Ossory noted in the 5th Century that animals have intrinsic rights because of their capacity to feel pleasure and pain. Butler's four-volume *Lives of the Saints* describes many saints as abstinent from childhood, never eating flesh-meats, never touching meat or wine, compassionate to all creatures, etc.

According to Father Ambrose Agius:

"Many of the saints understood God's creatures, and together they shared the pattern of obedience to law and praise of God that still leaves us wondering. The quickest way to understand is surely to bring our own lives as closely as possible into line with the intention of the Giver of all life, animate and inanimate."

The Reverend Alvin Hart, an Episcopalian priest in New York, says:

"Many Georgian saints were distinguished by their love for animals. St. John Zedazneli made friends with bears near his hermitage; St. Shio befriended a wolf; St. David of Garesja protected deer and birds from hunters, proclaiming, 'He whom I believe in and worship looks after and feeds all these creatures, to whom He has given birth.' Early Celtic saints, too, favored compassion for animals. Saints Wales, Cornwall and Brittany of Ireland in the 5th and 6th centuries AD went to great pains for their animal friends, healing them and praying for them as well."

St. Benedict, who founded the Benedictine Order in AD 529, permitted meat only in times of sickness, and made vegetarian foods the staple for his monks, teaching, "Nothing is more contrary to the Christian spirit than gluttony." The *Rule of St. Benedict* itself is a composite of ascetic teachings from previous traditions, such as St. Anthony's monasticism in Egypt, which called for abstinence from meat and wine.

Aegidius (c. 700) was a vegetarian who lived on herbs, water and the milk of a deer God sent to him. St. Werburgh of Chester made a deal with some geese that were damaging church property. Werburgh promised that no action would be taken against the geese if they left and ceased to cause trouble. But when one of her attendants unwittingly killed one of the geese, the others returned. They came back honking and protesting loudly, until St. Werburgh brought the animal back to life.

In the 7th century, the hermit monk St. Giles was an Athenian, who resided in a French forest, dwelling in a cave, and living on herbs, nuts, and fruits. One day the King of France came hunting in the forest. He pursued a young deer which took refuge in Giles' arms. The King was so impressed with Giles' holiness he begged forgiveness and built him a monastery. Boniface (672-754) wrote to Pope Zacharias that he had begun a monastery which followed the rules of strict abstinence, whose monks do not eat meat nor enjoy wine or other intoxicating drinks. St. Andrew lived on herbs, olives, oil and bread. He lived to be 105.

The early English mystic St. Guthlac of Crowland (673-714) is said to have been able to call birds in to feed from his hand. "Hast thou never learned in Holy Writ that he who led his life after God's will, the wild beasts and the wild birds have become more intimate with him?" he asked. St. Gudival of Ghent once brought a slaughtered sheep back to life "because he saw in it Christ led like a sheep to the slaughter."

After St. Macarius of Alexandria restored the sight of a young blind hyena, its mother, in gratitude, brought him some wool. Macarius chastised the hyena for stealing and killing a sheep. The hyena hung its head in shame and swore not to steal again.

St. Anselm of Canterbury (1033-1109) "was moved to feelings of compassion for animals, and he wept for them when he saw them caught in the hunter's net." St. Richard of Wyche, a vegetarian, was moved by the sight of animals taken to slaughter. "Poor innocent little creatures," he observed. "If you were reasoning beings and could speak, you would curse us. For we are the cause of your death, and what have you done to deserve it?"

Vegetarian writer Steven Rosen explains: "...over the centuries, there has arisen two distinct schools of Christian thought. The Aristotelian-Thomistic school and the Augustinian-Franciscan school. The Aristotelian-Thomistic school has, as its fundamental basis, the premise that animals are here for our pleasure—they have no purpose of their own. We can eat them, torture them in laboratories—anything...Unfortunately, modern Christianity embraces this form of their religion.

"The Augustinian-Franciscan school, however, teaches that we are all brothers and sisters under God's Fatherhood. Based largely on the world view of St. Francis and being platonic in nature, this school fits in very neatly with the vegetarian perspective."

It is said that St. Francis of Assisi (1182-1226) bought two lambs from a butcher and gave them the coat on his back to keep them warm; and that he bought two fish from a fishwoman and threw them back into the water. He even paid to ransom lambs that were being taken to their death, recalling the gentle Lamb who willingly went to slaughter (Isaiah 53:7; John 1:29) to pay the ransom of sinners.

"Be conscious, O man, of the wondrous state in which the Lord God has placed you," instructed Francis in his *Admonitions* (4), "for He created and formed you to the image of His beloved Son—and (yet) all the creatures under heaven, each according to its nature, serve know, and obey their Creator better than you." St. Francis felt a deep kinship with all creatures. He called them "brother," and "sister," knowing they came from the same Source as himself.

Francis revealed his fraternal love for the animal world during Christmas time 1223: "If I ever have the opportunity to talk with the emperor," he explained, "I'll beg him, for the love of God and me, to enact a special law: no one is to capture or kill our sisters the larks or do them any harm. Furthermore, all mayors and lords of castles and towns are required to scatter wheat and other grain on the roads outside the walls so that our sisters the larks and other birds might have something to eat on so festive a day.

"And on Christmas Eve, out of reverence for the Son of God, whom on that night the Virgin Mary placed in a manger between the ox and the ass, anyone having an ox or an ass is to feed it a generous portion of choice fodder. And, on Christmas Day, the rich are to give the poor the finest food in abundance."

Francis removed worms from a busy road and placed them on the roadside so they would not be crushed under human traffic. Once when he was sick and almost blind, mice ran over his table as he took his meals and over him while he slept. He regarded their disturbance as a "diabolical temptation," which he met with patience and restraint, indicating his compassion towards other living creatures.

St. Francis was once given a wild pheasant to eat, but he chose instead to keep it as a companion. On another occasion, he was given a fish, and on yet another, a waterfowl to eat, but he was moved by the natural beauty of these creatures and chose to set them free.

"Dearly beloved!" said Francis beginning a sermon after a severe illness, "I have to confess to God and you that...I have eaten cakes made with lard."

The *Catholic Encyclopedia* comments on this incident as follows: "St. Francis' gift of sympathy seems to have been wider even than St. Paul's, for we find to evidence in the great Apostle of a love for nature or for animals...

"Francis' love of creatures was not simply the offspring of a soft sentimental disposition. It arose from that deep and abiding sense of the presence of God. To him all are from one Father and all are real kin...hence, his deep sense of personal responsibility towards fellow creatures: the loving friend of all God's creatures."

Francis taught: "All things of creation are children of the Father and thus brothers of man...God wants us to help animals, if they need help. Every creature in distress has the same right to be protected."

According to Francis, a lack of mercy towards animals leads to a lack of mercy towards men: "If you have men who will exclude any of God's creatures from the shelter of compassion and pity, you will have men who will deal likewise with their fellow men."

One Franciscan monk, St. Anthony of Padua (1195-1231), who preached throughout France and Italy, is said to have attracted a group of fish that came to hear him preach. St. James of Venice, who lived during the 13th century, bought and released the birds sold in Italy as toys for children. It is said he "pitied the little birds of the Lord...his tender charity recoiled from all cruelty, even to the most diminutive of animals."

St. Bonaventure was a scholar and theologian who joined the Franciscan Order in 1243. He wrote *The Soul's Journey into God* and *The Life of St. Francis*, the latter documenting St. Francis' miracles with animals and love for all creation. Bonaventure taught that all creatures come from God and return to Him, and that the light of God shines through His different creatures in different ways:

"...For every creature is by its nature a kind of effigy and likeness of the eternal Wisdom. Therefore, open your eyes, alert the ears of your spirit, open your lips and apply your heart so that in all creatures you may see, hear, praise, love and worship, glorify and honor your God."

St. Bridget (1303?-1373) of Sweden, founder of the Brigittine Order, wrote in her *Revelations*:

"Let a man fear, above all, Me his God, and so much the gentler will he become towards My creatures and animals, on whom, on account of Me, their Creator, he ought to have compassion."

She raised pigs, and a wild boar is even said to have left its home in the forest to become her pet.

"The reason why God's servants love His creatures so deeply is that they realize how deeply Christ loves them," explained St. Catherine of Siena (1347-1380). "And this is the very character of love to love what is loved by those we love."

"Here I saw a great unity between Christ and us..." wrote Julian of Norwich (1360-?), "for when he was in pain we were in pain, and all creatures able to suffer pain suffered with him."

Christian mystic, Thomas A' Kempis (1380-1471) wrote in his devotional classic, *The Imitation of Christ*, that the soul desiring communion with God must be open to seeing, respecting and learning from all of God's creatures, including the nonhumans:

"...and if thy heart be straight with God," he wrote, "then every creature shall be to thee a mirror of life and a book of holy doctrine, for there is no creature so little or vile, but that showeth and representeth the goodness of God."

St. Thomas More (1478-1535), was an undersheriff of London and the speaker of the House of Commons before he was named Lord Chancellor of England. He refused to approve the divorce of Henry VIII from Catherine of Aragon. He also refused to sign the Act of Succession which placed the King's powers over those of the Church. For this he was imprisoned, tried for high treason, found guilty, and beheaded. More authored *Utopia*, a book which describes "the perfect commonwealth."

In *Utopia*, More abolished the killing of animals, stating that citizens should "kill no animal in sacrifice, nor (should) they think that God has delight in blood and slaughter, who has given life to animals to the intent they should live." A vegetarian, More spoke out primarily against butchering and meat-eating, but he also criticized those who would "waste" corn in the production of alcoholic beverages.

St. Filippo Neri spent his entire life protecting and rescuing other living creatures. Born in Florence in 1515, he went to Rome as a young man, and tried to live as an ascetic. He sold his books, giving away the money to the poor. He worked without pay in the city hospital, tending to the sick and the poor. He gave whatever he possessed to others.

St. Filippo loved the animals and could not bear to see them suffer. He took the mice caught in traps away from people's homes and set them free in the fields and stables. A vegetarian, he could not endure walking past a butcher shop. "Ah," he exclaimed. "If everyone were like me, no one would kill animals!"

According to E. Eyre-Smith, in an article from *The Ark*, "Montalembert's *Monks of the West* records in Vita Columbani, the Chronicler Jonas, writing within 25 years of the death of St. Columban, relates that this saint spent long periods in solitary contemplation and communion with the wild creatures of the forest, and insisted on his monks living, like himself, on the fruits of the earth, herbs and pulses. This indicates that in making rules for his followers in regard to non-meat eating, he was moved by his love and regard for the rest of God's creation."

St. Martin de Porres was born in 1579 in Lima, Peru, as the child of a Spaniard and Ana Velasquez, a black washerwoman. He joined the Dominican Order at the age of 24, and later established orphanages, hospitals and other charitable institutions. On one occasion, he told his superior, "charity knows no rules!" St. Martin's compassion extended to the lower animals, including even rats and mice. St. Martin healed and cared for stray dogs, cats, a mule, and even a vulture. He sometimes allowed the mosquitos to bite him, so that they might be fed, saying, "They, too, are God's creatures."

The Trappist monks of the Catholic Church practiced vegetarianism from the founding of their Order until the Second Vatican Council in the late 1960s. According to the Trappist rules, as formulated by Armand Jean de Rance (1626-1700), "in the dining hall nothing is layed out except: pulse, roots, cabbages, or milk, but never any fish...I hope I will move you more and more rigorously, when you discover that the use of simple and rough food has its origin with the holy apostles (James, Peter, Matthew).

"We can assure you that we have written nothing about this subject which was not believed, observed, proved good through antiquity, proved by historians and tradition, preserved and kept up to us by the holy monks."

A contemporary Benedictine monk, Brother David Steindl-Rast points out that the lives of the saints teach compassion towards all living beings. "Unfortunately," says Brother David, "Christians have their share of the exploitation of our environment and in the mistreatment of animals. Sometimes they have even tried to justify their crimes by texts from the Bible, misquoted out of context. But the genuine flavor of a tradition can best be discerned in its saints:

"All kinds of animals appear in Christian art to distinguish one saint from another. St. Menas has two camels; St. Ulrich has a rat; St. Bridgid has ducks and geese; St. Benedict, a raven; the list goes on and on. St. Hubert's attribute is a stag with a crucifix between its antlers. According to legend, this saint was a hunter but gave up his violent ways when he suddenly saw Christ in a stag he was about to shoot...Christ himself is called the Lamb of God."

According to Brother David, "...the survival of our planet depends on our sense of belonging—to all other humans, to dolphins caught in dragnets, to pigs and chickens and calves raised in animal concentration camps, to redwoods and rainforests, to kelp beds in our oceans, and to the ozone layer."

St. John of the Cross (1542-1591) wrote about God's beautifying the creatures:

"'God saw all the things that He had made and they were very good.' To behold them and find them very good was to make them very good in the Word, His Son. And not only did He communicate to them their being and their natural graces when he beheld them...but also in this image of His Son alone He left them clothed with beauty, communicating to them supernatural being. This was when He became man, and thus exalted man in the beauty of God, and consequently exalted all the creatures in him, since in uniting Himself with man He united Himself with the nature of them all...

"'If I be lifted up from the earth, I will draw all things to Myself.' And thus, in this lifting up the Incarnation of His Son, and in the glory of His resurrection according to the flesh, not only did the Father beautify the creatures in part, but we can say that He left them all clothed with beauty and dignity."

Fyodor Dostoevsky (1821-1881), in his literary classic, *The Brothers Karamazov*, depicted Father Zossima, a brother in the faith with St. Francis, teaching universal love as a natural result of Christian mysticism:

"Love all God's creation. Love every leaf, every ray of God's light! Love the animals, love the plants, love everything. If you love everything, you will perceive the divine mystery in things. Once you perceive it you will begin to comprehend it better every day. And you will come at last to love the whole world with an all-embracing love.

"Love the animals: God has given them the rudiments of thought and joy untroubled. Do not trouble it, don't harass them, don't deprive them of their happiness, don't work against God's intent. Man, do not pride yourself on your superiority to the animals; they are without sin, and you with your greatness defile the earth by your appearance on it, and leave the traces of your foulness after you..."

Roman Catholic Cardinal John Henry Newman (1801-90), wrote in 1870 that "cruelty to animals is as if a man did not love God." On another occasion, he asked:

"Now what is it that moves our very heart and sickens us so much at cruelty shown to poor brutes? I suppose this: first, that they have done us no harm; next, that they have no power whatever of resistance; it is the *cowardice and tyranny* of which they are the victims which make their sufferings so especially touching...there is something so very dreadful, so satanic, in tormenting those who have never harmed us and who cannot defend themselves; who are utterly in our power."

Cardinal Newman compared injustices against animals to the sacrifice, agony and death of Christ upon the cross:

"Think of your feelings at cruelty practiced upon brute animals and you will gain the sort of feeling which the history of Christ's cross and passion ought to excite within you. And let me add, this is in all cases one good use to which you may turn any...wanton and unfeeling acts shown towards the...animals; let them remind you, as a picture of Christ's sufferings. He who is higher than the angels, deigned to humble Himself even to the state of the brute creation..."

Another cardinal, Henry Edward Manning (1808-92), spoke out against cruelty to animals, especially experimentation upon animals. In a letter dated July 13, 1891, he wrote: "We owe ourselves the duty not to be brutal or cruel; and we owe to God the duty of treating all His creatures according to His own perfections of love and mercy." Bishop Westcott wrote, "Animals are in our power in a peculiar sense; they are committed by God to our sovereignty and we owe them a considerate regard for their rights. No animal life can be treated as a THING. Willful disrespect of the sanctities of physical life in one sphere bears its fruit in other and higher spheres."

Cardinal Francis Bourne (1861-1934) told children in Westminster Cathedral in April 1931: "There is even in kindness to animals a special merit in remembering that this kindness is obligatory upon us because God made the animals, and is therefore their creator, and, in a measure, His Fatherhood extends to them." Cardinal Arthur Hinsley (1865-1943), the former archbishop of Westminster, wrote that "the spirit of St. Francis is the Catholic spirit." According to Cardinal Hinsley, "Cruelty to animals is the degrading attitude of paganism."

Reverend Jean Gautier, a doctor in canon law, a director of the Grand Seminary in Paris (St. Sulpice), and a noted French authority on Roman Catholic philosophy, wrote in his book *A Priest and his Dog*: "For cruelty to defenseless beings we shall one day have to answer before Him who trieth the heart and the reins. Not with impunity is the weakness of animals abused."

In his 1957 book, *The Status of Animals in the Christian Religion*, author C.W. Hume wrote that the catechism children use for their first Communion and for their confirmation in France contains the answer, "it is not permissible for me to cause suffering to animals without good reason, to hurt them unnecessarily is an act of cruelty." British Jesuit Father John Bligh observed, "A man is not likely to be much of a Christian if he is not kind to animals."

A Roman Catholic priest, Msgr. LeRoy E. McWilliams of North Arlington, New Jersey, testified in

October 1962 in favor of legislation to reduce the sufferings of laboratory animals. He told congressional representatives:

"The first book of the Bible tell us that God created the animals and the birds, so they have the same Father as we do. God's Fatherhood extends to our 'lesser brethren.' All animals belong to God; He alone is their absolute owner. In our relations with them, we must emulate the divine attributes, the highest of which is mercy. God, their Father and Creator, loves them tenderly. He lends them to us and adjures us to use them as He Himself would do."

Msgr. McWilliams also issued a letter to all seventeen thousand Catholic pastors in the United States, calling upon them to understand "what Christianity imposes on humans as their clear obligation to animals."

Unfortunately, these are only isolated instances of concern for animals. "The Church should be a leader in the movement for the protection of animals, but it is not even in the procession," wrote Helen Jones of the National Catholic Society for Animal Welfare in 1966. "The attitude of the Church today toward the suffering of animals is for the most part one of utmost indifference." Voices within the Church calling for justice towards the animals have been few and far between.

Reverend Basil Wrighton, the chairman of the Catholic Study Circle for Animal Welfare in London, wrote in a 1965 article entitled, "The Golden Age Must Return: A Catholic's Views on Vegetarianism," that a vegetarian diet is not only consistent with, but actually required by the tenets of Christianity. He concluded that the killing of animals for food not only violates religious tenets, but brutalizes humans to the point where violence and warfare against other humans becomes inevitable.

In 1969, Reverend Kevin Daley, as chairman of the CSCAW in London, wrote that "the work of animal welfare" is an "essential part of the work of a Christian."

A strong condemnation of cruelty towards animals appeared in the March 10, 1966 issue of *L'Osserevatore della Domenica*, the official Vatican weekly newspaper. Written by the respected theologian, Msgr. Ferdinando Lambruschini, it read in part:

"Man's conduct with regard to animals should be regulated by right reason, which prohibits the infliction of purposeless pain and suffering on them. To ill treat them, and make them suffer without reason, is an act of deplorable cruelty to be condemned from a Christian point of view. To make them suffer for one's own pleasure is an exhibition of sadism which every moralist must denounce."

The 1967 *New Catholic Encyclopedia* took the position that while killing animals for food is acceptable and the mistreatment of animals may not be a mortal sin, wanton destruction of animal life is evil: irrational, unbeneficial and certainly not an example of positive spiritual development.

In his 1970 book *God's Animals* Reverend Don Ambrose Agius wrote: "It is a moral obligation for every Christian to fight cruelty to animals because the consequences of cruelty are destructive to the Christian order...The Bible...tells us that cruelty to animals is wicked and that it is opposed to God's will and intention...The duty of all Christians (is) to emulate God's attributes, especially that of mercy, in regard to animals. To be kind to animals is to emulate the loving kindness of God."

In his foreword to Reverend Agius' book, Cardinal John Heenan wrote: "Animals...have very positive rights because they are God's creatures. If we have to speak with absolute accuracy, we must say that God has the right to have all His creatures treated with respect...Only the perverted are guilty of deliberate cruelty to animals or, indeed, to children."

Vegetarianism, however, is still regarded by the Church as a form of abstinence; encouraged as a means to increase one's will power over mortal flesh and desires: "It is precisely because meat is so good that we do abstain from it," explained one Benedictine monk. "...to forego the use of meat makes one's meals somewhat less attractive and enjoyable." With simple living, a monk "will have greater spiritual freedom to attend to the things of the Spirit and of God."

Vladimir Lossky wrote about "Cosmic Awareness" and the teachings of St. Maximus in a 1973 religious text: *The Mystical Theology of the Eastern Church*. According to Lossky, the limitations of the creation are part of its intrinsic nature:

"[T]hey are problems to be resolved, obstacles to be surmounted on the way towards union with God. Man is not a being isolated from the rest of creation; by his very nature, he is bound up with the whole of the universe, and St. Paul bears witness that the whole creation await the future glory which will be revealed in the sons of God (Rom. viii, 18-22). This cosmic awareness has never been absent from Eastern spirituality, and is given expression in theology as well as in liturgical poetry, in iconography and, perhaps above all, in the ascetical writings of the masters of the spiritual life of the Eastern Church...

"In his way to union with God, man in no way leaves creatures aside, but gathers together in his love the whole cosmos disordered by sin, that it may at last be transfigured by grace."

Father Thomas Berry, a Catholic priest, author, and founder of the Riverdale Center of Religious Research in New York, wrote in 1987 that "vegetarianism is a way of life that we should all move toward for economic survival, physical well-being, and spiritual integrity."

As a second grade schoolboy, growing up in Petoskey, Michigan, Ron Pickarski had a "vision." He felt God was calling him to serve by abandoning everything and following Christ. His mother notes that as a youth, Ron Pickarski was introverted and had strong, spiritual inclinations. "He was serious about his God," she recalls. "He wasn't one of those kinds who drank and smoked pot."

At the age of 19, Ron entered Our Lady of the Angels seminary. Six years later, he took the vows of poverty, celibacy and obedience. "It would basically be easier to shoot myself than to leave the order," he admits. "It's a commitment between me and God. If I can't live up to a commitment I made to God, how can I live up to a commitment to anyone else? It's a commitment to a vision that is unfolding in everything that I'm doing," he says. "That whole vision is being lived out in my work as a food minister."

After his father died of cancer, Brother Ron experimented with different kinds of vegetarian diets, including raw foods, natural hygiene and macrobiotics. By this time, he had also become a master chef. Brother Ron studied at the Washburne Trade School for Chefs in Chicago, and graduated at the top of his class.

Brother Ron asked for a solo ministry—rather unusual for a Franciscan monk—and it was granted. His supervisors have compared his ministry to that of St. Francis of Assisi, the patron saint of animals and ecology. St. Francis loved nature and considered it God's gift to humanity.

Brother Ron combines his religious vocation with a career in vegetarian cooking. He considers himself a health missionary, teaching that a person who is healthy can better serve God. "Our bodies are temples of the Holy Spirit," he explains. "They are the vehicles by which we serve God. I think the consciousness of a person in a state of wellness is much higher than a person who is not." Brother Ron believes that God meant for us to eat a high-carbohydrate diet, and the best kind of high-carbohydrate diet is a vegetarian diet. A vegetarian diet promotes health, which puts one in the proper frame of mind to help others.

Brother Ron believes that if Jesus ate meat or fish, he did so seldomly, and always in the spirit of charity. He defines charity as putting someone else before oneself; encompassing love, respect and understanding. He gives an example from his own life:

"I was at a Christmas celebration last year that I was invited to by my lawyer. His mother, a sweet Italian lady, made this beautiful vegetarian ravioli with a dairy cream sauce. It was her Christmas present to me. I couldn't say, 'I'm a vegan (living entirely on plant foods). I'm not going to eat this.' I sat down, and I ate it and thoroughly enjoyed it. I partook of it in the same spirit in which she made it," he adds. "If a person knew I was a vegan and did it to defy me, then I'd say, 'Scratch off. I'm not going to eat it.'"

Prizing charity above everything else, Brother Ron is unimpressed with "self-righteous vegetarians" whose motives do not spring from the heart. "In Corinthians, he (Paul) says that we are just a clanging cymbal unless we act out of love...How many vegetarians out there are clanging cymbals?

"Quite frankly," he admits, "I would rather be a charitable consumer of meat than a self-righteous vegetarian, because it is love that will transform the world, not vegetarianism."

Nonetheless, Brother Ron does see vegetarianism as a natural consequence of divine love. "When people learn to love themselves and their fellow human beings, then and only then will vegetarianism predominate the universe. And the funny thing is, they will not perceive it as vegetarianism, just simply loving."

In an editorial that appeared on Christmas Day, 1988, *Washington Post* columnist Colman McCarthy, a prominent Catholic writer and a vegetarian, observed:

"A long raised but rarely answered question is this: If it was God's plan for Christ to be born among animals, why have most Christian theologians denied the value and rights of animals? Why no theology of the peaceable kingdom?...Animals in the stable at Bethlehem were a vision of the peaceable kingdom. Among theology's mysteries, this ought to be the easiest to fathom."

Mother Teresa, honored for her work amongst the poor with the 1979 Nobel Peace Prize, wrote in 1992 to Marlene Ryan, a former member of the National Alliance for Animals. Her letter reads:

"I am praying for you that God's blessing may be with you in all that you are doing to create concern for the animals which are often subjected to much cruelty. They, too, are created by the same loving Hand of God which created us. As we humans are gifted with intelligence which the animals lack, it is our duty to protect them and to promote their well being.

"We also owe it to them as they serve us with such wonderful docility and loyalty. A person who shows cruelty to these creatures cannot be kind to other humans also. Let us do all we can to become instruments of peace—where we are—the true peace that comes from loving and caring and respecting each person as a child of God—my brother—my sister."

In an article entitled "The Primacy of Nonviolence as a Virtue," appearing in *Embracing Earth: Catholic Approaches to Ecology* (1994), Brother Wayne Teasdale wrote:

"One key answer to a culture's preoccupation with violence is to teach, insist on, and *live* the value of nonviolence. It can be done successfully, and it has been done for more than 2,500 years by Jains and Buddhists.

"Neither Jainism nor Buddhism has ever supported war or personal violence; this nonviolence extends to all sentient beings. Christianity can learn something valuable from these traditions. This teaching on nonviolence has been incarnated in the lives of Mahatma Gandhi, Martin Luther King, Jr., and the Fourteenth Dalai Lama with significant results..."

According to Teasdale: "...it is necessary to elevate nonviolence to a noble place in our civilization of loving-compassion because nonviolence as *ahimsa* in the Hindu tradition, a tradition that seems to possess the most advanced understanding of nonviolence, *is* love! Love is the goal and ultimate nature of nonviolence as an inner disposition and commitment of the heart. It is the fulfillment of love and compassion in the social sphere, that is, in the normal course of relations among people in the matrix of society."

Brother Aelred (Robert Edmunds), a Catholic monk living in Australia, discusses the moral question of killing animals for food in his book *Encounter*. He points out that Jesus Christ greatly expanded the interpretation of the commandment "Thou shalt not kill" to include not getting angry without cause.

60

"My position is that Jesus' teachings on *mercy* in the *Beatitudes* require an *open-ended ethical inquiry*" writes Brother Aelred. "I ask, for example, how a Christian may speak of 'mercy' in the terms of Jesus Christ, and deny mercy to creatures of God who, as we do, experience fear and suffering. Isn't it the case that Jesus constantly went beyond the 'letter of the law' to its spirit?"

Brother Aelred quotes the prophecies of Isaiah (11:6-9, 65:25) concerning the coming Kingdom of Peace. "The passage sees a time when pain and bloodshed will be no more; when prey and devourer will be reconciled. What a vision! Even if the passage is seen as just poetic exaggeration, it is clear that there is hope for a future which will be *very different* to the world we know. And surely we, as Christians, must be part of this 'peace process.' Perhaps our main burden, as Christians, is to be *part of this message of hope and reconciliation.*"

Brother Aelred ends with the following:

"An Anglican Franciscan superior, in Australia, tells his novices that if they wish to eat flesh they must go out and themselves kill the animal. The moral responsibility must be theirs alone. I consider this a thoroughly sound position, and any Christian reading this article might well reflect on the brother's teaching. In conclusion, I must report a sad truth. My own Christian formation taught me many things of great value, but 'respect for all things living' was not part of that formation. It was other religious traditions and 'secular' insights which gave me teaching in this area."

chapter six
"A Tenderness Toward All Creatures"

Vegetarianism and concern for animals can be found in Protestant Christianity as well. Commenting on Deuteronomy 22:6, which forbids harming a mother-bird if her eggs or chicks are taken, Martin Luther (1483-1546) wrote: "What else does this law teach but that by the kind treatment of animals they are to learn gentleness and kindness? Otherwise it would seem to be a stupid ordinance not only to regulate a matter so unimportant, but also to promise happiness and a long life to those who keep it."

According to Luther, Adam "would not have used the creatures as we do today," but rather, "for the admiration of God and a holy joy." Referring to passages from Scripture concerning the redemption of the entire creation and the Kingdom of Peace, Luther taught that "the creatures are created for an end; for the glory that is to come." British historian William Lecky observed that, "Luther grew sad and thoughtful at a hare hunt, for it seemed to him to represent the pursuit of souls by the devil." Author Dix Harwood, in *Love for Animals*, depicts a grieving young girl being comforted by Luther. Luther assures her that her pet dog who died would certainly go to heaven. Luther tells her that in the "new heavens and new earth...all creatures will not only be harmless, but lovely and joyful...Why, then, should there not be little dogs in the new earth, whose skin might be as fair as gold, and their hair as bright as precious stones?"

Biblical teachings on human responsibilities towards animals were not lost on John Calvin (1509-1564). According to Calvin, animals exist within the framework of human justice: "But it must be remembered that men are required to practice justice even in dealing with animals. Solomon condemns injustice to our neighbours the more severely when he says, 'a just man cares well for his beasts' (Proverbs 12:10). In a word, we are to do what is right voluntarily and freely, and each of us is responsible for doing his duty."

John Wray (1627?-1705), the "father of English natural history," made the first systematic description and classification of animal and vegetable species. He wrote numerous works on botany, zoology, and theology. In 1691, Wray published *The Wisdom of God Manifest in the Works of His Creation*, which emphasized the sanctity and value of the natural world.

Wray advocated vegetarianism and made two points in his book. The first was that God can best be seen and understood in the study of His creation. "Let us then consider the works of God and observe the operation of His hands," wrote Wray. "Let us take notice of and admire His infinite goodness and wisdom in the formation of them. No creature in the sublunary world is capable of doing this except man, and yet we have been deficient therein." Wray's second point was that God placed animals here for their own sake, and not just for the pleasure of humans. Animals have their own intrinsic value. "If a good man be merciful to his beast, then surely a good God takes pleasure that all His creatures enjoy themselves that have life and sense and are capable of enjoying."

Thomas Tryon's lengthy *The Way to Health, Wealth, and Happiness* was published in 1691. Tryon defended vegetarianism as a physically and spiritually superior way of life. He came to this conclusion from his interpretation of the Bible as well as his understanding of Christianity. Tryon wrote against "that depraved custom of eating flesh and blood." The opening pages of his book begin with an eloquent plea for mercy towards the animals:

"Refrain at all times such foods as cannot be procured without violence and oppression, for know, that all the inferior creatures when hurt do cry and fend forth their complaints to their Maker...Be not insensible that every creature doth bear the image of the great Creator according to the nature of each, and that He is the vital power in all things. Therefore, let none take pleasure to offer violence to that life, lest he awaken the fierce wrath, and bring danger to his own soul. But let mercy and compassion dwell plentifully in your hearts, that you may be comprehended in the friendly principle of God's love and holy light. Be a friend to everything that's good, and then everything will be a friend to thee, and co-operate for thy good and welfare."

In *The Way*, Tryon (1634-1703) also condemned "Hunting, hawking, shooting, and all violent oppressive exercises..." On a separate occasion, he warned the first Quaker settlers of Pennsylvania that their "holy experiment" in peaceful living would fail unless they extended their Christian precepts of nonviolence to the animal kingdom:

"Does not bounteous Mother Earth furnish us with all sorts of food necessary for life?" he asked. "Though you will not fight with and kill those of your own species, yet I must be bold to tell you, that these lesser violences (as you call them) do proceed from the same root of wrath and bitterness as the greater do."

"Thanks be to God!" wrote John Wesley, founder of Methodism, to the Bishop of London in 1747. "Since the time I gave up the use of flesh-meats and wine, I have been delivered from all physical ills." Wesley was a vegetarian for spiritual reasons as well. He based his vegetarianism on the Biblical prophecies concerning the Kingdom of Peace, where "on the new earth, no creature will kill, or hurt, or give pain to any other." He further taught that animals "shall receive an ample amends for all their present sufferings."

Wesley's teachings placed an emphasis on inner religion and the effect of the Holy Spirit upon the consciousness of such followers. Wesley taught that animals will attain heaven: in the "general deliverance" from the evils of this world, animals would be given "vigor, strength and swiftness...to a far higher degree than they ever enjoyed."

Wesley urged parents to educate their children about compassion towards animals. He wrote: "I am persuaded you are not insensible of the pain given to every Christian, every humane heart, by those savage diversions, bull-baiting, cock-fighting, horse-racing, and hunting."

In 1786, Reverend Richard Dean, the curate of Middleton, published *An Essay on the Future Life of Brute Creatures*. He told his readers to treat animals with compassion, and not to "treat them as sticks, or stones, or things that cannot feel...Surely ...sensibility in brutes entitles them to a milder treatment than they usually meet from hard and unthinking wretches."

The Quakers have a long history of advocating kindness towards animals. In 1795, the Society of Friends (Quakers) in London passed a resolution condemning sport hunting. The resolution stated in part, "let our leisure be employed in serving our neighbor, and not in distressing, for our amusement, the creatures of God."

John Woolman (1720-72) was a Quaker preacher and abolitionist who traveled throughout the American colonies attacking slavery and cruelty to animals. Woolman wrote that he was "early convinced in my mind that true religion consisted in an inward life, wherein the heart doth love and reverence God the Creator and learn to exercise true justice and goodness, not only toward all men, but also toward the brute creatures..." Woolman's deep faith in God thus led to his reverence for all life. "Where the love of God is verily perfected and the true spirit of government watchfully attended to," he taught, "a tenderness toward all creatures made subject to us will be experienced, and a care felt in us that we do not lessen that sweetness of life in the animal creation which the great Creator intends for them."

Joshua Evans (1731-1798), a Quaker and a contemporary of Woolman's, stated that reverence for life was the moral basis of his vegetarianism. "I considered that life was sweet in all living creatures," he wrote, 'and taking it away became a very tender point with me...I believe my dear Master has been pleased to try my faith and obedience by teaching me that I ought no longer to partake of *anything that had life*."

The "Quaker poet" and abolitionist John Greenleaf Whittier (1807-92), wrote: "The sooner we recognize the fact that the mercy of the Almighty extends to every creature endowed with life, the better it will be for us as men and Christians."

The United Society for Believers in Christ's Second Appearance, also known as the Shakers, taught equality of the races and sexes, ecological conservation and compassion towards animals. The founder of the sect, Ann Lee (1736-84) came to America in 1774. She and her followers established the first Shakers colony at Watervliet, New York. Ann Lee is said to have taught that a person who mistreated animals could not be a Christian, and to have called for "justice and kindness to all the brute creation."

One of the most respected English theologians of the 18th century, William Paley (1743-1805), taught that killing animals for food was unjustifiable. Paley called the excuses used to justify killing animals "extremely lame" and even refuted the rationalizations concerning fishing.

Sermons Preached in Country Churches (London, 1880) contains a sermon entitled "Suffering and Glory" by F.D. Maurice (1805-72). It deals with the redemption of the entire creation:

> "But is it true that Death is the lord of any man or woman or child; of any beast or any insect; of any tree or flower? No. Death did not make them; and he who did make them, He who gave them life by whom their life has been renewed every hour, He has proved that He is stronger than death.

> "We wait for the deliverer of these bodies from their aches and torments; we wait for the day when Christ shall set them free from the bondage of death; when He shall make them like His glorious body. And as we hope for ourselves, so we hope for all those creatures who not for their own fault have been made subject to misery and death, who are not as sinful as we have been."

The founder and first secretary of the Royal Society for the Prevention of Cruelty to Animals (RSPCA) was an Anglican priest, the Reverend Arthur Broome. The RSPCA was originally founded as a Christian society "entirely based on the Christian Faith, and on Christian Principles," and sponsoring sermons on humane education in churches in London. The Society formed in 1824, and its first "Prospectus" spoke of the need to extend Christian charity and benevolence to the animals:

"Our country is distinguished by the number and variety of its benevolent institutions...all breathing the pure spirit of Christian charity...But shall we stop here? Is the moral circle perfect so long as any power of doing good remains? Or can the infliction of cruelty on any being which the Almighty has endued with feelings of pain and pleasure consist with genuine and true benevolence?"

This Prospectus was signed by many leading 19th century Christians including William Wilberforce, Richard Martin, G.A. Hatch, J. Bonner, and Dr. Heslop.

The Bible Christian Church was a 19th century movement teaching vegetarianism, abstinence from intoxication, and compassion for animals. The church began in England in 1800, requiring all its members to take vows of abstinence from meat and wine. One of its first converts, William Metcalfe (1788-1862), immigrated to Philadelphia in 1817 with forty-one followers to establish a church in America. Metcalfe cited numerous biblical references to support his thesis that humans were meant to follow a vegetarian diet for reasons of health and compassion for animals.

One of Metcalfe's converts, Sylvester Graham (1794-1851), was a Presbyterian minister and the originator of graham crackers. He had been healed through a vegetarian diet and advocated the use of unrefined, whole-wheat "graham" flour, from which graham crackers are now made. Graham was a temperance advocate who preached vegetarianism as a cure for those suffering from alcohol abuse. His regimen called for an abundance of fruits and vegetables in the diet, fresh air, moderate eating and plenty of exercise.

Beginning in 1830, Graham boardinghouses, societies and food stores spread across the land. A product of the Victorian period, Graham also wrote lectures on sexual chastity, warning that spices and rich foods heighten sexual desire, while sexual excesses amongst married couples lead to numerous afflictions. Graham influenced Amos Bronson Alcott (1799-1888) and Joseph Smith (1805-1844), founder of the Mormon Church.

Alcott was a teacher and a visionary influenced by the Quakers and by East Indian philosophy. He tried to make his vegetarian ideas a reality in his failed utopian experiment of Fruitlands (1841). He can be called the father of the Organic Food movement.

Kindness to animals can be found in the early teachings of the Church of Jesus Christ of Latter-day Saints, also known as the Mormon Church. Joseph Smith (1805-1844), who founded the Mormon Church in 1830, preached the humane treatment of animals:

> "God glorified Himself by saving all that His hands had made, whether beasts, fowls, fishes or men; and He will glorify Himself with them

> "Kindness to the whole animal creation and especially to all domestic animals is not only a virtue that should be developed but is the ABSO-LUTE DUTY OF MANKIND. Children should be taught that nature in all forms is our heavenly Father's Great Book of Life.

> "Furthermore, he who treats in a brutal manner a poor dumb animal, at that moment disqualifies himself for the companionship of the Holy Spirit."

It appears even poisonous snakes were to be treated with respect. An entry in Smith's diary dated May 26, 1834, describes poisonous snakes found in the encampment: "The brethren took the serpents carefully on sticks and carried them across the creek. I exhorted the brethren not to kill the serpent, bird or animal of any kind during our journey unless it became necessary to preserve ourselves from hunger."

According to Mormon theology, humans are held responsible for treatment of every animal in their care. In Joseph Smith's inspired version of the Bible, Genesis 9:11 reads: "Blood of animals shall not be shed only for meat to save your lives; and the blood of every beast I will require at your hands." Commenting on this verse, W. Cleon Skowsen writes in *First Two Thousand Years*, "God did not intend that the lives of animals should be subject to cruelty and abuse. The proper treatment of the animal kingdom is part of the human stewardship."

The Mormon scripture and Bible (*Doctrine and Covenants*, 49:21) says: "And woe be unto man that sheddeth blood or that wasteth flesh and hath no need." It further states, "Man has been entrusted with sovereignty over the animal kingdom that he may learn to govern as God rules, by the power of love and justice, and become fit for his eternal destiny as a ruler of worlds." (*Doctrine and Covenants*, Commentary, section 47, p. 361).

The Mormon Church has also advocated a mostly vegetarian diet as part of its philosophy of health and reverence for life. This began in 1833, when church founder Joseph Smith received a revelation of such a health code as God's will, emphasizing grains as the staple for one's diet. Meat is meant to be eaten only rarely, such as in times of famine or extreme cold, when animals will likely perish.

Brigham Young, who succeeded Joseph Smith as head of the Mormon Church in 1847, taught that animals are a sacred gift from God and humans are obliged to respect them: "If we maltreat our animals, or each other, the spirit within us, our traditions and the Bible, all agree in declaring it is wrong...The more kind we are to our animals, the more peace will increase."

David O. McKay, former president of the Mormon Church, explains humanity's duties and responsibilities towards animals as follows: "A true Latter-day Saint is kind to animals, is kind to every living thing, for God has created all...In all teaching, the element of love for all of the creatures of the earth can be emphasized, and thus religion imparted."

According to George Q. Cannon (1827-1901), "These birds and animals and fish cannot speak, but they can suffer, and our God who created them knows their sufferings, and will hold him who causes them to suffer unnecessarily to answer for it. It is a sin against their Creator.

"Children who are trained to respect the rights of the lower animals," taught Cannon, "will be more inclined to respect human rights and become good citizens. It has been observed that in places where special attention has been given in the public schools to the subject of kindness to animals, the percentage of crime has been lessened."

Joseph Fielding Smith, nephew of church founder Joseph Smith, and president of the Mormon Church from 1901 to 1918, has written:

> "It was intended that all creatures should be happy in their several elements. Therefore to take the life of these creatures wantonly is a sin before the Lord.
>
> "There is no inference in the scriptures that it is a privilege of men to slay birds or beasts or to catch fish wantonly
>
> "The domination the Lord gave man over the brute creations has been, to a very large extent, used selfishly, thoughtlessly, cruelly...
>
> "Kindness to the whole animal creation is not only a virtue that should be developed, but is the absolute duty of mankind...But with this dominion came the responsibility to treat with love and consideration every living thing...
>
> "Take not the life you cannot give. For all things have an equal right to live."

Hugh Nibley, a church leader in Utah, has written: "Man's domination is a call to service, not a license to exterminate. It is precisely because men now prey upon each other and shed the blood and waste the flesh of other creatures without need that the world lieth in sin."

German composer Richard Wagner (1813-1883) believed flesh-eating to be responsible for the downfall of man. He felt vegetarianism could help mankind return to Paradise. He wrote: "Plant life instead of animal life is the keystone of regeneration. Jesus used bread in place of flesh and wine in place of blood at the Lord's Supper."

General William Booth (1829-1912), founder of the Salvation Army, practiced and advocated vegetarianism. Booth never officially condemned flesh-eating as either cruelty or gluttony, but taught that abstinence from luxury is helpful to the cause of Christian charity. "It is a great delusion to suppose that flesh of any kind is essential to health," he insisted.

"If you want to pass from the consciousness of flesh into the consciousness of Spirit, you must withdraw your attention from the things of the flesh," taught Dr. Charles Filmore, founder of Unity. "You must recognize that there is but one universal life, one universal substance, one universal intelligence, and that every animal is contending for its life and is entitled to that life.

"But in the matter of animal slaughter, who countenances it or defends it after his eyes have been opened to the *unity of life*? Let us remember that the right kind of food will give our minds and our spirits opportunity to express that which is one with ideal life."

Founded in the 19th century at Lee's Summit, Missouri, the Unity School teaches that the time will come when man will look back upon eating animal flesh as he now looks upon cannibalism:

"As man unfolds spiritually he more and more perceives the necessity of fulfilling the divine law in every department of his life. From experience and observation Unity believes that somewhere along the way, as he develops spiritually, man comes to question seriously the rightness of meat as part of his diet. Man is naturally loathe to take life, even though the idea of killing animals for food has so long been sponsored by the race that he feels it is right and proper to do so.

"However, the Commandment, 'Thou shalt not kill,' considered in its fullest sense, includes the killing of animals...There is a kindred spirit in all living things—a love for life. Any man who considers honestly the oneness of life feels an aversion to eating meat: that is a reaction of his mind towards anything so foreign to the idea of universal life."

"The moral evils of a flesh diet are not less marked than are the physical ills," wrote Ellen White, founder of the Seventh-Day Adventist Church. "Flesh food is injurious to health, and whatever affects the body has a corresponding effect on the mind and soul."

Although Seventh-Day Adventists strongly recommend vegetarianism for reasons of health and nutrition, White also espoused the belief that kindness to animals should be a Christian duty. In *Ministry of Healing*, she urged the faithful to:

"Think of the cruelty that meat eating involves, and its effect on those who inflict and those who behold it. How it destroys the tenderness with which we should regard these creatures of God!"

In *Patriarchs and Prophets*, White referred to numerous passages in the Bible calling for kindness to animals, and concluded that humans will be judged according to how they fulfill their moral obligations to animals:

"It is because of man's sin that 'the whole creation groaneth and travaileth together in pain' (Romans 8:22). Surely, then, it becomes man to seek to lighten, instead of increasing, the weight of suffering which his transgression has brought upon God's creatures. He who will abuse animals because he has them in his power is both a coward and a tyrant. A disposition to cause pain, whether to our fellow men or to the brute creation, is satanic.

"Many do not realize that their cruelty will ever be known because the poor dumb animals cannot reveal it. But could the eyes of these men be opened, as were those of Balaam, they would see an angel of God standing as a witness to testify against them in the courts above.

"A record goes up to heaven, and a day is coming when judgement will be pronounced against those who abuse God's creatures."

In *Counsels on Diet and Foods*, White referred to the Garden of Eden, a Holy Sanctuary of God, where nothing would ever die, as the perfect example of humans in their natural state:

"God gave our first parents the food He designed that the race should eat. It was contrary to His plan to have the life of any creature taken. There was to be no death in Eden. The fruit of the tree in the garden was the food man's wants required."

"Tenderness accompanies all the might imparted by Spirit," wrote Mary Baker Eddy, founder of Christian Science, in *Science and Health with Key to the Scriptures*. "The individuality created by God is not carnivorous, as witness the millenial estate pictured by Isaiah (11:6-9). All of God's creatures, moving in the harmony of Science, are harmless, useful, indestructible. A realization of this grand verity was a source of strength to the ancient worthies. It supports Christian healing, and enables its possessor to emulate the example of Jesus. 'And God saw that it was good.'"

The Doukhobours were a sect of Russian Christians that originated in the 18th century. They lived as vegetarian pacifists and abstained from alcohol. Like the earliest Christians, they taught and practiced the renunciation of earthly possessions and worldly concerns in favor of a simple life of devotion to God.

These Christians had a profound influence upon Count Leo Tolstoy. "The vegetarian movement," wrote Tolstoy, "ought to fill with gladness the souls of all those who have at their heart the realization of God's Kingdom on earth." The Doukhobours passed on their traditions orally, through hymns and psalms. With the rise of communism and the Russian revolution in 1917, many Doukhobours emigrated to Canada.

Congregational minister Frederic Marvin preached a Christmas Eve sermon in 1899 entitled, "Christ among the Cattle." Marvin regarded Jesus' birth in the manger as that of God incarnate teaching humanity by dramatic example. Birth among the cattle was a sign for people all over the world to follow—a lesson teaching the need to show compassion towards the animals.

At the close of the 19th century, Reverend Thomas Timmins of Portsmouth, England, helped organize what may have been the first mass effort in America to teach kindness to animals. Reverend Timmins worked with George T. Angell (1823-1909) to organize American students into "Bands of Mercy," based on a similar movement taking place in England at the same time.

By 1912 there were over three million elementary school students enrolled in over 85,000 chapters. They all wore badges and pledged: "I will try to be kind to all living creatures, and try to protect them from cruel usage." This movement reached global proportions before declining after the Second World War.

In his 1923 work, *The Natural Diet of Man*, Dr. John Harvey Kellogg observed:

"The attitude of the Bible writers toward flesh-eating is the same as toward polygamy. Polygamy as well as flesh-eating was tolerated under the social and religious systems of the old Hebrews and even during the early centuries of the Christian era; but the first man, Adam, in his pristine state in the Garden of Eden was both a monogamist and a flesh-abstainer. If the Bible supports flesh-eating, it equally supports polygamy; for all the patriarchs had plural wives as well as concubines. Christian ethics enjoin a return to the Edenic example in matters matrimonial. Physiologic science as well as human experience call for a like return to Eden in matters dietetic."

An essay on "The Rights of Animals" by Dean William Ralph Inge (1860-1954) can be found in his 1926 book, *Lay Thoughts of a Dean*. It reads in part:

"Our ancestors sinned in ignorance; they were taught (as I deeply regret to say one great Christian Church still teaches) that the world, with all that it contains, was made for man, and that the lower orders of creation have no claims upon us. But we no longer have the excuse of saying that we do not know; we do know that organic life on this planet is all woven of one stuff, and if we are children of our Heavenly Father, it must be true, as Christ told us, that no sparrow falls to the ground without His care. The new knowledge has revolutionized our ideas of our relations to the other living creatures who share the world with us, and it is our duty to consider seriously what this knowledge should mean for us in matters of conduct."

Dean Inge is reported to have said, "Whether animals believe in a god I do not know, but I do know that they believe in a devil—the devil which is man."

Archbishop William Marlborough Carter of Cape Town (1850-1941) composed this prayer in 1929:

"O merciful Father, who hast given life to all things, and lovest all that
Thou hast made, pour into the hearts of men the spirit of Thy own

loving kindness, that they may show mercy to helpless creatures and
glorify Thee by that gentleness which is in accordance with Thy holy will."

According to Dietrich Bonhoeffer (1906-1945), in his *Christology:* "Christ is the new creature...Nature is not reconciled, like man and history, but it is redeemed for a new freedom...In the sacrament, Christ is the mediator between nature and God, and stands for all creatures before God."

"The day is surely dawning," wrote the Reverend V.A. Holmes-Gore, M.A., "when it will become clear that the idea of the Blessed Master giving His sanction to the barbaric habit of flesh-eating, is a tragic delusion, foisted upon the church by those who never knew Him."

Reverend Holmes-Gore called vegetarianism "absolutely necessary for the redemption of the planet. Indeed we cannot hope to rid the world of war, disease and a hundred other evils until we learn to show compassion to the creatures and refrain from taking their lives for food, clothing or pleasure.

"The church is powerless to free mankind from such evils as war, oppression and disease," insisted the Reverend Holmes-Gore, "because it does nothing to stop man's oppression of victimizing living creatures...Every evil action, whether it be done to a man, a woman, a child, or an animal will one day have its effect upon the transgressor. The rule that we reap what we sow is a Divine Law from which there is no escape.

"God is ever merciful," Reverend Holmes-Gore explained, "but He is also righteous, and if cruel men and women will learn compassion in no other way, then they will have to learn through suffering, even if it means suffering the same tortures that they have themselves inflicted. God is perfect Love, and He is never vengeful or vindictive, but the Divine Law of mercy and compassion cannot be broken without bringing tremendous repercussions upon the transgressor."

Reverend Holmes-Gore acknowledged that a great deal of social progress has been made, but injustices continue to flourish:

"...we have made many great reforms, but there remains much to be done. We have improved the lot of children, of prisoners, and of the poor beyond all recognition in the last hundred years. We have done something to mitigate the cruelties inflicted upon the creatures. But though some of the worst forms of torture have been made illegal, the welter of animal blood is greater than ever, and their sufferings are still appalling.

"What we need is not a reform of existing evils," concluded Reverend Holmes-Gore, "but a revolution in thought that will move Christians to show real compassion to all God's creatures. Many people claim to be lovers of animals who are very far from being so. *For a flesh-eater to claim to love animals is as if a cannibal expressed his devotion to the missionaries he consigns to the seething cauldron.*"

"Dear God," began the childhood prayers of Dr. Albert Schweitzer (1875-1965), "please protect and bless all living things. Keep them from evil and let them sleep in peace." This noted Protestant French theologian, music scholar, philosopher and missionary doctor in Africa won the Nobel Peace Prize in 1952.

Schweitzer preached an ethic of reverence for life: "Not until we extend the circle of compassion to include all living things shall we ourselves know peace." When a man questioned his philosophy, saying God created animals for man to eat, Schweitzer replied, "Not at all."

Schweitzer reflected, "How much effort it will take for us to get men to understand the words of Jesus, 'Blessed are the merciful,' and to bring them to the realization that their responsibility includes all creatures. But we must struggle with courage." According to Schweitzer, "We need a boundless ethics which will include the animals also." Schweitzer founded the Lambarene Hospital in French Equatorial Africa in 1913, managing it for many years. "I never go to a menagerie," he once wrote, "because I cannot endure the sight of the misery of the captive animals. The exhibiting of trained animals I abhor. What an amount of suffering and cruel punishment the poor creatures have to endure to give a few minutes of pleasure to men devoid of all thought and feeling for them." Schweitzer taught compassionate stewardship towards the animal kingdom: "We...are compelled by the commandment of love contained in our hearts and thoughts, and proclaimed by Jesus, to give rein to our natural sympathy to animals," he explained. "We are also compelled to help them and spare suffering as far as it is in our power."

In a sermon preached in Bath Abbey, the Reverend E.E. Bromwich, M.A., taught: "Our love of God should be extended as far as possible to all God's creatures, to our fellow human beings and to animals...In His love, God caused them all to exist, to express His feelings for beauty and order, and not merely to provide food and companionship for man. They are part of God's creation and it is God's will that they should be happy, quite as much as it is His will that we should be happy. The Christian ought to be bitterly ashamed for the unnecessary suffering that men still cause their animal brothers."

According to the Reverend Lloyd Putman: "In the beautiful story of creation in Genesis, God is pictured as the Creator of all Life—not just of man. To be sure, man is given 'dominion over the fish of the sea, and over the fowl of the air, and over every living thing that moveth upon the earth,' but far from being a brutal dominion, man is to view the animal world with a sense of stewardship and responsibility. If man lives recklessly and selfishly with no regard for animals, he is denying that God is to be seen as the creator of all life, and he is forgetting that God beheld not only man, but all creation and said that 'it was very good.' He is omitting the Biblical emphasis on man and animals sharing a common creation."

On June 5, 1958, the Reverend Norman Vincent Peale stated, "I do not believe a person can be a true Christian, and at the same time engage in cruel or inconsiderate treatment of animals." One of the leading Protestant thinkers of the 20th century, Karl Barth (1886-1968), wrote in *The Doctrine of Creation* (1961):

"If there is a freedom of man to kill animals, this signifies in any case the adoption of a qualified and in some sense enhanced responsibility. If that of his lordship over the living beast is serious enough, it takes on a new gravity when he sees himself compelled to suppress his lordship by depriving it of its life. He obviously cannot do this except under the pressure of necessity.

"Far less than all the other things which he dares to do in relation to animals, may this be ventured unthinkingly and as though it were self-evident. He must never treat this need for defensive and offensive action against the animal world as a natural one, nor include it as a normal element in his thinking or conduct. He must always shrink from this possibility even when he makes use of it.

"It always contains the sharp counter-question: who are you, man, to claim that you must venture this to maintain, support, enrich and beautify your own life? What is there in your life that you feel compelled to take this aggressive step in its favor? We cannot but be reminded of the perversion from which the whole historical existence of the creature suffers and the guilt which does not really reside in the beast but ultimately in man himself."

Responding to a question about the Kingdom of Peace, Donald Soper was of the opinion that Jesus, unlike his brother James, was neither a teetotaler nor a vegetarian, but, "I think probably, if He were here today, He would be both." In a 1963 article on "The Question of Vivisection," Soper concluded: "...let me suggest that Dr. Schweitzer's great claim that all life should be based on respect for personality has been too narrowly interpreted as being confined entirely to the personality of human beings. I believe that this creed 'respect for personality' must be applied to the whole of creation. I shouldn't be surprised if the Buddhists are nearer to an understanding of it than we are.

"When we apply this principle, we shall be facing innumerable problems, but I believe we shall be on the right track which leads finally to the end of violence and the achievement of a just social order which will leave none of God's creatures out of that Kingdom which it is our Father's good pleasure to give us."

A Book of Prayers (London, 1963) contains this prayer by Richard Tatlock:

"Almighty God who has ordained that man should have dominion over the beasts of the field and every living thing

"Grant us the help of Thy grace that we may see in this a great responsibility

"Give to all who deal with Thy creatures a compassionate heart:

"Visit with Thy justice those who are cruel to them, or hurt them needlessly;

"And make us ever thankful for the joy of their companionship

"For the sake of him who, at the last, will gather all things to himself, and make all things new again, even Jesus Christ, our Lord."

In 1970, the Church of England Board of Social Responsibility issued the following indictment of man's relationship with the animal kingdom:

"We make animals work for us, carry us, amuse us and earn money for us. We also make them die for us, sometimes in ways which would be rapidly rejected if we could readily see it done. In many fields we use them, not with gratitude and compassion, but with thoughtlessness, arrogance and complete selfishness."

In 1977, at an annual meeting in London of the Royal Society for the Prevention of Cruelty to Animals (RSPCA), Dr. Donald Coggan, the Archbishop of Canterbury, said: "Animals, as part of God's creation, have rights which must be respected. It behooves us always to be sensitive to their needs and to the reality of their pain."

"Honourable men may honourably disagree about some details of human treatment of the non-human," wrote Stephen Clark in his 1977 book, *The Moral Status of Animals,* "but vegetarianism is now as necessary a pledge of moral devotion as was the refusal of emperor-worship in the early church." According to Clark, eating animal flesh is "gluttony," and "Those who still eat flesh when they could do otherwise have no claim to be serious moralists."

"Clark's conclusion has real force and its power has yet to be sufficiently appreciated by fellow Christians," says the Reverend Andrew Linzey. "Far from seeing the possibility of widespread vegetarianism as a threat to Old Testament norms, Christians should rather welcome the fact that the Spirit is enabling us to make decisions so that we may more properly conform to the original Genesis picture of living in peace with creation."

The contemporary Christian attitude towards vegetarianism is perhaps best expressed by Kenneth Rose, in a 1984 essay entitled "The Lion Shall Eat Straw Like the Ox: The Bible and Vegetarianism."

"At present," Rose acknowledges, "vegetarianism among those who base their lives on the Bible is quite rare. Nevertheless, vegetarianism remains God's ultimate will. Since, according to the Bible, the goal of history is the transformation of the predatory principle in the principle of universal love, it seems reasonable to suppose that people who take the Bible seriously should strive to bring their lives into accordance with the righteousness and nonviolence that will prevail in God's kingdom. Surely we can't in this life fully escape the consequences of the Fall, but we can try, with God's grace, to live in accordance with God's perfect will.

"...no rational or scriptural reason can be discovered," Rose observes, "that would prohibit the teacher of Christian truth from encouraging believers to go beyond the concession to human weakness granted in Genesis 9:3 so that, even now, before the full dawning of God's kingdom of peace, they may begin living according to the ethics of that kingdom. To live in this way must be considered as part of God's ultimate intention for humanity, for how else can one account for the fact that the Bible both begins and ends in a kingdom where the sound of slaughter is unknown?

"For those of us who take the Bible seriously," Rose concludes, "our obedience to God will then become greater as it aspires to live out the vision of the peaceable kingdom the Bible points to. To the degree that we stop slaughtering innocent creatures for food, to that degree we will nullify the predatory principle, a principle that structures the injustices characteristic of this fallen age. And seeing all creatures with equal vision, we will enter more deeply into the kingdom of God."

In 1986, Dale and Judith Ostrander, ministers in the United Church of Christ issued a biblical call for stewardship, in which they concluded:

"For Christians the Scriptures contain the Word of God. And there is a particular conviction about Jesus Christ being the normative Word through whom all scriptural words are interpreted—the central meaning of Love and reconciliation of all creation. Therefore, all other biblical themes and all specific pieces of Scripture become authoritative for the Christian insofar as they affirm or are consistent with God's reconciling purpose.

"The role of Christians is to help God's reconciling purpose become a reality. This means, among other things, living out our calling to care for God's creation. It means taking seriously the interconnectedness of all life and our kinship with all living things. If Christians accept God's loving dominion, then, created in God's likeness, we are called to exercise our given 'dominion' over creation with the same kind of love. And if the great commandment is to love God, we must love God also through the complex ecological relationship of all living things.

"To misuse our delegated authority over the creation in exploitative, abusive, cruel or wasteful ways is to live as if we did not love God. We are led, therefore, as Christians to raise questions about our attitudes toward and treatment of animals. A growing number of 'voices crying in the wilderness' are calling us to take more seriously the ways in which we are despoiling the Earth and threatening its ability to sustain and support life. These voices are calling us to rethink our attitudes and our treatment of animals as we consider anew what it means to be faithful stewards of creation."

In 1987, the Reverend Carolyn J. Michael Riley declared Unity Church in Huntington, N.Y. a fur-free zone. Reverend Riley, a vegetarian since 1982, remains committed to her position. "I really do believe," she says, "that everyone is able that much more to feel the Spirit, because there are no longer vibrations of death." Reverend Riley says she wants to "help raise the consciousness of the suffering going on in the animal kingdom."

According to the Reverend James E. Caroll, an Episcopal priest in Van Nuys, California, "A committed Christian, who knows what his religion is about, will never kill an animal needlessly. Above all, he will do his utmost to put a stop to any kind of cruelty to any animal. A Christian who participates in or gives consent to cruelty to animals had better reexamine his religion or else drop the name Christian."

In 1992, members of Los Angeles' First Unitarian Church agreed to serve vegetarian meals at the church's weekly Sunday lunch. This decision was made as a protest against animal cruelty and the environmental damage caused by the livestock industry.

Vegetarianism and ethical concern for animals are consistent with Protestant Christianity:

"It is not a question of palate, of custom, of expediency, but of right," wrote the Reverend J. Tyssul-Davies, B.A., on the subject of vegetarianism. "As a mere Christian Minister, I have had to make my decision. My palate was on the side of custom; my intellect argued for the expedient; but my higher reason and conscience left me no alternative. Our Lord came to give life, and we do not follow Him by taking life needlessly. So, I was compelled, against myself, to eschew carnivorism."

The Reverend George Laughton taught that: "The practice of kindness towards dumb creatures is a sign of development to the higher reaches of intelligence and sympathy. For, mark you, in every place there are those who are giving of their time and thought and energy to the work of protecting from cruelty and needless suffering the beasts of the field and streets. These are the people who make the earth clean and sweet and more like what God intended it to be."

chapter seven
Christianity and Animal Rights

"There is no religion without love, and people may talk as much as they like about their religion, but if it does not teach them to be kind to beasts as well as man, it is all a sham."

— *Anna Sewell*
author, Black Beauty

"I care not for a man's religion whose dog or cat are not the better for it...I am in favor of animal rights as well as human rights. That is the way of a whole human being."

— *Abraham Lincoln*

French philosopher and mathematician Rene Descartes (1596-1650) taught that animals are simply machines, without souls, reason or feeling. The cry of a dog in pain, according to Descartes, is merely a mechanical noise, like the creak of a wheel. His beliefs found acceptance in ecclesiastical and scientific circles. Science was progressing quite rapidly in the 17th century; Descartes effectively removed all moral objections to animal experimentation.

One voice of objection was that of Henry More (1614-1687). In a series of letters with Descartes, More wrote that no one can prove animals lack souls or do not experience an afterlife. He regarded animal souls and immortality as consistent with the inherent goodness of God. He wrote that people deny the animals souls and an afterlife out of "narrowness of spirit, out of overmuch self-love, and contempt of other creatures."

More wrote further that this world was not made for man alone, but for other living creatures as well. He taught that God loves the animals and is concerned about their welfare and happiness. More believed that humans were meant to rule over the animals with compassionate stewardship. He quoted Proverbs 12:10 from the Old Testament: "The good man is merciful to his beasts."

A distinguished philosopher and an eloquent writer, More believed unrestrained human violence and abuse towards animals would cause humans to likewise deal with one another. "I think that he that slights the life or welfare of a brute Creature," wrote More, "is naturally so unjust, that if outward laws did not restrain him, he would be as cruel to Man."

In 1776, Dr. Humphrey Primatt, an Anglican priest, published *A Dissertation on the Duty of Mercy and the Sin of Cruelty to Brute Animals.* This may have been the first book devoted to kindness to animals. Dr. Primatt believed that cruelty towards animals leads inevitably to human violence: "if all the barbarous customs and practices still subsisting amongst us were decreed to be as illegal as they are sinful, we should not hear of so many shocking murders and acts as we now do."

According to Primatt, "Love is the great Hinge upon which universal Nature turns. The Creation is a transcript of the divine Goodness; and every leaf in the book of Nature reads us a lecture on the wisdom and benevolence of its great Author...upon this principle, every creature of God is good in its kind; that is, it is such as it ought to be."

Primatt drew no distinction between the sufferings of animals and those of men: "Pain is pain, whether it is inflicted on man or on beast; and the creature that suffers it, whether man or beast, being sensible of the misery of it whilst it lasts, suffers *Evil*..."

Primatt wrote with a vision of universal emancipation: "It has pleased God the Father of all men, to cover some men with white skins, and others with black skins; but as there is neither merit nor demerit in complexion, the *white man*, nonwithstanding the barbarity of custom and prejudice, can have no right, by virtue of his *colour*, to enslave and tyrannize over a *black* man...

"Now, if amongst men, the differences of their powers of the mind, and of their complexion, stature, and accidents of fortune, do not give any one man a right to abuse or insult any other man on account of these differences; for the same reason, a man can have no natural right to abuse and torment a beast, merely because a beast has not the mental powers of a man.

"For, such as the man is, he is but as God made him; and the very same is true of the beast. Neither of them can lay claim to any intrinsic *Merit*, for being such as they are; for, before they were created, it was impossible that either of them could deserve; and at their creation, their shapes, perfections or defects were invariably fixed, and their bounds set which they cannot pass.

"And being such, neither more nor less than God made them, there is no more demerit in a beast being a beast, than there is merit in a man being a man; that is, there is neither merit nor demerit in either of them.

"We may pretend to what religion we please," Primatt concluded, "but cruelty is atheism. We may boast of Christianity; but cruelty is infidelity. We may trust to our orthodoxy; but cruelty is the worst of heresies.

"The religion of Jesus Christ originated in the mercy of God; and it was the gracious design of it to promote peace to every creature on earth, and to create a spirit of universal benevolence or goodwill in men.

"And it has pleased God therein to display the riches of His own goodness and mercy towards us; and the revealer of His blessed will, the author and finisher of our faith, hath commanded us to be merciful, as our Father is also merciful, the obligation upon Christians becomes the stronger; and it is our bounded duty, in an especial manner, and above all other people, to extend the precept of mercy to every object of it. For, indeed, a cruel Christian is a monster of ingratitude, a scandal to his profession and beareth the name of Christ in vain..."

Christian writer C.S. Lewis noted that animals were included in the first Passover. The application of the "blood of the lamb" on the doorposts, not only saved a man and his family from death that night in Egypt, it saved his animals as well. Lewis put forth a rational argument concerning the resurrection of animals in *The Problem of Pain*. His 1947 essay, "A Case for Abolition," attacked vivisection (animal experimentation) and reads as follows:

"Once the old Christian idea of a total difference in kind between man and beast has been abandoned, then *no argument for experiments on animals can be found which is not also an argument for experiments on inferior men*. If we cut up beasts simply because they cannot prevent us and because we're backing up our own side in the struggle for existence, it is only logical to cut up imbeciles, criminals, enemies, or capitalists for the same reason. Indeed, experiments on men have already begun. We all hear that Nazi scientists have done them. We all suspect that our own scientists may begin to do so, in secret, at any moment.

"The victory of vivisection marks a great advance in the triumph of ruthless, non-moral utilitarianism over the old world of ethical law; a triumph in which we, as well as animals, are already the victims, and of which Dachau and Hiroshima mark the more recent achievements. In justifying cruelty to animals we put ourselves also on the animal level. We choose the jungle and must abide by our choice."

"I am not a Christian," wrote one animal rights activist in *Animals, Men and Morals* (1971), "but I find it incomprehensible that those who preach a doctrine of love and compassion can believe that the material pleasures of meat-eating justify the slaughter it requires."

In 1977, at an annual meeting in London of the Royal Society for the Prevention of Cruelty to Animals (RSPCA), Dr. Donald Coggan, the Archbishop of Canterbury, said, "Animals, as part of God's creation, have rights which must be respected. It behooves us always to be sensitive to their needs and to the reality of their pain."

Dr. L. Charles Birch, an Australian "eco-philosopher," has long urged the churches to preach conservation of nature and respect for other living creatures. In July 1979 he argued at a conference of the World Council of Churches in Cambridge, Massachussetts, that all living creatures should be valued because of their "capacity for feeling." Dr. Birch has also condemned factory farming—the overcrowded, confinement methods of raising and killing animals for food—as "unethical," and declared that "the animal rights movement should be supported by all Christians."

Christians have mobilized on abortion, euthanasia, capital punishment and other sanctity-of-life issues. While a rational case can be made for the rights of preborn humans, a stronger, more immediate and compelling secular case exists for the rights of animals. Animals are highly complex creatures, possessing a brain, a central nervous system and a sophisticated mental life. Animals *suffer* at the hands of their human tormentors and exhibit such "human" behaviors and feelings as fear and physical pain, defense of their children, pair bonding, group/tribal loyalty, grief at the loss of loved ones, joy, jealousy, competition, territoriality, and cooperation.

Can organized religion give its massive support to the struggle for animal rights? Today we find churches spearheading social change, calling for civil rights, the protection of unborn children, an end to human rights abuses in other countries, etc. This has not always been the case. It has often been said that on issues such as women's rights and human slavery, religion has impeded social progress.

The church of the past never considered slavery to be a moral evil. The Protestant churches of Virginia, South Carolina, and other southern states actually passed resolutions in favor of the human slave traffic.

Human slavery was called "by Divine Appointment," "a Divine institution," "a moral relation," "God's institution," "not immoral," but "founded in right." The slave trade was called "legal," "licit," "in accordance with humane principles" and "the laws of revealed religion."

New Testament verses calling for obedience and subservience on the part of slaves (Titus 2:9-10; Ephesians 6:5-9; Colossians 3:22-25; I Peter 2:18-25) and respect for the master (I Timothy 6:1-2; Ephesians 6:5-9) were often cited in order to justify human slavery. Many of Jesus' parables refer to human slaves. Paul's epistle to Philemon concerns a runaway slave returned to his master.

"Paul's outright endorsement of slavery should be an undying embarrassment to Christianity as long as they hold the entire New Testament to be the word of God," says contemporary Quaker physician Dr. Charles P. Vaclavik. "Without a doubt, the American slaveholders quoted Paul again and again to substantiate their right to hold slaves.

"The moralist movement to abolish slavery had to go to non-Biblical sources to demonstrate the immoral nature of slavery. The abolitionists could not turn to Christian sources to condemn slavery, for Christianity had become the bastion of the evil practice through its endorsement by the Apostle Paul. Only the Old Testament gave the abolitionist any Biblical support in his effort to free the slaves. 'You shall not surrender to his master a slave who has taken refuge with you.' (Deuteronomy 23:15) What a pittance of material opposing slavery from a book supposedly representing the word of God."

In 1852 Josiah Priest wrote *Bible Defense of Slavery*. Others claimed blacks were subhuman. Buckner H. Payne, calling himself "Ariel," wrote in 1867, "the tempter in the Garden of Eden...was a beast, a talking beast...the negro." Ariel argued that since the negro was not part of Noah's family, he must have been a beast. Eight souls were saved on the ark, therefore, the negro must be a beast, and "consequently he has no soul to be saved."

The status of animals in contemporary human society is not unlike that of human slaves in centuries past. Quoting Isaiah 61:1, Luke 4:18, Colossians 3:11 or any other biblical passages in favor of liberty, equality and an end to human slavery in the 18th century would have been met with the same kind of response animal rights activists receive today (e.g., II Corinthians 12:8-9) if they cite biblical passages in favor of vegetarianism and compassion towards animals.

Dr. Tom Regan, the foremost intellectual leader of the animal rights movement and author of *The Case for Animal Rights*, notes that animals "have beliefs and desires; perception, memory, and a sense of the future, including their own future; and emotion life together with feelings of pleasure and pain; preference and welfare interests; the ability to initiate action in pursuit of their desires and goals; a psycho-physical identity over time; and an individual welfare in the sense that their experiential life fares well or ill for them, logically independently of their being the object of anyone else's interests."

Similarly, research psychologist Dr. Theodore Barber, writes in his 1993 book, *The Human Nature of Birds*, that birds are intelligent beings, capable of flexible thought, judgement, and the ability to express opinions, desires, and choices just as humans do. According to Dr. Barber, birds can make and use tools; work with abstract concepts; exhibit grief, joy, compassion and altruism; create musical compositions, and perform intricate mathematical calculations in navigation.

If animals have rights, then the widespread misconception amongst Christians, that compassion for animals and vegetarianism are solely "Jewish" concerns, becomes as absurd as saying, "it's only wrong to own slaves if you're a Quaker." Suffering and injustice concern us all. Christian clergy have begun to seriously address the issue of animal rights. The Reverend Dr. S. Parkes Cadman has been quoted as saying:

"Life in any form is our perpetual responsibility. Its abuse degrades those who practice it; its rightful usage is a signal token of genuine manhood. If there be a superintending Justice, surely It takes account of the injuries and sufferings of helpless yet animate creation. Let us be perfectly clear about the spirituality of the issue before us. We have abolished human bondage because it cursed those who imposed it almost more than those who endured it. It is now our bounded duty to abolish the brutal and ferocious oppression of those creatures of our common Father which share with man the mystery of life...this theme is nothing if not spiritual: an acid test of our relation to the Deity of love and compassion."

In a 1985 paper entitled "The Status of Animals in the Christian Tradition" (based on a September 1984 talk at a Quaker study center entitled "Non-violence: Extending the Concept to Animals"), the Reverend Andrew Linzey redefined the traditional understanding of human "dominion" over the animal kingdom:

"...scholarly research in the modern period interprets the notion of dominion in terms of early kingship theology in which man is to act as God's vice-regent in creation, that is with authority, but under divine moral rule. We are therefore not given absolute or arbitrary power over animals but entrusted with God-like power which must be exercised with responsibility and restraint.

"...for centuries Christians have misinterpreted their own scripture and have read into it implications that were simply not there. The idea that human beings have absolute rights over creation is therefore eclipsed. The vital issue that now confronts moral theologians is how far and to what extent we may use animal life and for what purposes."

After citing Scripture and many positive instances of concern for animals in the Christian tradition, Reverend Linzey concludes that the Christian basis for animal rights includes the following points:

1. Animals are fellow creatures with us and belong to God.

2. Animals have value to God independently of their value or use to us.

3. Animals exist in a covenant relationship with God and mankind and therefore there is a moral bond between us.

4. Human beings are set in a position of responsibility to animals.

5. Jesus Christ is our moral exemplar in his sacrifice of love for creation.

6. God's redeeming love extends to all creation.

7. We have duties to animals derived from our relationship of responsibility to them.

In a sermon preached in York Minster, September 28, 1986, John Austin Baker, the Bishop of Salisbury, England, attacked the overcrowded confinement methods of raising and killing animals for food, choosing as his example, the treatment of chickens.

"Is there any credit balance for the battery hen, denied almost all natural functioning, all normal environment, lapsing steadily into deformity and disease, for the whole of her existence?" he asked. "It is in the battery shed and the broiler house, not in the wild, that we find the true parallel to Auschwitz. Auschwitz is a purely human invention."

On another occasion, Bishop Baker taught: "By far the most important duty of all Christians in the cause of animal welfare is to cultivate this capacity to see; to see things with the heart of God, and so to suffer with other creatures."

On World Prayer Day for Animals, October 4, 1986, Bishop Baker preached against indifference to animal pain and lauded the animal welfare movement: "To shut your mind, heart, imagination to the sufferings of others is to begin slowly but inexorably to die. It is to cease by inches from being human, to become in the end capable of nothing generous or unselfish—or sometimes capable of anything, however terrible. You in the animal welfare movement are among those who may yet save our society from becoming spiritually deaf, blind and dead, and so from the doom that will justly follow..."

According to Bishop Baker: "...Rights, whether animal or human, have only one sure foundation: that God loves us all and rejoices in us all. We humans are called to share with God in fulfilling the work of love toward all creatures...the true glory of the strong is to give themselves for the cherishing of the weak."

In October, 1986, on the Feast Day of St. Francis, the Very Reverend James Morton in the Cathedral of St. John the Divine, New York City, made this observation: "We don't own animals, any more than we don't own trees or own mountains or seas or, indeed, each other. We don't own our wives or our husbands or our friends or our lovers. We respect and behold and we celebrate trees and mountains and seas and husbands and wives and lovers and children and friends and animals...Our souls must be poor—must be open—in order to be able to receive, to behold, to enter into communion with, but not to possess. Our poverty of soul allows animals to thrive and to shine and be free and radiate God's glory."

A 1980 United Nations report states that women constitute *half* the world's population, perform nearly *two-thirds* of its work hours, yet receive *one-tenth* of the world's income and own less than *one-hundredth* of the world's property. The impact of the women's movement upon the church is being heralded as a Second Reformation. Women are now being ordained as priests, pastors and ministers, while patriarchal references to the Almighty as "Father" are replaced with the gender-neutral "Parent." Jesus Christ is designated the "Child of God." The words of Scripture—perhaps, more accurately, the words of the apostle Paul—on this subject are seen today not as a divine revelation, but rather as an embarrassment from centuries past:

"Let the women keep silent in the churches, for they are not allowed to speak. Instead, they must, as the Law says, be in subordination. If they wish to learn something, let them inquire of their own husbands at home; for it is improper for a woman to speak in church...let a woman learn quietly with complete submission. I do not allow a woman to teach, neither to domineer over a man; instead she is to keep still. For Adam was first formed, then Eve. And Adam was not deceived, but the woman, since she was deceived, experienced the transgression. She will, however, be kept safe through the child-bearing, if with self-control she continues in faith and love and consecration." (I Corinthians 14:34-35; I Timothy 2:11-15)

Many churches now claim these instructions were merely temporary frameworks used to build churches in the first century pagan world—they are not to be taken as universal absolutes for all eternity. If churches, Scripture and Christianity can adapt and be redefined or reinterpreted in a changing world to end injustices towards women, they can certainly do the same towards animals.

The International Network for Religion and Animals (INRA) was founded in 1985 by Virginia Bouraquardez. Its educational and religious programs are meant to "bring religious principles to bear upon humanity's attitude towards the treatment of our animal kin...and, through leadership, materials, and programs, to successfully interact with clergy and laity from many religious traditions."

According to the INRA:

"Religion counsels the powerful to be merciful and kind to those weaker than themselves, and most of humankind is at least nominally religious. But there is a ghastly paradox. Far from showing mercy, humanity uses its dominion over other animal species to pen them in cruel close confinement; to trap, club, and harpoon them; to poison, mutilate, and shock them in the name of science; to kill them by the billions; and even to blind them in excruciating pain to test cosmetics.

"Some of these abuses are due to mistaken understandings of religious principles; others, to a failure to apply those principles. Scriptures need to be fully researched concerning the relationship of humans to nonhuman animals, and to the entire ecological structure of Nature. Misinterpretations of scripture taken out of context, or based upon questionable theological assumptions need to be re-examined."

In the winter of 1990, INRA's Executive Director, the Reverend Dr. Marc A. Wessels of the United Church of Christ wrote: "As a Christian clergyman who speaks of having compassion for other creatures and who actively declares the need for humans to develop an ethic that gives reverence for all of life, I hope that others will open their eyes, hearts and minds to the responsibility of loving care for God's creatures."

In a pamphlet entitled "The Spiritual Link Between Humans and Animals," Reverend Wessels writes: "We recognize that many animal rights activists and ecologists are highly critical of Christians because of our relative failure thus far adequately to defend animals and to preserve the natural environment. Yet there are positive signs of a growing movement of Christian activists and theologians who are committed to the process of ecological stewardship and animal liberation.

"Individual Christians and groups on a variety of levels, including denominational, ecumenical, national and international, have begun the delayed process of seriously considering and practically addressing the question of Christian responsibility for animals. Because of the debate surrounding the 'rights' of animals, some Christians are considering the tenets of their faith in search for an appropriate ethical response."

According to Reverend Wessels, "The most important teaching which Jesus shared was the need for people to love God with their whole self and to love their neighbor as they loved themselves. Jesus expanded the concept of neighbor to include those who were normally excluded, and it is therefore not too farfetched for us to consider the animals as our neighbors.

"To think about animals as our brothers and sisters is not a new or radical idea. By extending the idea of neighbor, the love of neighbor includes love of, compassion for, and advocacy of animals. There are many historical examples of Christians who thought along those lines, besides the familiar illustration of St.

Francis. An abbreviated listing of some of those individuals worthy of study and emulation includes Saint Blaise, Saint Comgall, Saint Cuthbert, Saint Gerasimus, Saint Giles, and Saint Jerome, to name but a few."

Reverend Wessels notes that: "In the Bible, which we understand as the divine revelation of God, there is ample evidence of the vastness and goodness of God toward animals. The Scriptures announce God as the creator of all life, the One responsible for calling life into being and placing it in an ordered fashion which reflects God's glory. Humans and animals are a part of this arrangement. Humanity has a special relationship with particular duties to God's created order, a connection to the animals by which they are morally bound by God's covenant with them.

"According to the Scriptures, Christians are called to respect the life of animals and to be ethically engaged in protecting the life and liberty of all sentient creatures. As that is the case, human needs and rights do not usurp an animal's intrinsic rights, nor should they deny the basic liberty of either individual animals or specific species. If the Christian call can be understood as being a command to be righteous, then Christians must have a higher regard for the lives of animals.

"Jesus' life was one of compassion and liberation," explains Reverend Wessels, "his ministry was one which understood and expressed the needs of the oppressed. Especially in the past decade, Christians have been reminded that their faith requires them to take seriously the cries of the oppressed.

"Theologians such as Gutierrez, Miranda, and Hinkelammert have defined the Christian message as one which liberates lives and transforms social patterns of oppression. That concept of Christianity which sees God as the creator of the universe and the One who seeks justice is not exclusive; immunity from cruelty and injustice is not only a human desire or need—the animal kingdom also needs liberation."

A growing number of Christian theologians, clergy and activists are beginning to take a stand in favor of animal rights. In a pamphlet entitled "Christian Considerations on Laboratory Animals," Reverend Marc Wessels notes that in laboratories animals cease to be persons and become "tools of research." He cites William French of Loyala University as having made the same observation at a gathering of Christian ethicists at Duke University—a conference entitled "Good News for Animals?"

On Earth Day, 1990, Reverend Wessels observed: "It is a fact that no significant social reform has yet taken place in this country without the voice of the religious community being heard. The endeavors of the abolition of slavery; the women's suffrage movement; the emergence of the pacifist tradition during World War I; the struggles to support civil rights, labor unions, and migrant farm workers; and the anti-nuclear and peace movements have all succeeded in part because of the power and support of organized religion. Such authority and energy is required by individual Christians and the institutional church today if the liberation of animals is to become a reality."

The Reverend Dr. Andrew Linzey's 1987 book, *Christianity and the Rights of Animals*, may be regarded as a landmark in Christian theology as well as in the animal rights movement. Linzey responds to criticism from many of the intellectual leaders of the animal rights and environmental movements—Peter Singer, Richard Ryder, Maureen Duffy, Lynn White, Jr.—that Christianity has excluded nonhumans from moral concern, that Christian churches are consequently agents of oppression, and that Christian doctrines are thus responsible for the roots of the current ecological crisis.

"We do not have books devoted to a consideration of animals," he acknowledges. "We do not have clearly worked-out systematic views on animals. These are signs of the problem. The thinking, or at least the vast bulk of it, *has yet to be done.*"

Dr. Tom Regan calls Reverend Linzey, an Anglican clergyman, "the foremost theologian working in the field of animal/human relations." *Christianity and the Rights of Animals*, a must-read for all Christians, certainly clears the ground.

According to Reverend Linzey:

"It does seem somewhat disingenuous for Christians to speak so solidly for human rights and then query the appropriateness of rights language when it comes to animals...the Christian basis for animal rights is bound to be different in crucial respects from that of secular philosophy. But because Christians (as we see it) have a good, even superior, basis for animal rights, that in no way precludes others from utilizing the terminology."

Linzey acknowledges that the gospel is ambiguous on ethical questions such as animal rights. "When it comes to wanting to know the attitude that Jesus may have taken to a range of pressing moral issues today, we are often at a loss to know precise answers. But we can at least be clear about the contours. The lordship of Christ is expressed in service. He is the one who washes dirty feet, heals the sick, releases individuals from oppression, both spiritual and physical, feeds the hungry, and teaches his followers the way of costly loving..."

Linzey justifies compassion for animals through the example of Christ. "If God's self-revealed life in Jesus is the model of how Christians should behave and if, crucially, divine power is expressed in service, how can we disregard even 'the least among us'? It may be that in the light of Christ we are bound to say that the weakest have in fact the greater claim upon us.

"In some ways," Linzey continues, "Christian thinking is already oriented in this direction. What is it that so appalls us about cruelty to children or oppression of the vulnerable, but that these things are betrayals of relationships of special care and special trust? Likewise, and even more so, in the case of animals who are mostly defenceless before us.

"Slowly but surely," Linzey explains, "having grasped the notion of dominion means stewardship, we are now for the first time seeing how demanding our lordship over creation is really meant to be. Where once we thought we had the cheapest ride, we are now beginning to see that we have the costliest responsibilities...Lordship without service is indeed tyranny."

Discussing the finer points between human "dominion" over animals, versus humane stewardship, Linzey says, "the whole point about stewardship is that the stewards should value what God has given as highly as they value themselves. To be placed in a relationship of special care and special protection is hardly a license for tyranny or even... 'benevolent despotism.' If we fail to grasp the necessarily sacrificial nature of lordship as revealed in Christ, we shall hardly begin to make good stewards, even of those beings we regard as 'inferior.'"

Linzey sees divine reconciliation through Christ. The "hidden purpose" of God in Christ was "determined beforehand," and consists of bringing "all in heaven and on earth" into a "unity in Christ." (Ephesians 1:9-11) Linzey notes that in Ephesians, as in Colossians and Romans, the creation is "foreordained in Christ."

"Since it is through man's curse that the creation has become estranged from its Creator," Linzey asserts, "it is only right that one important step along the road to recovery is that man himself should be redeemed. The salvation of human beings is in this way a pointer to the salvation of all creation...For it must be the special role of humans within God's creation to hasten the very process of redemption, by the power of the Spirit for which God has destined it.

"Human beings must be healed," Linzey insists, "because it is *their* violence and disorder which has been let loose on the world. Through humans, liberated for God, we can glimpse the possibility of world redemption. Can it really be so difficult to grasp that the God who performs the demanding and costly task of redeeming sinful man will not also be able to restore the involuntary animal creation, which groans under the weight of another's burden?"

Linzey thus sees Jesus Christ as the only hope for animal liberation. "In Christ, God has borne our sufferings, actually entered into them in the flesh so that we may be liberated from them (and all pain and all death) and secure, by his grace, eternal redemption.

"In principle the question of how an almighty, loving God can allow suffering in a mouse is no different to the same question that may be posed about man. Of course there are important differences between men and mice, but there are no morally relevant ones when it comes to pain and suffering. It is for this reason alone that we need to hold fast to those cosmic strands of the biblical material which speak of the inclusive nature of Christ's sacrifice and redeeming work."

Linzey finds two justifications for a Christian case for vegetarianism:

"The first is that killing is a morally significant matter. While justifiable in principle, it can only be practically justified where there is real need for human nourishment. Christian vegetarians do not have to claim that it is always and absolutely wrong to kill in order to eat. It could well be that there were, and are, some situations in which meat-eating was and is essential in order to survive. Geographical consider-ations alone make it difficult to envisiage life in Palestine at the time of Christ without some primitive fishing industry. But the crucial point is that where we are *free to do otherwise* the killing of Spirit-filled individuals requires moral justification. It *may* be justifiable, but only when human nourishment clearly requires it, and even then it remains an inevitable consequence of sin.

"The second point," Linzey explains, "is that misappropriation occurs when humans do not recognize that the life of an animal belongs to God, not to them. Here it seems to me that Christian vegetarianism is well-founded. For while it may have been possible in the past to rear animals with personal care and consideration for their well-being and to dispatch them with the humble and scrupulous recognition that their life should only be taken in times of necessity, such conditions are abnormal today."

In *Christianity and the Rights of Animals*, the Reverend Dr. Andrew Linzey not only makes a very sound Christian theological case for animal rights, but states further that animal slavery may be abolished on the same grounds that were used in biblical times to abolish human sacrifice and infanticide:

"...it may be argued that humans have a right to their culture and their way of life. What would we be, it may be questioned, without our land and history and ways of life? In general, culture is valuable. But it is also the case that there can be evil cultures, or at least cherished traditions which perpetuate injustice or tyranny.

"The Greeks, for example, despite all their outstanding contributions to learning did not appear to recognize the immorality of (human) slavery. There can be elements within every culture that are simply not worth defending, not only slavery, but also infanticide and human sacrifice."

"With God, all things are possible." (Matthew 19:26; Mark 10:27; Luke 18:27) Linzey urges Christian readers to think in terms of future possibilities. "For to be committed to Jesus involves being committed not only to his earthly ministry in the past but also to his living Spirit in whose power new possibilities are continually opened up for us in the present. All things have yet to be made new in Christ and we have yet to become perfect as our Father in heaven is perfect. Making peace is a dynamic possibility through the Spirit."

Frances Arnetta founded Christians Helping Animals and People Inc. (CHAP), a New York-based ministry. "I believe Jesus Christ is the only hope for ending cruelty towards animals," she says. The end of animal cruelty will coincide with Jesus' Second Coming, when the Kingdom of Peace will reign. Arnetta lives her life in preparation for that day. Arnetta cites Psalm 50:10-11 and Revelations 4:11, insisting animals belong to God and are not here for human exploitation.

"Compassion towards people and compassion towards animals are not mutually exclusive," Arnetta writes. "A truly sympathetic person cannot turn his or her feelings on and off like a faucet, depending on the species, race, sex or creed of the victim. God teaches us in Psalm 36:6 and in Matthew 6:26 and 10:29 that his compassion encompasses all creatures, human and animal. Shall we not imitate our Heavenly Father?"

In a pamphlet entitled *Animal Rights: A Biblical View*, Arnetta cites Genesis 1:20-22. God creates animals and blesses them; animals have the right to be blessed by God. After creating the nonhuman world,

God "saw that it was good." (Genesis 1:25) "Here, God gave the animals their own intrinsic value; the Creator and Lord of the universe called them good! Now they had the right to be viewed as individuals with inherent qualities of goodness and worth, independent of human beings, who had not yet been created!

"Next," Arnetta continues, "God brought the animals to Adam to be named. This naming gave status to the animals...God saw to it that every living creature had a name. (Genesis 2:19) here God gave them the right to personhood and respect...God has also used the animals as His messengers. The first time Noah sent forth the dove from the ark, her return told him that the waters had not receded enough for the occupants of the ark to leave it. The second time she returned with an olive leaf, telling him that the waters were abated. During the drought and resulting famine in Israel under Ahab's reign, God sent ravens to feed the prophet Elijah. (I Kings 17:4-6)"

On the issue of animal sacrifice, Arnetta notes that, "Without the shedding of innocent blood, there can be no forgiveness of sin (Hebrews 9:22). I believe that death was the price exacted by Satan for the return of creation into fellowship with God...The sacrificial animal was an Old Testament symbol of Christ, the Redeemer: 'Except ye eat the flesh of the Son of Man and drink His blood, ye shall have no life in you.' (John 6:53) I believe God dearly loves the animals, because they are innocent—only their innocent blood could cover sin until Jesus shed His innocent blood to wash away sin. With Jesus' death, the need for animal sacrifice was done away with."

Arnetta supports this position, as well as her view that animals are included in God's kingdom, by citing John 3:16:

"'For God so loved the world (not just humankind), that He gave His only begotten Son...' The word 'world' used here in the original Greek means 'cosmos'—all of creation! (See also I Corinthians 15:16-28 and Colossians 1:15-20). And so, through Jesus Christ, the animals have a right to eternal life!

"Revelations 5:13 tells of the coming worship of Jesus," explains Arnetta. "And every creature which is in heaven, and on the earth, and under the earth, and such as are in the sea, and all that are in them, heard I saying, 'Blessing and honour and glory and power be unto Him that sitteth upon the throne, and unto the Lamb (Jesus) for ever and ever.'"

Arnetta examines numerous passages from both the Old and New Testaments and concludes that God has given the animals many rights:

1. The right to His blessing

2. Their own intrinsic worth

3. The right to personhood

4. The right to a voice—either their own or ours

5. The right to eternal life

6. The right to be included in the covenants of God

7. The right to life

8. The right to freedom from fear, pain, and suffering

9. The right not to be overworked

10. The right to mercy and compassion

11. The right to shelter and comfort

12. The right to worship God, however they are able

Arnetta regards animal rights not as a kind of "good works," but rather as a fundamental Christian concern: "Why worry about the unwanted unborn? Why worry about the starving peoples of the world? Here's why: We are to 'occupy' until Jesus returns...the salvation of souls is our first priority. But we can't help souls if we're one-dimensional. Jesus commands us to feed the hungry, clothe the naked, visit the imprisoned, and in general practice all the works of mercy.

"In our present world," Arnetta admits, "human problems will never be solved. Jesus said, 'For ye have the poor always with you...' (Matthew 26:11) What we must do is try to relieve suffering wherever we find it, regardless of the nature of the victim, until Jesus comes back. Only His return will eliminate all suffering forever (see Isaiah 11:6-9).

"Revelations 12:12 specifically states that the devil causes suffering to animals, and Ephesians 4:27 warns us not to give him any place. Genesis 1:20-25 declares that as God created each creature 'He saw that it was good.' In this way, God gave every creature its own intrinsic worth, before man was even created...Some years ago, the FBI did a study on the link between a child's cruelty to animals and his/her tendency toward violent crime in adulthood. A direct relationship was proven beyond doubt..."

According to Arnetta, "As humanism and speciesism took hold in the 'Age of Reason,' Descartes declared that animals are only machines. And so, Western civilization took a tragic detour from Biblical compassion—a detour that is with us to this day."

Arnetta rejects the idea that biblically-based respect for the sanctity of all life will lead to pantheism or the deification of animals, as is the case with certain non-Christian faiths. "When we Christians are *compassionate* to animals," she says, "we are imitating our Heavenly Father. If non-Christian people are leading the way in respect for the lives of animals, it is because we Christians have failed to be the light Jesus commanded us to be. We should be an example of boundless mercy."

In a pamphlet entitled *What the Bible Says About Vegetarianism: God's Best for All Concerned*, Arnetta writes that Christians should be "harmless as doves," and describes vegetarianism as "God's best for good health," "God's best for the environment," and "God's best to feed the hungry."

She writes: "Vegetarianism is the diet that will once again be given by God. Jews look forward to that time as the coming of the Messiah; Christians see it as the *return* of the Messiah—Jesus Christ. It is prophesied in Isaiah 11:1-9 and in Isaiah 65—a time when, under His lordship, predator and prey will lie down side by side in peace and once again enjoy the green herb and the fruit of the seed-bearing tree.

"In the New Testament, Revelation 21:4 describes this as the time when 'God shall wipe away all tears from their eyes; and there shall be no more death, neither sorrow, nor crying, neither shall there be any more pain: for the former things are passed away.'

"Not only is it totally Scriptural to be a vegetarian," Arnetta concludes, "but when done in service to the true and living God, it may well be as close to a heavenly lifestyle as one can get!"

Clive Hollands of the St. Andrew Animal Fund in England, wrote in a 1987 paper entitled "The Animal Kingdom and the Kingdom of God" that animal rights "is an issue of strict justice," and one that calls for Christian compassion:

"As Christians we believe that God gave us dominion over His Creation and we used that authority, not to protect and safeguard the natural world, but to destroy and pollute the environment and, worse, we have deprived animals of the dignity and respect which is due to all that has life.

"Let us then thank God for the unending wonder of the created world, for the oneness of all life—for the Integrity of Creation. Let us pray for all living creatures, those in the wild that may never even see man and in whose very being worship their Creator.

"Let us think and pray especially for all those animals who do know man, who are in the service of man, and who suffer at the hands of man. Let us pray to the God who knows of the fall of a single sparrow, that the suffering, pain and fear of all animals may be eased.

"Finally, let us pray for all those who work to protect animals that their efforts may be rewarded and the time may come when animals are granted the dignity and respect which is their due as living beings created by the same hand that fashioned you and me."

The Glauberg Confession is a theological statement of faith made before a God whose love extends to all His creatures. It reads as follows:

"We confess before God, the Creator of the Animals, and before our fellow Men; We have failed as Christians, because we forgot the animals in our faith.

"As theologians we were not prepared to stand up against scientific and philosophical trends inimical to life with the Theology of Creation. We have betrayed the diaconical mission of Jesus, and not served our least brethren, the animals.

"As pastors we were scared to give room to animals in our churches and parishes.

"As the Church, we were deaf to the 'groaning in travail' of our mistreated and exploited fellow-creatures.

"We justify the *Glauberg Confession* theologically.

"We read the statements in the Bible about Creation and regard for our fellow-creatures with new eyes and new interest. We know how tied up we are with Nature, linked with every living thing—and under the same threat.

"The rediscovery of the theology of Creation has also turned our regard upon the animals, our poorest brothers and sisters. We perceive that as theologically thinking and working Christians we owe them a change of attitude.

"We justify our *Confession* pastorally.

"For years many people actively engaged in animal welfare have been waiting for us ministers of religion to take up the cause of animal rights. Many of them have quit the Church in disappointment because no clear witness was given for the animals in the field of theology, in the Church's social work or in the parishes, either in word or in deed. The task of winning back the trust of these people who dedicate their time, money, energy and sometimes their health to reconciliation with the animals, is a pastoral challenge to us."

Reverend Marc Wessels says of *The Glauberg Confession*:

"It speaks simply but eloquently on behalf of those who have determined that they will no longer support a theology of human dictatorship that is against God's other creatures...

"This brief statement was written during the spring of 1988 and was signed by both Roman Catholic and Protestant clergy who participated in its framing.

"It was signed by men and women of religious orders, as well as by laity. Both academics and average church members have indicated their support for the document by signing it.

"Growing numbers of people around the globe are also adding their own personal declaration of support by forwarding their names to the covenors of the confession."

> "Increasingly, during this century Christians have come to understand the gospel, the Good News, in terms of freedom, both freedom *from* oppression and freedom *for* life with God and others. Too often, however, this freedom has been limited to human beings, excluding most other creatures, as well as the earth.
>
> "This freedom *cannot* be so limited because if we destroy other species and the ecosystem, human beings cannot live. This freedom *should* not be so limited because other creatures, both species and individuals, deserve to live in and for themselves and for God. Therefore, we call on

Christians as well as other people of good will to work towards the
liberation of life, *all* life."

— World Council of Churches
"The Liberation of Life," 1988

In "The Liberation of Life," the World Council of Churches, a politically left-liberal organization with worldwide influence, has taken the strongest animal protection position of any Christian body.

This document urges parishioners to avoid cosmetics and household items that have been tested on animals; to buy "cruelty-free" products, instead. This document urges parishioners to boycott animal furs and skins, and purchase "cruelty-free" clothing as a humane alternative. This document asks that meat, eggs and dairy products be purchased from sources where the animals have not been subject to over-crowding, confinement and abuse, and reminds parishioners they are free to avoid such products alto-gether. Parishioners are also asked not to patronize any form of entertainment that treats animals as mere objects of human usage.

In a paper presented before the Conference on Creation Theology and Environmental Ethics at the World Council of Churches in Annecy, France in September, 1988, Dr. Tom Regan expressed opposition to discrimination based upon genetic differences:

"...biological differences *inside* the species *Homo sapiens* do not justify radically different treatment among those individual humans who differ biologically (for example, in terms of sex, or skin color, or chromosome count). Why, then, should biological differences *outside* our species count morally? If having one eye or deformed limbs do not disqualify a human being from moral consideration equal to that given to those humans who are more fortunate, how can it be rational to disqualify a rat or a wolf from equal moral consideration because, unlike us, they have paws and a tail?"

Dr. Regan concluded: "...the whole fabric of Christian *agape* is woven from the threads of sacrificial acts. To abstain, on principle, from eating animals, therefore, although it is not the end-all, can be the begin-all of our conscientious effort to journey back to (or toward) Eden, can be one way (among others) to re-establish or create that relationship to the earth which, if Genesis 1 is to be trusted, was part of God's original hopes for and plans in creation.

"It is the integrity of this creation we seek to understand and aspire to honor. In the choice of our food, I believe, we see, not in a glass darkly, but face to face, a small but not unimportant part of both the challenge and the promise of Christianity and animal rights."

In a 1989 interview, Reverend Linzey insisted, "...my primary loyalty is to God, and not to the church. You see, I don't think the claims of the church and the claims of God are identical...The church is a very human institution, a frail human institution, and it often gets things wrong. Indeed, it's worse than that. It's often a stumbling block and often a scandal."

Linzey expressed optimism from a study of history: "Let's take your issue of slavery. If you go back in history, say 200 years, you'll find intelligent, conscientious, loving Christians defending slavery, because they hardly gave it two thoughts. If they were pressed, they might have said, 'Slavery is part of progress, part of the Christianization of the dark races.'

"A hundred or perhaps as little as 50 years later, what you suddenly find is that the very same Christian community that provided one of the major ideological defenses of slavery had begun to change its mind...here is a classic example of where the Christian tradition has been a force for slavery and a force for liberation.

"Now, just think of the difficulties that those early Christian abolitionists had to face. Scripture defended slavery. For instance, in *Leviticus* 25, you're commanded to take the child of a stranger as a slave...St. Paul simply said that those who were Christian slaves should be better Christians. Almost unanimously, apart from St. Gregory, the church fathers defended slavery, and for almost 1800 years, Christians defended and supported slavery. So, in other words, the change that took place within the Christian community on slavery is not just significant, it is historically astounding.

"Now, I give that example because I believe the case of animals is in many ways entirely analogous. We treat animals today precisely as we treated slaves, and the theological arguments are often entirely the same or have the same root. I believe the movement for animal rights is the most significant movement in Christianity, morally, since the emancipation of the slaves. And it provides just as many difficulties for the institutional church..."

Christians have found themselves unable to agree upon many pressing moral issues—including abortion. Exodus 21:22-24 says if two men are fighting and one injures a pregnant woman and the child is killed, he shall repay her according to the degree of injury inflicted upon her, *and not the fetus.* On the other hand, the *Didache* (Apostolic Church teaching) forbade abortion.

"There has to be a frank recognition that the Christian church is divided on every moral issue under the sun: nuclear weapons, divorce, homosexuality, capital punishment, animals, etc.," says Reverend Linzey. "I don't think it's desirable or possible for Christians to agree upon *every* moral issue. And, therefore, I think within the church we have no alternative but to work within diversity."

In a 1989 article entitled, "Re-examining the Christian Scriptures," Rick Dunkerly of Christ Lutheran Church notes that, "Beginning with the Old Testament, animals are mentioned and included everywhere...and in significant areas."

According to Dunkerly, God's solution to the problem of human loneliness "was to bring the animals to the man for personalized naming and for a restorative, unconditional, and loving relationship with them all. Animals are specifically included in the covenant given by God to Noah in the aftermath of the Flood, with God as the sole contracting party.

"Animals portray Jesus Christ in the covenant with Abraham: Three animals are included as the intermediary. Each animal is a willing servant of man and each was to be three years old; the same duration as the earthly ministry of the Messiah."

Dunkerly cites Romans 8:18-25, which describes the entire creation awaiting redemption:

"What Saint Paul is saying in the Romans 8 passage is that the death of Jesus upon the cross not only redeems every human being who willingly appropriates it unto him/herself, it also redeemed the entire creation as well, including the animals who were subjugated to the Adamic curse without choice on their part...each element of the ancient Curse would be reversed...Satan would be denied all aspects of victory.

"In light of this," he concludes, "...the Bible-believing Christian, should, of all people, be on the frontline in the struggle for animal welfare and rights. We who are Christians should be treating the animal creation now as it will be treated then, at Christ's second coming. It will not now be perfect, but it must be substantial, otherwise we have missed our calling, and we grieve the One we call 'Lord,' who was born in a stable surrounded by animals simply because He chose it that way." Dunkerly teaches Bible studies at his home church and is actively involved in animal rescue projects.

1991 marked the publication (in England) of *Using the Bible Today*, a collection of essays by distinguished clergy, theologians, and Christian writers on the relevance of the Bible to contemporary issues such as ecology, human suffering, animal rights, the inner city, war and psychology. An essay by the Reverend Andrew Linzey, "The Bible and Killing for Food" makes the following observations:

"...we have first of all to appreciate that those who made up the community whose spokesperson wrote Genesis 1 were not themselves vegetarian. Few appreciate that Genesis 1 and 2 are themselves the products of much later reflection by the biblical writers themselves. How is it then that the very people who were not themselves vegetarian imagined a beginning of time when all who lived were vegetarian by divine command?

"To appreciate this perspective we need to recall the major elements of the first creation saga. God creates a world of great diversity and fertility. Every living creature is given life and space (Genesis 1:9-10, 24-25). Earth to live on and blessing to enable life itself (1:22). Living creatures are pronounced good (1:25). Humans are made in God's image (1:27) given dominion (1:26-29), and then prescribed a vegetarian diet (1:29-30). God then pronounces that everything was 'very good' (1:31). Together the whole creation rests on the Sabbath with God (2:2-3).

"When examined in this way, we should see immediately that Genesis 1 describes a state of paradisal existence. There is no hint of violence between or among different species. Dominion, so often interpreted as justifying killing, actually precedes the command to be vegetarian. Herb-eating dominion is hardly a license for tyranny. The answer seems to be that even though the early Hebrews were neither pacifists nor vegetarians, they were deeply convinced of the view that violence between humans and animals, and indeed between animal species themselves, was not God's original will for creation.

"But if this is true, how are we to reconcile Genesis 1 with Genesis 9, the vision of original peacefulness with the apparent legitimacy of killing for food? The answer seems to be that as the Hebrews began to construct the story of early human beginnings, they were struck by the prevalence and enormity of human wickedness.

"The stories of Adam and Eve, Cain and Abel, Noah and his descendants are all testimonies to the inability of humankind to fulfill the providential purposes of God in creation. The issue is made explicit in the story of Noah: Now the earth was corrupt in God's sight, and the earth was filled with violence. And God saw the earth, and behold, it was corrupt; for all flesh had corrupted their way upon the earth. And God said to Noah, 'I have determined to make an end of all flesh; for the earth is filled with violence through them.'" (Genesis 6:11-14)

"The radical message of the Noah story (so often overlooked by commentators) is that God would rather not have us be at all if we must be violent. It is violence itself within every part of creation that is the pre-eminent mark of corruption and sinfulness. It is not for nothing that God concludes: 'I am sorry that I have made them.' (Genesis 6:7)

"It is in *this* context—subsequent to the Fall and the Flood—that we need to understand the permission to kill for food in Genesis 9. It reflects entirely the situation of the biblical writers at the time they were writing. Killing—of both humans as well as animals—was simply inevitable given the world as it is and human nature as it is. Corruption and wickedness had made a mess of God's highest hopes for creation. There just had to be some accommodation to human sinfulness...

"For many students of the Bible this seems to have settled the matter of whether humans can be justified in killing animals for food. In the end, it has been thought, God allows it. And there can be no doubt that throughout the centuries this view has prevailed. Meat eating has become the norm. Vegetarians, especially Christian vegetarians, have survived from century to century to find themselves a rather beleaguered minority."

Reverend Linzey explains, however, that the permission to kill for food given in Genesis 9 is far from unconditional or absolute—it carries with it the prohibition against consuming the blood of a slain creature.

"At first sight these qualificatory lines might be seen as obliterating the permission itself. After all, who can take animal life without the shedding of blood? Who can kill without the taking of blood, that is the life itself? In asking these questions we move to the heart of the problem. For the early Hebrews life was symbolized by, and even constituted by, blood itself. To kill *was* to take blood. And yet it is precisely *this* permission which is denied.

"...Rereading these verses in the light of their original context should go rather like this: The world in which you live has been corrupted. And yet God has not given up on you. God has signified a new relationship—a covenant with you—despite all your violence and unworthiness...What was previously forbidden can now—in the present circumstances—be allowed. You may kill for food. But you may kill only on the understanding that you remember that the life you kill is not your own—it belongs to God. You must not misappropriate what is not your own. As you kill what is not your own—either animal or human life—so you need to remember that for every life you kill you are personally accountable to God."

Linzey studies the messianic prophecies concerning the future Kingdom of Peace: "It seems...while the early Hebrews were neither vegetarians nor pacifists, the ideal of the peaceable kingdom was never lost sight of. In the end, it was believed, the world would one day be restored according to God's original will for all creation...we have no biblical warrant for claiming killing as God's will. God's will is for peace.

"We need to remember that even though Genesis 9 gives permission to kill for food it does so only on the basis that we do not misappropriate God-given life. Genesis 9 posits divine reckoning for the life of every beast taken under this new dispensation (9:5)."

Linzey concludes his essay by examining the current trends in vegetarianism and animal rights in contemporary society: "...it often comes as a surprise for Christians to realize that the modern vegetarian movement was strongly biblical in origin. Inspired by the original command in Genesis 1, an Anglican priest...founded the Bible Christian Church in 1809 and made vegetarianism compulsory among its members. The founding of this Church in the United Kingdom and its sister Church in the United States by William Metcalfe, effectively heralded the beginning of the modern vegetarian movement."

Reverend Linzey further elaborates upon themes discussed in *Christianity and the Rights of Animals* in his 1991 paper "The Moral Priority of the Weak: The Theological Basis of Animal Liberation."

Linzey agrees with Australian philosopher Peter Singer that there are no morally relevant differences between humans and animals, and asks: "What is the theological insight that makes Christians claim humans as superior or as possessing special status? In what does this specific value of humans consist?

"...any decent theological insight must be grounded in God and in particular God's attitude towards creation. And that insight can properly be summed up in one word: *generosity*. The special value of humankind consists wholly and exclusively in the generosity of God, Creator, Reconciler and Redeemer. This idea is of course a perennial theme throughout the Old and New Testaments, is found consistently in the work of the Fathers, and reaches its richest expression in the theology of Karl Barth."

Linzey observes that "here is a God supreme above all who in Christ humbles himself to identify with and suffer for the weakly and frail creature...if it is true that this paradigm of generous costly service is at the heart of the Christian proclamation then it must also be the paradigm for the exercise of human dominion over the animal world. We do well to remind ourselves of that ethical imperative arising from early Christian reflection upon the work and person of Jesus:

> "Take to heart among yourselves what you find in Christ Jesus: He was in
> the form of God; yet he laid no claim to equality with God, but made
> himself nothing, assuming the form of a slave.

> "Bearing the human likeness, sharing the human lot, he humbled him-
> self, and was obedient even to the point of death, death on a cross."

> — *Philippians 2:5-9*

"If we 'take to heart' this paradigm of generosity we can perceive moral meaning in our relationship of power over the nonhuman creation...The obligation is always and everywhere on the 'higher' to sacrifice for the 'lower'; for the strong, powerful and rich to give to those who are vulnerable, poor or powerless. This is not some by-theme of the moral example of Jesus, it is rather central to the demands of the kingdom, indeed those who minister to the needs of the vulnerable and the weak minister to Christ himself:

> "I was hungry and you gave me food, I was thirsty and you gave me drink, I was naked and you clothed me, I was sick and you visited me. I was in prison and you came to me."
>
> — *Matthew 25:35-37*

"In this respect, it is the sheer vulnerability and powerlessness of animals, and correspondingly our absolute power over them which strengthens and compels the response of moral generosity. I suggest that we are to be present to creation as Christ is present to us. When we speak of human superiority, we speak of such a thing properly only and insofar as we speak of not only Christlike lordship but also Christlike service. There can be no lordship without service and no service without lordship. Our special value in creation consists in being of special value to others."

In a 1991 article entitled "Hunting: What Scripture Says," Rick Dunkerly observes:

"There are four hunters mentioned in the Bible: three in Genesis and one in Revelation. The first hunter is named Nimrod in Genesis 10:8-9. He is the son of Cush and founder of the Babylonian Empire, the empire that opposes God throughout Scripture and is destroyed in the Book of Revelation. In Micah 5:6, God's enemies are said to dwell in the land of Nimrod. Many highly reputable evangelical scholars such as Barnhouse, Pink and Scofield regard Nimrod as a prototype of the anti-Christ.

"The second hunter is Ishmael, Abraham's 'son of the flesh' by the handmaiden, Hagar. His birth is covered in Genesis 16 and his occupation in 21:20. Ishmael's unfavorable standing in Scripture is amplified by Paul in Galatians 4:22-31.

"The third hunter, Esau, is also mentioned in the New Testament. His occupation is contrasted with his brother (Jacob) in Genesis 25:27. In Hebrews 12:16 he is equated with a 'profane person' (KJV). He is a model of a person without faith in God. Again, Paul elucidates upon this model unfavorably in Romans 9:8-13, ending with the paraphrase of Malachi 1:2-3: 'Jacob have I loved, but Esau have I hated.'

"The fourth hunter is found in Revelation 6:2, the rider of the white horse with the hunting bow. Scholars have also identified him as the so-called anti-Christ. Taken as a group, then, hunters fare poorly in the Bible. Two model God's adversary and two model the person who lives his life without God.

"In Scripture," notes Dunkerly, "the contrast of the hunter is the shepherd, the man who gently tends his animals and knows them fully. The shepherds of the Bible are Abel, Jacob, Joseph, Moses and David. Beginning in the 23rd Psalm, Jesus is identified as 'the Good Shepherd.'

"As for hunting itself, both the Psalms and Proverbs frequently identify it with the hunter of souls, Satan. His devices are often called 'traps' and 'snares,' his victims 'prey.' Thus, in examining a biblical stance on the issue of hunting, we see the context is always negative, always dark in contrast to light...premeditated killing, death, harm, destruction. All of these are ramifications of the Fall. When Christ returns, all of these things will be ended...

"Of all people," Dunkerly concludes, "Christians should not be the destroyers. We should be the healers and reconcilers. We must show NOW how it will be THEN in the Peaceable Kingdom of Isaiah 11:6 where 'the wolf shall lie down with the lamb...and a little child shall lead them.' We can begin now within our homes and churches by teaching our children respect and love for all of God's creation..."

"We do not know how to celebrate, rejoice, and give thanks for the beautiful world God has made," wrote the Reverend Dr. Andrew Linzey in 1992. "If we treat it as trash it is because so many of us still imagine the world as just that. For too long Christian churches have colluded in a doctrine that the earth is half-evil, or unworthy, or—most ludicrous of all—'unspiritual.'

"The church needs to teach reverence for life as a major aspect of Christian ethics...So much of Christian ethics is pathetically narrow and absurdly individualistic... One of the major problems with St. Francis...is that the church has not taken any practical notice of him. St. Francis preached a doctrine of self-renunciation, whereas the church today remains concerned with its own respectability. St. Francis lived a life of poverty, whereas the modern church is as ever concerned about money. St. Francis, like Jesus, associated with the outcasts and the lepers, whereas the church today consists predominately of the middle class."

Linzey cites Paul's epistle to the Romans, which describes the creation itself in a state of childbirth. "The creation itself will be set free from its bondage to decay and obtain the glorious liberty of the children of God." According to the Christian scheme of things, Linzey explains, "the world is going somewhere. It is not destined for eternal, endless suffering and pain. It has a destiny. Like us, it is not born to die eternally.

"The fundamental thing to grasp," Linzey declares, "is that we have responsibility to cooperate with God in the creation of a new world." Linzey quotes St. Isaac the Syrian's response to the question, "What is a charitable heart?"

> "It is a heart which is burning with love for the whole creation, for men, for the birds, for the animals...for all creatures.
>
> "He who has such a heart cannot see, or call to mind, a creature without his eyes being filled with tears by reason of the immense compassion which seizes his heart; a heart which is softened and can no longer bear to see or learn from others of any suffering, even the smallest pain, being inflicted upon any creature.
>
> "That is why such a man never ceases to pray also for the animals...He will pray even for the reptiles, moved by an infinite pity which reigns in the hearts of those who are becoming united with God."

"I believe then that the church must wake up to a new kind of ministry," Linzey concludes, "not just to Christians or to human beings, but to the whole world of suffering creatures. It must be our human, Christian task to heal the suffering in the world."

Linzey notes that "humans are made in the image of God, given dominion, and then told to follow a vegetarian diet (Genesis 1:29). Herb-eating dominion is not despotism." However, Linzey acknowledges the need for a new theology, an *animal liberation theology*, which would revolutionize our understanding of humanity's place in creation and relationship to other species, just as the Copernican picture of a sun-centered universe replaced the earth-centered picture.

"We need a concept of ourselves in the universe not as the master species but as the servant species—as the one given responsibility for the whole and the good of the whole. We must move from the idea that animals were given to us and made for us, to the idea that we were made for creation, to serve it and ensure its continuance. This actually is little more than the theology of Genesis chapter two. The Garden is made beautiful and abounds with life: humans are created specifically to 'take care of it.' (Genesis 2:15)

"A great wickedness of the Christian tradition," observes Reverend Linzey, "is that, at this very point, where it could have been a source of great blessing and life; it has turned out to be a source of cursing and death. I refer here to the way Christian theology has allowed itself to promulgate notions that animals have no rights; that they are put here for our use; that animals have no more moral status than sticks and stones.

"Animal rights in this sense is a religious problem. It is about how the Christian tradition in particular has failed to realize the God-given rights of God-given life. Animal rights remains an urgent question of theology.

"Every year," says Dr. Linzey, "I receive hundreds of anguished letters from Christians who are so distressed by the insensitivity to animals shown by mainstream churches that they have left them or on the verge of doing so. Of course, I understand why they have left the churches and in this matter, as in all else, conscience can be the only guide. But if all the Christians committed to animal rights leave the church, where will that leave the churches?

"The time is long overdue to take the issue of animal rights to the churches with renewed vigor. I don't pretend it's easy but I do think it's essential—not, I add, because the churches are some of the best institutions in society but rather because they are some of the worst. The more the churches are allowed to be left to one side in the struggle for animal rights, the more they will remain forever on the other side.

"I derive hope from the Gospel preaching," Linzey concludes, "that the same God who draws us to such affinity and intimacy with suffering creatures declared that reality on a Cross in Calvary. Unless all Christian preaching has been utterly mistaken, the God who becomes incarnate and crucified is the one who has taken the side of the oppressed and the suffering of the world—however the churches may actually behave."

The Bible teaches God's love and compassion for humans, animals and all creation; beginning and ending in a vegetarian paradise. Christianity teaches not just the redemption of man, but that of the entire creation. Jesus taught nonviolence and performed acts of mercy and self-sacrifice. Jesus opposed the buying and selling of animals for sacrifice in the Temple. He substituted a sacrament of bread and drink offered to God in place of such a ritual, and finally offered *himself* as a divine sacrifice before God. Christ is the savior of all flesh-and-blood creatures. All flesh shall be redeemed, and the entire creation awaits resurrection.

According to church history, the first apostles, including Jesus' very own brother, were vegetarian. The New Testament teaches compassion, mercy, repentance, faith in God, baptism, rejoicing, refraining from gratifying fleshly cravings (Romans 13:14), and not being a slave to one's bodily appetites (Philippians 3:19).

Some of the most distinguished figures in the history of Christianity have been vegetarian or at least sympathetic to animal rights. Many Christian thinkers are beginning to seriously address the moral issue of animal rights. The Catholic periodical *America* has run articles on animal rights, as has the Protestant publication *Christian Century*. Compassion towards animals—to the point of not killing and eating them merely to satisfy one's taste buds—is consistent with Christian teaching.

Perhaps the real question true believers should be asking themselves on issues such as animal rights and vegetarianism is not, "Why should Christians abstain from certain foods?" but rather, "Why should Christians want to unnecessarily harm or kill God's innocent creatures in the first place?"

chapter eight
Animals Have Souls

One widespread rationalization in Christian circles, often used to justify humanity's mistreatment of animals, is the erroneous belief that humans alone possess immortal souls, and only humans, therefore, are worthy of moral consideration. The 19th century German philosopher, Arthur Schopenhauer, condemned such a philosophy in his *On the Basis of Morality.*

"Because Christian morality leaves animals out of account," wrote Schopenhauer, "they are at once outlawed in philosophical morals; they are mere 'things,' mere means to any ends whatsoever. They can therefore be used for vivisection, hunting, coursing, bullfights, and horse racing, and can be whipped to death as they struggle along with heavy carts of stone. Shame on such a morality that is worthy of pariahs, and that fails to recognize the eternal essence that exists in every living thing, and shines forth with inscrutable significance from all eyes that see the sun!"

According to the Bible, animals have souls. Texts such as Genesis 1:21,24 are often mistranslated to read "living creatures." The exact Hebrew used in reference to animals throughout the Bible is "*nephesh chayah,*" or "living soul." This is how the phrase has been translated in Genesis 2:7 and in four hundred other places in the Old Testament. Thus, Genesis 1:30 should more accurately read: "And to every beast of the earth, and to every fowl of the air, and to everything that creepeth upon the earth, *wherein there is a living soul,* I have given every green herb for meat."

God breathed the "breath of life" into man, and caused him to become a living soul. (Genesis 2:7) Animals have the same "breath of life" as do humans. (Genesis 7:15, 22) Numbers 16:22 refers to the Lord as "the God of spirits of all flesh." In Numbers 31:28, God commands Moses to divide up among the people the cattle, sheep, asses and human prisoners captured in battle and to give to the Lord "one soul of five hundred" of both humans and animals alike. Psalm 104 says God provides for animals and their ensoulment.

> "O Lord, how innumerable are Thy works; in wisdom Thou hast made them all! The earth is full of Thy well-made creations. All these look to Thee to furnish their timely feed. When Thou providest for them, they gather it. Thou openest Thy hand, and they are satisfied with good things. When Thou hidest Thy face, they are struck with despair. When Thou cuttest off their breath, in death they return to their dust. Thou sendest Thy Spirit and more are created, and Thou dost replenish the surface of the earth."

Similarly, the apocryphal *Book of Judith* praises God, saying, "Let every creature serve You, for You spoke and they were made. You sent forth Your Spirit and they were created." Job 12:10 teaches that in God's hand "is the soul of every living thing, and the breath of all mankind."

Ecclesiastes 3:19-20 says humans have no advantage over animals: "They all draw the same breath...all came from the dust, and to dust all return."

The verse that immediately follows asks, "Who knows if the spirit of man goes upward, and the spirit of the beast goes down to the earth?" The exact Hebrew word for "spirit," "*ruach,*" is used in connection with animals as well as humans. Ecclesiastes 12:7 concludes that "the spirit shall return unto God who gave it."

This position was taken by Paul, who called himself an apostle to the gentiles. Paul spoke of God as the "giver of life and breath and all things to everyone." (Acts 17:25) In his epistle to the Romans 8:18-25, Paul wrote that the entire creation, and not just mankind, is awaiting redemption.

Revelations 16:3 also refers to the souls of animals: "The second angel poured out his bowl upon the sea, so that it turned to blood as of a corpse, and every living soul that was in the sea died." The exact Greek word for soul, "*psyche*," was used in the original texts.

English theologian Joseph Butler (1692-1752), a contemporary of John Wesley's, was born in a Presbyterian family, joined the Church of England, and eventually became a bishop and dean of St. Paul's. In his 1736 work, *The Analogy of Religion*, Bishop Butler became one of the first clergymen to teach the immortality of animal souls. "Neither can we find anything in the whole analogy of Nature to afford even the slightest presumption that animals ever lose their living powers, much less that they lose them by death," he wrote.

The Reverend John George Wood (1827-89) was an eloquent and prolific writer on the subject of animals. A popular lecturer on the subject of natural history, he wrote several books as well, such as *My Feathered Friends* and *Man and Beast—Here and Hereafter*. Wood believed most people were cruel to animals because they were unaware that the creatures possessed immortal souls and would enjoy eternal life.

One of the most scholarly studies on the issue of animal souls was undertaken by Elijah D. Buckner in his 1903 book *The Immortality of Animals*. He concluded: "...The Bible, without the shadow of a doubt, recognizes that animals have living souls the same as man. Most of the quotations given are represented as having been spoken by the Creator Himself, and he certainly knows whether or not He gave to man and lower animals alike a living soul, which of course means an immortal soul."

Influenced by Aristotle, Augustine and Aquinas, the Church of Rome maintains that animals lack souls or divinity, even though such a doctrine contradicts many biblical passages. Previously, during the Synod of Macon (585 AD), the Church had debated whether or not *women* have souls! Women in the Western world are finally being recognized as persons in every sense of the word—social, political and spiritual. Animals have yet to be given the same kind of moral consideration.

Pope Innocent VIII of the Renaissance required that when witches were burned, their cats be burned with them; Pope Pius IX of the 19th century forbade the formation of an SPCA in Rome, declaring humans had no duty to animals; Pope Pius XII of World War II stated that when animals are killed in slaughter-houses or laboratories, "...their cries should not arouse unreasonable compassion any more than do red-hot metals undergoing the blows of the hammer;" and Pope Paul VI in 1972, by blessing a batallion of Spanish bullfighters, became the first Pope to bestow his benediction upon one cruelty even the Church had condemned.

In *Christianity and the Rights of Animals*, the Reverend Andrew Linzey responds to the widespread Christian misconception that animals have no souls by taking it to its logical conclusion:

"But let us suppose for a moment that it could be shown that animals lack immortal souls, does it follow that their moral status is correspondingly weakened? It is difficult to see in what sense it could be. If animals are not to be recompensed with an eternal life, how much more difficult must it be to justify their temporal sufferings?

"If, for an animal, this life is all that he can have, the moral gravity of any premature termination is thereby increased rather than lessened...In short, if we invoke the traditional argument against animals based on soullessness, we are not exonerated from the need for proper moral justification.

"Indeed, if the traditional view is upheld, the question has to be: How far can any proposed aim justify to the animal concerned what would seem to be a *greater* deprivation or injury than if the same were inflicted on a human being?"

"Mark Twain remarked long ago that human beings have a lot to learn from the Higher Animals," writes Unitarian minister Gary Kowalski, in his 1991 book, *The Souls of Animals*. "Just because they haven't invented static cling, ICBM's, or television evangelists doesn't mean they aren't spiritually evolved."

Kowalski's definition of "spiritually evolved" includes "the development of a moral sense, the appreciation of beauty, the capacity for creativity, and the awareness of one's self within a larger universe as well as a sense of mystery and wonder about it all. These are the most precious gifts we possess...

"I am a parish minister by vocation," Kowalski explains. "My work involves the intangible and perhaps undefinable realm of spirit. I pray with the dying and counsel the bereaved. I take part in the joy of parents christening their newborns and welcoming fresh life into the world.

"I occasionally help people think through moral quandries and make ethical decisions, and I also share a responsibility for educating the young, helping them realize their inborn potential for reverence and compassion. Week after week I stand before my congregation and try to talk about the greatest riddles of human existence. In recent years, however, I have become aware that human beings are not the only animals on this planet that participate in affairs of the spirit."

Kowalski notes that animals are aware of death. They have a sense of their own mortality, and grieve at the loss of companions. Animals possess language, musical abilities, a sense of the mysterious, creativity and playfulness. Animals possess a sense of right and wrong; they are capable of fidelity, altruism, and even self-sacrifice.

"Animals, like us, are microcosms," says Kowalski. "They too care and have feelings; they too dream and create; they too are adventuresome and curious about their world. They too reflect the glory of the whole.

"Can we open our hearts to the animals? Can we greet them as our soul mates, beings like ourselves who possess dignity and depth? To do so, we must learn to revere and respect the creatures, who, like us, are a part of God's beloved creation, and to cherish the amazing planet that sustains our mutual existence.

"Animals," Kowalski concludes, "are living souls. They are not things. They are not objects. Neither are they human. Yet they mourn. They love. They dance. They suffer. They know the peaks and chasms of being."

chapter nine
Animal Rights and Civil Rights

In his 1975 book, *Animal Liberation*, Australian philosopher Peter Singer writes that the "tyranny of human over nonhuman animals" is "causing an amount of pain and suffering that can only be compared with that which resulted from the centuries of tyranny by white humans over black humans."

Singer favorably compares animal liberation with women's liberation, black liberation, and movements on behalf of Native Americans and Hispanics. He optimistically observes: "...the environmental movement...has led people to think about our relations with other animals in a way that seemed impossible only a decade ago.

"To date, environmentalists have been more concerned with wildlife and endangered species than with animals in general, but it is not too big a jump from the thought that it is wrong to treat whales as giant vessels filled with oil and blubber to the thought that it is wrong to treat (animals) as machines for converting grains to flesh."

Abraham Lincoln said: "I care not for a man's religion whose dog or cat are not the better for it...I am in favor of animal rights as well as human rights. That is the way of a whole human being."

Supporters of civil rights should be supportive of animal rights. Many of the moral and theological arguments used today to oppress animals were once used to oppress blacks. Buckner H. Payne, calling himself "Ariel," wrote in 1867, that "the tempter in the Garden of Eden...was a beast, a talking beast...the negro." Ariel argued that since the negro was not part of Noah's family, he must have been a beast. Eight souls were saved on the ark, therefore, the negro must be a beast, and "consequently he has no soul to be saved."

In her preface to Marjorie Spiegel's *The Dreaded Comparison: Human and Animal Slavery*, Alice Walker, author of *The Color Purple*, writes: "The animals of this world exist for their own reasons. They were not made for humans any more than black people were made for whites or women for men..."

At a rally in San Francisco protesting the use of animals in medical research, former Alameda County supervisor John George said, "My people were the first laboratory animals in America." Black Americans suffered at the hands of research scientists just as animals continue to do today.

In 1968, civil rights leader Dick Gregory compared humanity's treatment of animals to the conditions in America's inner cities:

"Animals and humans suffer and die alike. If you had to kill your own hog before you ate it, most likely you would not be able to do it. To hear the hog scream, to see the blood spill, to see the baby being taken away from its momma, and to see the look of death in the animal's eye would turn your stomach. So you get the man at the packing house to do the killing for you.

"In like manner, if the wealthy aristocrats who are perpetuating conditions in the ghetto actually heard the screams of ghetto suffering, or saw the slow death of hungry little kids, or witnessed the strangulation of manhood and dignity, they could not continue the killing. But the wealthy are protected from such horror...If you can justify killing to eat meat, you can justify the conditions of the ghetto. I cannot justify either one."

Gregory credits the Judeo-Christian ethic and the teachings of Dr. Martin Luther King, Jr. with having caused him to become a vegetarian. In 1973, he drew a connection between vegetarianism and nonviolent civil disobedience:

"...the philosophy of nonviolence, which I learned from Dr. Martin Luther King, Jr. during my involvement in the civil rights movement was first responsible for my change in diet. I became a vegetarian in 1965. I had been a participant in all of the 'major' and most of the 'minor' civil rights demonstrations of the early sixties, including the March on Washington and the Selma to Montgomery March.

"Under the leadership of Dr. King, I became totally committed to nonviolence, and I was convinced that nonviolence meant opposition to killing in any form. I felt the commandment 'Thou shalt not kill' applied to human beings not only in their dealings with each other—war, lynching, assassination, murder and the like—but in their practice of killing animals for food or sport. Animals and humans suffer and die alike...Violence causes the same pain, the same spilling of blood, the same stench of death, the same arrogant, cruel and brutal taking of life."

In a 1979 interview, Gregory explained: "Because of the civil rights movement, I decided I couldn't be thoroughly nonviolent and participate in the destruction of animals for my dinner...I didn't become a vegetarian for health reasons; I became a vegetarian strictly for moral reasons...Vegetarianism will definitely become a people's movement."

When asked if humans will ultimately have to answer to a Supreme Being for their exploitation of animals, Gregory replied, "I think we answer for that every time we go to the hospital with cancer and other diseases."

Gregory has also expressed the opinion that the plight of the poor will improve as humans cease to slaughter animals: "I would say that the treatment of animals has something to do with the treatment of people. The Europeans have always regarded their slaves and the people they have colonized as animals."

Since the 1980s, Dick Gregory has been involved in the anti-drug campaign. In his first major civil rights sermon at the Holt Street Baptist Church in Montgomery, Dr. Martin Luther King, Jr. said: "If we are wrong, Jesus of Nazareth was merely a utopian dreamer...If we are wrong, justice is a lie!" These words apply equally well to the struggle for animal rights. Bruce Friedrich of People for the Ethical Treatment of Animals (PETA) reports that under Gregory's influence, Dexter Scott King—head of the Martin Luther King, Jr. Center for Nonviolence in Atlanta, and son of the slain civil rights leader—and King's widow, Coretta Scott King, have both become committed vegetarians.

Peter Singer concludes in *Animal Liberation* that "by ceasing to rear and kill animals for food, we can make extra food available for humans that, properly distributed, would eliminate starvation and malnutrition from this planet. Animal liberation is human liberation, too." The animal rights movement should be supported by all caring Americans.

chapter ten
"Nonviolence or Nonexistence"

When the soldiers asked John the Baptist, "And what shall we do?" he replied, "Do violence to no man, neither accuse any falsely; and be content with your wages." Since they could not remain soldiers and practice nonviolence, this passage suggests he told them to put down their weapons and seek a peaceful profession.

Jesus, in his Sermon on the Mount, said: "Blessed are the peacemakers, for they shall be called the children of God." (Matthew 5:9) Expressing concern for God's children, he said, "Blessed are they which are persecuted for righteousness sake; for theirs is the kingdom of heaven."

"In concrete and vivid precepts," writes Professor G.J. Heering in *The Fall of Christianity*, "the Sermon on the Mount set forth the character and conduct of those who really follow Jesus: of those who may really be called God's children; of those who shall submit to the rule of God, of those who shall enter His Kingdom; in short, of true Christians: the pure in heart, the meek, the peacemakers, those who hunger and thirst after righteousness, and are willing to suffer for its sake. They are the salt of the earth and the light of the world.

"And then follow the commandments; 'Ye shall keep yourselves from murder but also from revenge. And in place of an eye for an eye and a tooth for a tooth, resist not that which is evil; but whosoever smiteth thee on thy right cheek, turn to him the other also.' Can one find one little implication in these words that does not plead for peace or that does not shrink from violence in every degree or form?

"Jesus does not give detached commands. He brings you whole being and doing and suffering under the compulsion of one single principle. 'Ye have heard that it was said, Thou shalt love thy neighbor and hate thine enemy, but I say unto you: love your enemies, do good to them that hate you, bless them that curse you, pray for them that despitefully use you and persecute you: that ye may be sons of your Father which is in heaven.' (Matthew 5:43-45; Luke 6:27-38)

"'Love even your enemy!' This is the highest demand that can ever be made. *This love of enemy is not just one virtue among many, but the fairest flower of all human conduct.*

"It is recognized that these commands though lay stress on the inward disposition and have not the force of law, were certainly meant as concrete instructions for the followers of Jesus. They had to be obeyed. Their carrying out was counted on. Behind these injunctions, which admit no cleavage between conduct and character, stands the newly sent Ambassador of God with His 'But I say unto you.'

"Not only the war of aggression but also defensive warfare is ruled out by the Sermon on the Mount...the gospel condemns war...We have primarily to recognize, however hard it may be to do so, that the waging of war has no place in the moral and spiritual teachings of Jesus.

"Hippolytus, second century Christian father and historian, wrote what he considered the Apostolic tradition and so the authentic Christian teaching, maintained, that when he applied for admission to the Christian fellowship, a soldier must refuse to kill men, even if he were commanded by his superiors to do so and also must not take an oath.

"Justin Martyr, the principle apologist of the early church (Cir. AD 150) writes that:

"'Christians seek no earthly realm, but a heavenly, and that this will be a realm of peace. The prophecy of Isaiah—that swords shall be beaten into plowshares and spears to pruning hooks begins to find fulfillment in the missions of Christians. For we refrain from the making of war on our enemies, but gladly go to death for Christ's sake. Christians are warriors of a different world, peaceful fighters. For

Caesar's soldiers possess nothing which they can lose more precious than their life, while our love goes out to that eternal life which God will give.'"

The apostle Paul taught that Christian warfare is spiritual. (Romans 13:12) According to Professor Heering: "Origen, the great Christian father of the second century, would hear nothing of earthly military service: he regarded it as wholly forbidden:

"'We Christians no longer take up sword against nation, nor do we learn war any more, having become children of peace for the sake of Jesus who is our leader. We do not serve as soldiers under the Emperor, even though he requires it.

"'Persons who possess authority to kill, or soldiers, should not kill at all, even when it is commanded of them. Every one who receives a distinctive leading position, or a magisterial power, and does not clothe himself in the weaponlessness of which is becoming to the Gospel, should be separated from the flock.'"

Although he was the son of a military officer, the early Christian father Tertullian (AD 200) was opposed to militarism and violence. Professor Heering observes: "The question Tertullian faces is not whether a Christian may be a soldier, but even whether a soldier may be allowed within the church. He answers 'No.' The soldier who becomes a Christian ought to leave the army. 'One soul cannot be true to two lords—God and Caesar. How shall a Christian man wage war; nay, how shall he even be a soldier in peace time, without the sword, which the Lord has taken away?—for in disarming Peter he ungirded every soldier.'"

The great church father Cyprian, Bishop of Carthage, denounced war and wrote:

"The whole earth is drenched in adversaries' blood, and if murder is committed, privately it is a crime, but if it happens with State authority, courage is the name for it: not the goodness of the cause, but the greatness of the cruelty makes the abominations blameless."

Attacking even capital punishment, Cyprian wrote: "Christians are not allowed to kill, it is not permitted to guiltless to put even the guilty to death."

The Christian writer Lactantius of Bithinia wrote about the Sixth Commandment ("Thou shalt not kill") as follows:

"When God prohibits killing, he not only forbids us to commit brigandage, which is not allowed even by public laws, but he warns us not to do even those things which are legal among men. And so it will not be lawful for a just man to serve as a soldier for justice itself is his military service, nor to accuse anyone of a capital offense, because it makes no difference whether they kill with a sword or with a word, since killing itself is forbidden."

Erasmus, a fifteenth century Christian father, scholar and theologian, considered it a sacrelige for a soldier to stitch the cross on his standard. "The cross," he said, "is the banner and standard of Him who has overcome and triumphed, not by fighting and slaying, but by His own bitter death. With the cross do ye deprive the life of your brother, whose life was rescued by the cross?

"O, you cruel, shameless lips: how dare ye call Father whilst ye rob your brother of Life?

"'Hallowed by Thy name': how can the name of God be more dishonored than by war?

"'Thy kingdom come': will ye pray thus while ye scraple at nought and shrink from no bloodshed, however great?

"'Thy will be done on earth as it is in heaven': God desires peace and ye make war.

"Ye pray your common Father for daily bread, and meantime ye burn all your brother's rye and corn.

"How shamefully will ye say: 'Forgive us our trespasses as we forgive them who trespass against us, while ye desire nothing else but to slay and to do mischief.

"Ye pray that ye may not come into danger or temptation and ye lead your brother into every sort of danger and temptation."

In her 1991 essay, "The Bible and Peace and War," Ursula King asks, "how are we to explain that Jesus, the founder of Christianity, is often called 'the Prince of Peace' and yet Western civilization so deeply shaped by the Christian story which is clearly pacifist in origin and essence, has become so militaristic from an early stage in its history?"

King quotes Christian pacifist John Ferguson from his 1977 study *War and Peace in the World's Religions*:

"The historic association of the Christian faith with nations of commercial enterprise, imperialistic expansion and technological advancement has meant that Christian peoples, although their faith is one of the most pacifistic in its origins, have a record of military activity second to none."

According to King, "In the early church, pacifism was the dominant position up to the reign of Constantine, when Christianity became a state religion. Until then no Christian author approved of Christian participation in battle, whereas in AD 314 the Council of Arles decreed that Christians who gave up their arms in time of peace should be excommunicated."

In *Theology and Social Structure*, Robin Gill has written:

"The situation of the pre-Constantinian church appears all the more remarkable when it is realised that no major Christian church or denomination has been consistently pacifist since Constantine. Indeed, Christian pacifism has been largely confined to a small group of sects, such as the Quakers, Anabaptists, Mennonites, Brethren and Jehovah's Witnesses. Further, pacifists within the churches, as distinct from sects, have in times of war been barely tolerated by their fellow Christians."

Dr. Martin Luther King, Jr. once said that in today's world the choice is either nonviolence or nonexistence.

These quotes against killing and war and in favor of pacifism also serve to indicate that religiously-based nonviolence towards animals as well as humans is not at all extreme or absurd, but rather, consistent with the Christian doctrines expressed above. History reveals to us that the earliest Christians were both pacifists *and* vegetarians. Ethical vegetarianism is, in itself, a form of pacifism—nonviolence towards animals.

chapter eleven
"...Kill Not a Living Creature"

Islam is a global faith. Nearly one person in seven in the world today—some 800 million people in over 75 countries—is a Muslim. Islam is, quite possibly, the fastest-growing religion on the globe. Introduced among the Arabs in the 7th century, Islam spread rapidly throughout the Middle East, North Africa and South Asia. Within a century, Islam controlled an empire larger than that of Rome or Alexander. "*Islam*" means "submission"—to God.

"There is no God but Allah, and Mohammed is His messenger."

A solemn recitation of this confession of faith is required of every Muslim. According to Islamic tradition, the archangel Gabriel appeared to Mohammed in 610 AD and imparted to him the wisdom of the Koran, or "Recital." At first, Mohammed was afraid he was going insane or was possessed by an evil spirit. But he soon became convinced this calling was truly from God.

Muslims revere the Koran's "*surahs*" or chapters as the literal word of God, superceding all previous revelations (including the Bible) and correcting the alleged theological "errors" that had crept into Judaism and Christianity. The Koran itself is somewhat smaller than the New Testament.

Mohammed taught that Jews and Christians have been worshipping Allah under a different name. The Koran recognizes Adam, Noah, Abraham, Moses, John the Baptist, Jesus and other biblical personalities as genuine prophets through whom God spoke. Whereas the Jewish people are said to be descended from Abraham through Isaac, Mohammed's family lineage is traced to Abraham through the patriarch's grandson Kedar, son of Ishmael (Genesis 25:13).

Muslims, however, regard Mohammed (570-632 AD) as the greatest and last (or "seal") of the prophets. Muslims deny the divinity of Jesus, as well as his crucifixion and resurrection. "They do blaspheme who say: 'God is Christ the son of Mary'...Christ was merely an apostle," the Koran asserts.

Despite the high status accorded to Mohammed, Muslims do not worship him as a divine figure. For this reason, Muslims dislike being called "Mohammedans," for the term implies they worship Mohammed. "We of Islam," they will carefully point out, "are monotheists. People of one God, like the Jews. We honor Moses and Jesus as prophets. And we honor Mohammed as the final and greatest prophet. But we do not worship him. We worship only one God: Allah."

Muslims pray towards the holy city of Mecca five times each day. On Friday, Muslims observe a special day of public prayer in the mosque. During the entire holy month of Ramadan, the ninth month of the Muslim year, Muslims fast during daylight hours. Muslims are also expected to make a "*hajj*" or pilgrimage to the sacred city of Mecca at least once in their lifetime, if it is at all possible. Almsgiving to the poor, aged and orphans is another obligation required of Muslims. A yearly 2.5 percent "*zakat*" tax is levied against one's total assets. In addition to these major directives, the Koran forbids gambling, the eating of carrion, the consumption of animal blood, foods offered to pagan gods and idols (compare Genesis 9:3; Acts 15), pork and alcohol. The Koran vividly describes punishment in hell and reward in paradise.

The "*Sharia*," or Islamic Law has been condemned in the West as cruel and barbaric. The penalty for habitual thievery may be loss of a hand. The penalty for premarital sex may be 100 lashes in public. The Islamic codes of justice, however, are not that different from the civil and criminal laws found in Exodus

21-23. Muslim countries have significantly lower crime rates than the Western nations.

Many Muslims, too, are alarmed at the resurgence of Islamic fundamentalism sweeping the Middle East. In an interview before his assassination, Anwar Sadat, President of Egypt, pointed out that the brutality of the Khomeini regime in Iran could not be called true "Islam" any more than the Crusades or the Inquisition could be called genuine "Christianity." The taking of hostages—especially diplomatic ones—is clearly forbidden in Islamic tradition. "I do not break treaties, nor do I make prisoners of envoys," Mohammed insisted. Many Muslims saw the taking of American hostages by Iran in 1979 as an embarrassment to Islam.

Mohammed actually advanced the status of women significantly, offering them greater honor than most societies of his time. "O men, respect women who have borne you as mothers," teaches the Koran. Muslim women were given civil and property rights—a revolutionary step in the Arab world. The practice of wearing a "*chador*" or a veil is not mandated by the Koran; this cultural practice appeared centuries after Mohammed. The Koran merely asks women to dress "modestly." As far as polygamy is concerned, few Muslim males have more than one wife. The Koran allows four—*if* the husband can afford to provide and care for them, and *if* he can treat them without partiality.

When the Muslims conquered India, they attacked what they misunderstood to be idolatry and polytheism. Many Hindu temples were destroyed. On doctrinal issues, Muslims oppose the Christian worship of the Trinity, which they term "the triple God." As in Judaism, God is a solitary Being, who has no equal. Muslims see the Trinitarian concept of God as disguised polytheism and, therefore, sacrilegious. The Catholic veneration of saints and use of images in worship is also regarded as idolatry and polytheism by Muslims.

Devout Muslims see the rampant sinful behavior of the Western nations: drunkenness, fornication, greed, homosexuality, gambling, adultery, carousing, indecency, drug abuse, abortion, pornography, uncleanliness, crime, etc. and wonder why these things happen in supposedly "Christian" cultures! Has the West rejected God's word? Most Christians in the West, of course, have long ago abandoned practicing their faith; today, they merely profess it. Modernization and secularization may inevitably cause followers of Islam and many of the world's other faiths to do the same. At present, however, Islam is regarded more as a way of life than as an armchair theology.

> "...but to hunt...is forbidden you, so long as ye are on the pilgrimage. Be mindful of your duty to Allah, unto Whom you will all be gathered."
>
> — *Koran, surah 5, verse 96*

Islam teaches that in Mecca, the birthplace of Mohammed, no creature can be slaughtered and that perfect harmony should exist between all living beings. Muslim pilgrims approach Mecca wearing a shroud ("*ihram*"). From the moment they wear this religious cloth, absolutely no killing is allowed. Mosquitos, lice, grasshoppers, and other living creatures must also be protected. If a pilgrim sees an insect on the ground, he will motion to stop his comrades from accidentally stepping on it. Islam teaches respect for animals and nature; the Islamic tradition has much to say about humanity's relationship with the animal world.

> "Whoever is kind to the creatures of God is kind to himself."
>
> — *the Prophet Mohammed*

> "There is not an animal on the earth, nor a flying creature flying on two

wings, but they are all peoples like unto you."

— *Koran, surah 6, verse 38*

The Koran (Majeed 55:10-12) teaches that God assigned the earth "to all living creatures," and humanity is ordered not to "spread corruption on earth, after it has been put in order." (Majeed 7:56) "Seest thou not that it is God whose praises are celebrated by all beings in heaven and on earth, and by the birds with extended wings?" asks the Koran. "Each one knows its prayer and psalm. And God is aware of what they do." (Majeed 24:41) The Koran calls the pagan practice of slitting the ears of animals "devilish acts." Mohammed is recorded as having told his followers, "it behooves you to treat the animals gently." (Majeed 4:118-19, 5:103)

About Mohammed, the English Arabic scholar, David Margoliouth (1858-1940), has written: "His humanity extended itself to the lower creation. He forbade the employment of towing birds as targets for marksmen and remonstrated those who ill-treated their camels. When some of his followers had set fire to an anthill, he compelled them to extinguish it. Acts of cruelty were swept away by him."

In one popular tradition ("*Hadith*"), Mohammed is said to have rebuked his followers for failing to show compassion. "But we do show compassion," they responded, "to our wives, children and relatives." The Prophet insisted, "It is not this to which I refer. I am speaking of *universal* mercy." According to tradition (*Hadith Mishkat* 3:1392), Mohammed taught that "all creatures are like a family of God; and He loves the most those who are the most beneficent to His family."

Providing food and drink for animals, Mohammed explained, "are among those virtuous gestures which draw us one step nearer to God," and "everyone who shows clemency, even towards a mere bird under the knife, will find God's clemency towards him on Doomsday."

Awakening from rest one afternoon, Mohammed found a small, sick cat sound asleep on the fringe of his cloak. The Prophet cut off his garment, allowing the cat to sleep undisturbed. "Is this a man who would advocate the unnecessary slaughter of harmless beasts?" asks writer Steven Rosen. "Show sympathy to others," taught Mohammed, "especially to those who are weaker than you."

Islamic scholar Dr. M. Hafiz Syed records the following traditions from the life and teachings of Mohammed:

> The Prophet passed by certain people who were shooting arrows at a ram and hated that, saying, "Maim not the brute beasts."

> The Prophet, seen wiping the face of his horse with his wrapper, said, "At night I received a reprimand from God in regard to my horse."

> A man once robbed some eggs from the nest of a bird, whereupon the Prophet had them restored to the nest. "Fear God in these dumb animals," said the Prophet, "and ride them when they are fit to be ridden—and get off them when they are tired."

> "Verily, are there rewards for our doing good to quadrupeds and giving them water to drink?" asked the disciples. And the Prophet answered, "There are rewards for benefitting every animal having a moist liver." (i.e., everyone alive!)

The Prophet spoke of the rewards and punishments one would receive depending on one's treatment of animals. He once told his companions he had a vision of a woman being punished in hell because she had starved a cat to death. "A good deed done to an animal is as meritorious as a good deed done to a human being," taught Mohammed, "while an act of cruelty to an animal is as bad as an act of cruelty to a human being."

On another occasion, the Prophet is recorded as having said, "He who takes pity even on a sparrow and spares its life, God will be merciful to him on the Day of Judgement...There is no man who kills even a sparrow, or anything smaller, without a justifiable cause, but God will question him about it."

Again, Mohammed is said to have taught that, "one who kills even a sparrow or anything smaller without a justifiable reason will be answerable to Allah." Muslim literature even records the Prophet forbidding the use of animal skins.

Mohammed took pity on beasts of burden. He forbade the beating of animals, as well as branding, striking, or painting them on the face. When the Prophet encountered a donkey that had been branded on the face, he exclaimed, "May Allah condemn the one who branded it." According to Mohammed, some animals were better than their riders. "Verily, there exist among the ridden ones some who are indeed better than their riders, and who praise their Lord more worthily."

According to Islamic scholar B.A. Masri, "All kinds of animal fights are strictly forbidden in Islam." Mohammed forbade using living creatures as targets, and went so far as to condemn putting animals in cages, calling it "a great sin for man to imprison those animals which are in his power."

Mohammed even classified the unnecessary slaughter of animals as one of the seven deadly sins. "Avoid the seven abominations," he said, then referring to a verse from the Koran, "And kill not a living creature, which Allah has made sancrosanct, except for a justifiable reason."

Dr. Masri writes that: "According to the spirit and overall teachings of Islam, causing avoidable pain and suffering to the defenseless and innocent creatures of God is not justifiable under any circumstances."

On the issue of animal experimentation, Dr. Masri points out that: "Many of the experiments that are being done on animals in the name of scientific research and education are not really necessary and are sheer cruelty. Such experiments are a contradiction in terms of the Islamic teachings...According to Islam, all life is sancrosant and has a right to protection and preservation."

Like the Bible, the Koran also describes God's blessings to mankind as essentially vegetarian, in verses similar to Genesis 1:29:

> "Therewith He causes crops to grow for you, and the olive and the date-palm and grapes and all kinds of fruit. Lo! Herein is indeed a portent for people who reflect."
>
> — *Koran, surah 16, verse 11*

> "A token unto them is the dead earth. We revive it, and We bring forth from it grain—so that they will eat thereof. And We have placed therein gardens of the date-palm and grapes, and We have caused springs of water to gush forth therein. That they may not eat of the fruit thereof and their hands created it not. Will they not, then, give thanks?"
>
> — *Koran, surah 36, verses 33-35*

> "Let man reflect on the food he eats: how We poured out the rain abundantly, and split the earth into fissures, and how We then made the grains to grow, and vines and reeds, olives and palms and gardens and fruits and pastures—an enjoyment for you and your cattle to delight in.

"It is God who sends down water out of the sky, and with it quickens the earth after it is dead. Surely, in that is a sign for people who have ears to hear. In cattle, too, there is a lesson for you: We give you to drink of what is in their bellies, between filth and blood—pure milk, sweet to those who drink.

"And We give you the fruits of the palms and the vines from which you derive sweet-tasting liquid and fair provision. Indeed, this is a sign for men of understanding.

"And your Lord inspires the bees, saying, 'Build your homes in the mountains, in the trees and in the thatch of roots, then feed on every kind of fruit and follow the ways of your Lord, so easy to go upon.' Then there comes forth out of their bellies a liquid of various colors wherein is healing for men. Truly, this is a sign for people who reflect."

Dr. M. Hafiz Syed writes that the Prophet taught worshippers who eat animal flesh to wash out their mouths before going to pray. It is a Muslim custom to clean one's mouth before prayer, but many biographers record Mohammed giving this instruction only in regards to meat, and not to any other kind of food.

Mohammed's earliest biographers wrote that he preferred vegetarian foods. The Prophet enjoyed milk diluted with water, yogurt with butter or nuts, and cucumbers with dates. His favorite fruits, which he would often subsist on for weeks at a time, were pomegranates, grapes and figs. He liked soaked, crushed dates as a morning drink.

The Prophet was especially fond of honey. He would eat it mixed with vinegar. Mohammed is quoted as having said that in a home where there is honey and vinegar, there will be the blessings of the Lord. He enjoyed a preparation known as "hees," made from butter, dates and yogurt. "Where there is an abundance of vegetables," said the Prophet, "hosts of angels will descend on that place."

Mohammed did not directly forbid the killing of animals for food, but he taught that such killing should be done as humanely as possible. "If you must kill," he conceded, "kill without torture." The laws governing the "humane slaughter" of animals for food in Islam are similar to those found in Judaism. The knife must be "razor sharp," to cause as little pain to the animal as possible. The knife should not be sharpened in the presence of the animal about to be killed. An animal must not be slaughtered in the presence of other animals. In order to prevent harm to an animal that may still be alive, it is forbidden to skin or slice an animal carcass until it is cold, i.e., when *rigor mortis* has set in.

The Koran clearly evokes compassion and mercy towards animals. Islamic mystics, such as the Sufis, regard vegetarianism as a high spiritual ideal. One contemporary Sufi master explains, "If you understand the '*qurban*' (ritual slaughter and Islamic dietary laws) from within with wisdom, its purpose is to reduce this killing. But if you look at it from outside, it is meant to supply desire with food, to supply the craving of the base desires..."

As in the Jewish tradition, animal life partakes of the sacred, and the ritual and humane slaughter of animals is regarded as a divine concession to human lust and brutality. Like the Bible, the Koran (22:37) also teaches the futility of animal sacrifice as a means of worship. "Their flesh will never reach Allah, nor yet their blood—but your devotion and piety will reach Him."

The death of the Prophet Mohammed put flesh-eating in its proper perspective. It is said a non-Muslim woman invited Mohammed and his companions to a meal and served them poisoned meat. By the gift of prophecy, Mohammed knew the flesh was poisoned. He alone ate it, and ordered his companions not to do so.

Although Mohammed was not in the habit of eating foods prepared by non-Muslims, on this occasion he did. Struck down by the poisoned meat, he was ill for nearly two years before dying in 632 AD. Some scholars believe Mohammed deliberately ate the poisoned meat to teach his followers to moral wrong of flesh-eating, recalling passages from the biblical Book of Numbers (11:4-34).

The traditional understanding of the Islamic dietary laws is that Muslims are meant to eat wholesome foods. The Koran (surah 7, verse 157) teaches that "He (Mohammed) makes lawful to them the good things of life and he forbids them the bad things." Al-Ghazzali (1058-1111), one of Islam's most distinguished philosophers, wrote in his book *Ihya Ulum ul-Din*: "Eating the meat of a cow causes disease ('*marz*'), its milk is health ('*safa*') and its clarified butter ('*ghee*') is medicine ('*dava*'). Compassionate eating leads to compassionate living." Compassion in Islam should extend to the animals.

Rabi'a al Adawiyya was born in 717 AD in Basra, in what is now known as Iraq. During childhood, her parents died, and she was sold into slavery. Rabi'a was a Sufi, a member of a mystical sect that preaches total love of God and total union with Him. After her release from slavery, she went to the desert for prayer and meditation. She returned to Basra, leading a life of voluntary poverty and simplicity. She refused gifts of money and riches as well as many offers of marriage. Her life was marked by acts of kindness towards humans and animals alike. When she was in the mountains, the animals gathered around her: deer, gazelles, mountain goats and wild donkeys. In her presence, they were trusting and fearless.

Once, when another Sufi teacher, Hasan-al-Basri approached her, the animals ran away. He asked her why the animals gathered around her, but ran from him. Rabi'a responded by asking him what he had eaten. "Onions fried in fat," he replied. "You eat their fat!" exclaimed Rabi'a. "Why should they not flee from you?"

"Share thy water with the early birds
For this is a worthwhile deed
The birds do no harm nor sin
But beware and fear thy kind.

"Freeing an insect is kinder
Than giving money to the needy
There is no difference between releasing
The deformed black creature,
And the black prince of Kinda,
Ready to be crowned.

"Both deserve living, for their lives are precious
And seeking to live is a continual struggle."

These are the teachings of Abu l'Ala, a blind poet, born in Syria in 973 AD. He originally planned to live as a vegetarian ascetic, but his fame spread, and disciples and students all came to him. He was surrounded by people who wanted to learn from him. He used his eloquence with words to speak on behalf of the oppressed.

Abu l'Ala called for religious equality, urging Jews, Christians and Muslims to respect one another's faiths and to act with good will towards one another. He opposed tyranny, and taught that rulers and princes are servants of the people.

"My heart bleeds for the cruelty toward
The poor burro, who stubbornly endures
But also gets whipped for resting because of
the excessive burden on his back."

Abu l'Ala was a vegetarian out of compassion for animals. "Neither eat the sea creatures," he taught, "for this is cruel. Nor seek nor desire thy food from the painful slaughtering of animals." Abu l'Ala also objected to the use of fur, leather, milk, honey and eggs, because they involve abusing or taking things from animals.

The Koran teaches compassion and mercy. Each of its 114 chapters, except one, begin, "Allah is merciful and compassionate." The name of God used most often in the Koran is "al-Rahim," which means "the All-Compassionate." Mohammed taught love and respect for nature, compassion for animals and condemned the needless suffering and death of other living creatures. Vegetarianism and animal rights are consistent with Islam.

chapter twelve
"Show Kindness to Animals"

The Baha'i faith began in 19th century Persia (Iran) as an offshoot of the Shi'ite branch of Islam. Today, there are an estimated five million members of the Baha'i faith in some twenty thousand Baha'i communities in over 150 countries throughout the world. Regrettably, the Baha'i religion is now outlawed and persecuted as a heresy in the very country of its birth.

The founder of the Baha'i religion, Baha'u'llah ("Glory of God," 1817-92), taught that all the world's religions should unite and that the human race are one people under God. Animals and the rest of creation are seen as part of the unity of the earth and the cosmos. Abdu'l-Baha (1844-1921), Baha'u'llah's eldest son and successor, indicated that although humans occupy a position in the universe that is "higher and nobler" than nature, and humans are "rulers over nature's sphere and province," nature is nonetheless to be given respect. According to Abdu'l-Baha, "the Lord of all mankind hath fashioned this human realm to be a Garden of Eden, an earthly paradise."

Baha'u'llah has been quoted as saying: "Not a single atom in the entire universe can be found which doth not declare the evidences of His might, which doth not glorify His holy name...So perfect and comprehensive is His creation that no mind nor heart, however keen or pure, can ever grasp the nature of the most insignificant of His creatures."

Compassion for animals is a fundamental tenet of the Baha'i faith. Baha'u'llah called upon humanity to "show kindness to animals," and wrote: "Look not upon the creatures of God except with the eyes of kindliness and mercy, for Our loving providence hath pervaded all created things." Abdu'l-Baha wrote that "tenderness and loving-kindness (to animals) are basic principles of God's heavenly kingdom.

"Briefly," explained, Abdu'l-Baha, "it is not only their fellow human beings that the beloved of God must treat with mercy and compassion, rather must they show forth the utmost loving-kindness to every living creature. For in all physical respects, and where the animal spirit is concerned, the selfsame feelings are shared by animals and man...What difference is there when it cometh to physical sensations? The feelings are the same whether you inflict pain on man or beast. There is no difference here whatsoever.

"And indeed you do worse to harm an animal, for man hath a language, and he can lodge a complaint... But the hapless beast is mute, able neither to express its hurt nor take its case to the authorities... Therefore, it is essential that ye show forth the utmost consideration to the animal, and that ye be even kinder to him than to your fellow-man."

Abdu'l-Baha also recognized the value of a humane education:

"Train your children from their earliest days to be infinitely tender and loving to animals. If an animal be sick, let the children try to heal it, if it be hungry, let them feed it, if thirsty, let them quench its thirst, if weary, let them see that it rests."

The Baha'i faith endorses vegetarianism. An article appearing in the *American Baha'i* concluded:

"Regarding the eating of animal flesh and abstinence therefrom...he (man) is not in need of meat, nor is he obliged to eat it. Even without eating meat, he would live with the utmost vigor and energy...Truly, the killing of animals and the eating of their meat is somewhat contrary to pity and compassion, and if one can content oneself with cereals, fruits, oil and nuts, such as pistachios, almonds and so on, it would undoubtedly be better and more pleasing."

An article entitled "Conservation of the Earth's Resources," appeared in the "Baha'i National Review" in the January 1990 issue of the *American Baha'i*. Respect for nature is part of the Baha'i faith:

"Nature is held in high regard. Baha'u'llah states that the contemplation of nature creates an awareness of the 'signs' and 'tokens' of God and constitutes proof of His existence. Thus:

> "...Every time I lift mine eyes unto Thy heaven, I call to mind Thine incomparable glory and greatness; and every time I turn my gaze to Thine earth, I am made to recognize the evidences of Thy power and the tokens of Thy bounty.

> "And when I behold the sea, I find that it speaketh to me of Thy majesty, and of the potency of Thy might, and of Thy sovereignty and Thy grandeur. And at whatever time I contemplate the mountains, I am led to discover the ensigns of Thy victory and the standards of Thine omnipotence.

> "Nature reflects the 'names and attributes of God.' It is the expression of 'God's Will...in...the contingent world.' Baha'u'llah writes: 'Nature in its essence is the embodiment of My Name, the Maker, the Creator. Nature...is a dispensation of Providence ordained by the Ordainer, the All-Wise.'"

Robert A. White, in an article for the *Journal of Baha'i Studies*, entitled, "Spiritual Foundations for an Ecologically Stable Society," concluded:

"An attitude an awe and gratitude towards the earth is part of attaining spiritual humility...the soul is refreshed and revitalized by contact with the beauty, mystery, and grandeur of nature." The Baha'i faith espouses a reverence for all life.

chapter thirteen
"No Bloodshed or Slaughter"

Ancient Greece, more than any other culture or society in human history, has come to be seen as the basis of Western civilization. According to Dr. T.Z. Lavine: "It may be said that the Western world has had a long-standing love affair with...Athens, as our ideal and model...than to any other city in all of human history, except possibly Jerusalem. But we relate to Jerusalem not as an ideal city, but only in devotion to the great persons who lived there and to the sacred events that happened there.

"Why the long love affair with the ancient city of Athens? Athens is our ideal as the first democracy, and as a city devoted to human excellence in mind and body, to philosophy, the arts and science, and to the cultivation of the art of living..." The ancient Greco-Roman civilization had a tradition of poets and philosophers advocating moral and ethical consideration for animals—even to the point of not eating them.

The Greek poet Hesiod (800 BC) espoused vegetarianism. In passages 109-201 of *Works and Days*, he wrote that the first race of humans, the golden race, was created by the gods of Olympus under the rule of Cronus. These humans were free from sorrow, toil and grief. They did not have to labor for food: the earth spontaneously gave them nourishment. Humans in the golden age were vegetarian. Hesiod suggests that gods and men freely mixed, and even shared their meals together. Death in this age was comparable to going to sleep.

This golden age of rule under Cronus eventually gave way to rule under Zeus. A new race of silver men appeared. These were not descendants of the original golden race, but a new creation. This race was foolish and impious, and did not offer sacrifices to the gods. Zeus thus destroyed them and created a third race, a race of bronze. The bronze race was fond of violence. They did not eat bread, and they eventually destroyed each other.

The fourth race appeared in what was called the age of heroes. This age was characterized by demi-gods who died in battle and were rewarded for their heroism. The fifth and current race indicates the further deterioration of humanity. This is the age of iron. It is a time of anxiety, toil, sorrow, war and false pride. The human race in this age is described by Hesiod as the worst of races, and he expressed the desire to have been born in an earlier age.

Yet the centuries ahead brought a spiritual and intellectual awakening across the globe. In Egypt, Pharaoh Necho caused Africa to be circumnavigated. Zoroaster appeared in Persia, Confucius and Lao-Tzu in China, the Hebrew prophets in Israel, and the Buddha in India. In Ionia, it was the time of Thales, Anaximander and Pythagoras.

Pythagoras (570-470 BC) was born on the island colony of Samos. Historian Dr. Martin A. Larson describes him as "A universal genius...He made important contributions to music and astronomy; he was a metaphysician, a natural philosopher, a social revolutionary, a political organizer, and the universal theologian. He was one of those all-embracing intellects which appears at rare intervals." Pythagoras' biographer Diogenes Laertius records that he did not "neglect medicine;" his followers contributed to medical wisdom. In the history of religion, Pythagoras was the first person to teach the concepts of reincarnation, heaven and hell to the Western world.

Diogenes Laertius writes that Pythagoras warned that all who did not accept his teachings would suffer torment in the afterlife, while promising his followers the spiritual kingdom. According to the early Christian father Eusebius: "Pythagoras...declared...that the doctrines which he had received...were a personal revelation to himself from God."

Pythagoras was driven from his native Samos in 529 BC when the tyrant Polycrates declared him a subversive. He went to Croton in Italy, established a school of philosophy, and lectured to classes of up to six hundred students. He founded a monastic order that soon became very influential. It was basically a religious sect made up of dedicated saints practicing vegetarianism, voluntary poverty and chastity. In less that two decades, the Pythagoreans were numerous and powerful enough to take political power without having to resort to force or violence. History shows that when the Pythagoreans were attacked and massacred in Magna Grecia in 450 BC, they practiced nonviolence and did not resist their aggressors.

Ancient and modern historians alike acknowledge that Pythagoras was vegetarian. This was the conclusion of Plutarch, Ovid, Diogenes Laertius and Iamblichus in ancient times, and it is the conclusion of scholars today. Nor was vegetarianism loosely connected with the Pythagorean philosophy—it was an integral part of it.

"Oh, my fellow men!" exclaimed Pythagoras. "Do not defile your bodies with sinful foods. We have corn. We have apples bending down the branches with their weight, and grapes swelling on the vines. There are sweet flavored herbs and vegetables which can be cooked and softened over the fire. Nor are you denied milk or thyme-scented honey. The earth affords you a lavish supply of riches, of innocent foods, and offers you banquets that involve no bloodshed or slaughter."

Pythagoras' meals consisted of honeycomb, millet or barley bread, and vegetables. He would pay fishermen to throw their catch back into the sea. Ironically, he claimed to have been a fisherman in a previous life. He abhorred animal sacrifice and wine, and would only sacrifice cakes, honey, and frankincense to the gods. He revered the altar at Delos because it was free from blood sacrifices. Upon it, he offered flour, meal, and cakes made without the use of fire. Pythagoras would not associate with cooks or hunters.

According to Iamblichus, Pythagoras taught his followers not to kill even a flea, especially in a temple. He not only showed respect for gods, humans, and animals, but also for the trees, which were not to be destroyed, unless absolutely necessary. It is said Pythagoras pet an eagle, told an ox not to trample a bean field, and fed a ferocious bear barley and acorns, telling it not to attack humans any more.

Pythagoras not only taught transmigration of the soul, or reincarnation, but even claimed to remember his previous lives. It is said Pythagoras once stopped a man from beating a dog, because in the dog's yelping he recognized the voice of an old friend. For Pythagoras, killing animals for food meant causing suffering or death to living creatures just as worthy of moral concern as human beings, and who may also have been human in previous lifetimes.

The Roman poet Ovid (43 BC - 18 AD), quoted Pythagoras in the 15th chapter of *Metamorphosis* as follows: "Our souls are immortal, and are ever received into new homes where they live and dwell, when they have left their previous abode...All things change, but nothing dies; the spirit wanders hither and tither, taking possession of what limbs it pleases, passing from beasts into human beings, or again our human spirit passes into beasts, but never at any time does it perish...Alas, what wickedness to swallow flesh into our own flesh, to fatten our greedy bodies by cramming in other bodies, to have one living creature fed by the death of another!"

If souls can transmigrate from one species to another, and all souls are of the same nature, then the unnecessarily killing animals is as morally indefensible as the unnecessary killing of human beings. Pythagoras may have also drawn a parallel between the plight of animals in human hands, and the fate of humans in the hands of the gods. We humans would suffer should the gods unnecessarily kill or torment us; we should likewise treat the animal world with mercy.

Local tradition says Pythagoras spent time living in a cave on Mount Kerkis in Samos. He was the first person in the history of the world to deduce that the Earth is a sphere. He may have reached this conclusion by comparing the Earth to the Sun and the Moon, or perhaps he noticed the curved shadow of the Earth upon the Moon during a lunar eclipse, or he may have seen that when ships depart and recede over the horizon, their masts disappear last.

The famous "Pythagorean theorem" is now known to have been mathematical knowledge long before Pythagoras. Square roots and cube roots and the "Pythagorean" theorem are mentioned in the *Sulbha Sutràs* of Bodhayana, in India. (700 BC) Bodhayana also calculated the areas of triangles, circles, trapezoids and determined the value of pi = 3.14136 in measuring and constructing temple altars. Some scholars believe Pythagoras may have received his wisdom from the East.

What was significant about Pythagoras' approach, however, was that he did more than list examples of this theorem: he developed a method of mathematical proof of the theorem, based on deduction. Our modern tradition of mathematical proof, the basis for every kind of science, originated in the West with Pythagoras. Whereas classical Indian mathematics tended to be intuitive, the Greeks established a tradition of rigorous mathematical proofs. Pythagoras further taught that the world is well-ordered, harmonious, and may be comprehended through human reason. He was the first person to use the word "*cosmos*" to denote a fathomable universe. According to Pythagoras, the laws of nature could be deduced purely by thought.

During the Renaissance and the age of Enlightenment, Kepler and Newton thought of the world in terms of harmony—the order and beauty of planetary motion and the existence of mathematical laws explaining such motion, and from them came our modern scientific belief that the entire universe can be measured, quantified, and explained in terms of mathematical relationships. These ideas began with Pythagoras. "Chemistry is simply numbers," said Dr. Carl Sagan, "an idea Pythagoras would have liked."

Pythagorean science was far more theoretical than experimental. However, one of Pythagoras' students, Alcmaeon, is the first person known to have dissected a human body. He further identified arteries and veins, discovered the optic nerve and the eustachian tubes, and declared the brain to be the seat of the intellect. This final contention was denied by Aristotle, who placed intelligence in the heart. Alcmaeon also founded the science of embryology.

The Pythagoreans also contributed to medical ethics through the Oath of Hippocrates. Hippocrates was a physician who lived in the 5th century BC. In a treatise entitled "The Sacred Disease," he maintained that epilepsy and other illnesses were not the result of evil spirits or angry gods, but due to natural causes.

Hippocrates has been called the "Father of Medicine," the "wisest and greatest practitioner of his art," and the "most important and most complete medical personality of antiquity." Before Hippocrates, the physician studied plants and animals and had a working knowledge of both harmful and beneficial remedies. He could simultaneously heal some patients while killing others. Hippocrates believed in the sanctity of life and called other physicians to the highest ethical standards and conduct.

"Throughout the primitive world, the doctor and the sorcerer tended to be the same person," observed anthropologist Margaret Mead. "He with the power to kill had the power to cure, including especially the undoing of his own killing activities. He who had the power to cure would necessarily also be able to kill." According to Mead, the Oath of Hippocrates marked a turning point in the history of Western civilization because "for the first time in our tradition" it caused "a complete separation between curing and killing." The Oath reads:

> "I swear by Apollo Physician, by Asclepius...I will use treatment to help
> the sick according to my ability and judgement, but never with a view to
> injury and wrong-doing. Neither will I administer a poison to anybody
> when asked to do so, nor will I suggest such a course.

"Similarly, I will not give to a woman a pessary to cause abortion...Into whatsoever houses I enter, I will enter to help the sick, and I will abstain from all intentional wrong-doing and harm, especially from abusing the bodies of man or woman, bond or free."

"With the Greeks," concluded Dr. Mead, "the distinction was made clear. One profession, the followers of Asclepius, were to be dedicated completely to life under all circumstances, regardless of the rank, age, or intellect—the life of a slave, the life of the Emperor, the life of a foreign man, the life of a defective child."

The United States Supreme Court in 1973, noted that the Oath of Hippocrates "echoes Pythagorean doctrines." Dr. Herbert Ratner observes that in ancient Greece, "medicine emerged as the prototype of the learned professions. The contribution of Hippocrates, the father of medicine, was to incorporate the rights of the patient, as well as the obligations of the physician, into the Oath. Hippocrates' profound grasp of the nature of a learned profession serving one of man's basic needs makes the Hippocratic Oath one of the great documents and classics of man, a fact not only signified by its universal inclusion in collections of the great books of Western civilization, but by the universal veneration accorded it by physicians, singly and collectively, throughout the ages...the Oath, properly constituted, becomes the one hope of preserving the unconfused role of the physician as healer."

At the end of the Second World War, during the Nuremberg Doctors' Trial, twenty physicians were tried for crimes against humanity. In this case, the crimes were committed in the euthanasia wards and concentration camps of the Third Reich. Physicians there had become executioners as well as healers. American medical science consultant Dr. Andrew C. Ivy said, "The moral imperative of the Oath of Hippocrates I believe is necessary for the survival of the scientific and technical philosophy of medicine."

The Oath of Hippocrates and its modern equivalent, the Declaration of Geneva, enacted by the World Medical Association in 1948, are frequently cited by the American Medical Association in its prohibition against medical participation in legally authorized executions. A code of conduct for physicians as healers, as well as concern for the rights and well-being of the patient, originated with Hippocrates and the Pythagorean tradition.

Despite these and many other outstanding contributions to ethics, medicine, music, astronomy, geometry and general science, mathematics dominated Pythagorean thought. The Pythagoreans were mathematicians as well as mystics. Pythagoras taught that the laws of Nature could be deduced through logic and reason. They delighted in the absolute certainty of mathematics, and found in it a pure and undefiled realm accessible to the human intellect. They believed that in mathematics they had glimpsed a perfect reality, a realm of the gods, of which our own world is but an imperfect reflection.

Pythagorean theology was dualistic; it contrasted this corruptible, earthly sphere with a pure and divine realm. One's higher nature, the eternal soul, is entangled in temporal flesh. The body is like a tomb. The soul must not become a slave to the body and its lusts. One must not fall prey to the demands of the flesh.

Pythagoreanism exerted a profound influence upon Plato, and, later, Christian theology. In Plato's famous parable of the cave, prisoners are tied to stakes so they can only see shadows of passerby and believe the shadows to be real—unaware of the higher reality that is accessible if they would merely turn their heads. The Pythagorean concept of a perfect and mystical world, unseen by the senses, and inaccessible to flesh and blood was also readily accepted by the early Christians.

History tells us there were two classes of Pythagoreans. The *akousmatikoi* heard the teachings of the Master and followed them to a degree, but were never initiated into the deeper levels of mysticism. By contrast, the *mathematikoi* were strict Pythagoreans, living as ascetics, and observing the holy way of life taught by the Master. Pythagoras established a monastic order at Croton that soon became a vegetarian colony. After the massacre in Magna Grecia in 450 BC, the political fortunes of the Pythagoreans declined. By 350 BC, Pythagoreanism had become more of a religious sect than a philosophical school of thought. As a religion, Pythagoreanism continued to attract spiritual seekers for over seven centuries.

Pythagorean thought was familiar to the leadership of the early Christian church. The Christian father Justin Martyr wrote that when he was a youth seeking spiritual enlightenment, he first went to the Pythagoreans. A "celebrated" Pythagorean teacher told him, however, that before he could be initiated into any kind of mysticism, he would first have to master music, geometry and astronomy.

Discouraged, he turned to the Platonists. Their way of life may have been equally demanding. Jesus' demands upon anyone wishing to become his disciple are well-known. These did not deter Justin Martyr from eventually converting to Christianity.

Although the Pythagoreans acknowledged the minor gods of the Greek pantheon, they also recognized a Supreme Being. According to authorities within the early Christian church, the Pythagoreans were monotheists:

"God is one; and He is not...outside of the frame of things, but within it; but, in all the entireness of His being is in the whole circle of existence...the mind and vital power of the whole world," wrote Clement of Alexandria in *Exhortation* VI, quoting Pythagoras. The Pythagoreans held a pantheistic concept of God, recognizing His omnipresent Spirit, but with no knowledge of His personal qualities—a concept which the Stoics were to adopt. Like the Jews and the Zoroastrians, the Pythagoreans consequently forbade the worship of images and statues.

First century Pythagoreanism is described in detail in *The Life of Apollonius of Tyana*. The ancient texts records this neoplatonic philosopher and miracle worker having a divine birth, absorbing the wisdom of Pythagoras, practicing celibacy, vegetarianism, as well as voluntary poverty; healing the sick, restoring sight to the blind, exorcising demons, foretelling the future, and teaching the innermost secrets of religion. Finally, the text says he never died, but went directly to heaven in a physical assumption.

The philosopher Empodocles (5th century BC) wrote that the ancients were much more fortunate than modern man because they were vegetarian and there was neither animal sacrifices nor war. He described humanity in previous ages using statues, pictures, perfumes and honey in their worship. They did not offer animals, Empodocles maintained, because to kill an animal for sacrifice or food is the greatest moral wrong. Empodocles described these ancient races as gentle to animals and birds as well as to each other. Empodocles was greatly influenced by Pythagorean doctrine. He believed in the transmigration of souls:

> "For I was once already boy and girl,
> Thicket and bird, and mute fish in the waves
> All things doth Nature change,
> Enwrapping souls
> In unfamiliar tunics of the flesh"

Because of reincarnation and the equality of all living beings, Empodocles felt flesh-eating was comparable to cannibalism. "Will ye not cease from this great din of slaughter?" he once wrote. "Will ye not see, unthinking as ye are, how ye rend one another unbeknoweth?" With a vision of eternal souls endlessly clothed in new bodies, Empodocles compared flesh-eating to fathers unknowingly killing their sons, and children similarly killing their parents:

> "The father lifteth for the stroke of death

His own dear son within a changed form...
Each slits the throat and in his halls prepares
A horrible repast. Thus too the son
Seizes the father, children the mother seize,
And...eat their own dear flesh."

Belief in the golden age and vegetarianism existed outside the Pythagorean tradition. The Cynic, Crates (4th century BC), wrote a poem linking nonviolence to vegetarianism, and expressing the hope for a vegetarian utopia. Dicaerchus' *Life in Greece* has been called the first cultural history of a people. Dicaerchus, who lived in the late 4th century BC, did not believe in reincarnation, the soul, or the afterlife. Nonetheless, he also wrote in favor of ethical vegetarianism, insisting it is morally wrong to cause unnecessary suffering to a being that can experience pain.

In her book, *From Socrates to Sartre: The Philosophic Quest*, Dr. T.Z. Lavine writes:

"Plato is the most celebrated, honored and revered of all the philosophers of the Western world. He lived in Athens...in the fourth century before Christ...He is said to be the greatest of the philosophers which Western civilization has produced; he is said to be the father of Western philosophy; the son of the god Apollo...

"The British philosopher and mathematician Alfred North Whitehead said of him that the history of Western philosophy is only a series of footnotes to Plato. The American poet and philosopher Ralph Waldo Emerson said, 'Plato is philosophy, and philosophy is Plato...Out of Plato come all things that are still written and debated among men of thought.'"

According to Diogenes Laertius, Plato (427-347 BC) began as a follower of Socrates. After Socrates' death, he became the pupil of the leading Pythagoreans of his day—Philolaus, Eurytas, Archytas, and others. Plato was also the greatest collector of Pythagorean literature in antiquity. Ovid attributed Plato's great longevity to his "moral purity, temperance, and natural food diet of herbs, berries, nuts, grains and the wild plants...which the earth, the best of mothers, produces."

An economic link between flesh-eating and war can be found in Plato's *Republic*. Plato records a dialogue between Socrates and Glaucon in which Socrates extols the peace and happiness that come to people eating a vegetarian diet. The citizens, Socrates says, will feast upon barley meal, wheat flour, salt, olives, cheese, onions, greens, figs, chickpeas, beans, myrtle berries and acorns. These are the foods of peace and good health: "And with such a diet they may be expected to live in peace and health to a good old age, and bequeath a similar life to their children after them."

Glaucon does not believe people will be satisfied with such fare. He insists that people will desire the "ordinary conveniences of life," including animal flesh. He asks Socrates what foods would be eaten if he were not founding a Republic but a city of pigs. Pigs are omnivores, they can be made to eat even the flesh of their own kind, and they experience inebriation on alcohol.

Socrates responds: "The true state I believe to be the one we have described—the healthy state, as it were. But if it is your pleasure that we contemplate also a fevered state, there is nothing to hinder." Socrates then proceeds to stock the once ideal state with swineherds, huntsmen, and "cattle in great number." The dialogue continues. Socrates asks Glaucon:

"...and there will be animals of many other kinds, if people eat them?"

"Certainly."

"And living in this way we shall have much greater need of physicians than before?"

"Much greater."

"And the country which was enough to support the original inhabitants will be too small now, and not enough?"

"Quite true."

"Then a slice of our neighbor's land will be wanted by us for pasture and tillage, and they will want a slice of ours, if, like ourselves, they exceed the limit of necessity, and give themselves up to the unlimited accumulation of wealth?"

"That, Socrates, will be inevitable."

"And so we shall go to war, Glaucon. Shall we not?"

"Most certainly," replies Glaucon.

Critics of Plato, reading the rest of the *Republic*, have complained that Plato's "ideal" society is a militaristic or fascist state, with censorship and a rigidly controlled economy. Plato would hardly disagree with these critics; what they have failed to observe is that the state which he describes is not his idea—it is merely a result of Glaucon's demand for meat, which Socrates himself disavows.

Philosophy professor Daniel Dombrowski says, "That the Republic was to be a vegetarian city is one of the best-kept secrets in the history of philosophy." (*Republic* 369d-373e)

Plato also developed a theory that it would not be possible to have a just and good society until kings were philosophers or until philosophers became kings. In this way, the leaders would have a true understanding of justice and virtue, and would be able to rule properly for the benefit of all the citizens. According to Plato, the ideal society consists of three classes of men: the governing class, the military class, and the mercantile class.

Perhaps because he lived in a slave state, Plato failed to recognize laborers as a fourth, or working class. However, he did teach that people fall into different classes according to their talents and abilities, rather than as a result of their birth. Plato taught further that women are recognized as equals with men in the ideal society, and may also become rulers, soldiers, or merchants.

In Plato's ideal state, the guardian (ruling) class and the military class are trained to be just and virtuous. They must live like members of an ascetic religious order. They have no worldly possessions or private property, nor do they have any dealings with money. Sex and marriage in these classes exist solely for the sake of procreation. They take their meals communally, the food itself is simple, and consumed in moderation.

Plato infers that the guardian class, which consists entirely of philosophers, should be vegetarian. In the *Republic*, he depicts what history would be if philosophers of the golden age were to rule, and in the *Statesman*, he describes the people of the golden age as vegetarian. In the *Statesman*, the Eleatic Stranger, who is the hero of the dialogue, describes an age similar to the creation account found in Genesis 1, in which "God was supreme governor...So it befell that savagery was nowhere to be found nor preying of creature on creature, nor did war rage nor any strife whatsoever...they had fruits without stint from trees and bushes; these needed no cultivation but sprang up of themselves out of the ground without man's toil." (*Statesman* 271e, 272a)

According to Plato, vegetarianism was divinely ordained. In the *Timaeus*, Plato says the gods created certain kinds of life to be our food:

"These are the trees and plants and seeds which have been improved by cultivation and are now domesticated among us; anciently there were only the wild kinds, which are older than the cultivated."

(*Timaeus* 77a) These kinds of life were especially created "to be food for us." (77c) Plato also makes a passing reference to "the fruits of the earth or herb of the field, which God planted to be our daily food." (80d)

In Plato's *Laws* (713), an analogy is made between Cronus' daemons ruling over men and human shepherds tending animals. The lesson implied here is that dominion over lesser beings is not an automatic license for exploitation. It would be unthinkable that Cronus' assistants should eat men just because they themselves are godlike or superhuman in nature. Human "dominion" over the animal kingdom must likewise be questioned.

Plato's writings contain frequent references to reincarnation. The souls of animals and the souls of men are taught to be of equal worth. This is made clear in the story of Er. (*Republic* 614-621) In this story, souls with human bodies become animals in their next life, while souls clothed in animal bodies become human.

Plato presented detailed accounts of reincarnation in many of his other writings. (*Phaedrus* 248c; *Phaedo* 81-83, 85a; *Meno* 81b; *Timaeus* 90e-91c, etc.) According to Plato, pure souls have fallen from the plane of absolute reality because of sensual desire, and have taken on physical bodies.

First, the fallen souls are embodied in human forms. Of these, the highest is that of the philosopher, who delights in higher knowledge, and lives on the level of the mind, rather than the body. As long as he remains caught up in the heavenly spheres, he returns to eternal life and existence. But if he becomes entangled in carnal desires, he will descend into the animal kingdom.

Plato believed gluttons and drunkards could easily become asses in future lifetimes, cruel and violent people may take birth as hawks or wolves, and blind followers of social convention may be reborn as bees or ants. Eventually, the soul will again receive another human body, and with it another opportunity to seek first the spiritual kingdom, righteousness, and eternal life.

Plato wrote about ethics, politics, justice, knowledge, virtue, the soul, rebirth, judgement, heaven, hell, monastic living, and a transcendent realm of goodness. The early church historian Eusebius observed: "Plato, more than anyone else, shared in the philosophy of Pythagoras." Early church father Justin Martyr is known to have said repeatedly that Plato must have been versed in Christian prophecy.

Aristotle (384-322 BC) was a student of Plato's who became a leading philosopher with his own school of thought. Theophrastus, a student of Aristotle, taught that grass was the most ancient kind of offering made to the gods. This was followed later by trees, and eventually fruits, barley, frankincense, and so forth. The sacrifice of animals came much later. According to Theophrastus, a vegetarian, this defiled the pure religion.

Porphyry (3rd century AD), wrote in his masterpiece *De Abstentia* that Theophrastus regarded vegetarianism as a return to primeval perfection. Theophrastus taught that the most ancient libations were performed with sobriety. Water was initially offered, and only in later times did the offerings consist of honey, oil, and wine. When animal sacrifices began, not only did meat-eating become widespread, but so did atheism, as a reaction against the anger of the gods for deliberately killing animals. (*De Abstentia* 2:7,20,32)

Theophrastus also regarded vegetarianism as a matter of ethics. To kill animals unnecessarily is unjust. (*De Abstentia* 2:11-12) He suggested that war, pestilence and damaged crops may have caused humans to start killing animals for food, but in a world where fruits, grains, nuts, and vegetables are in abundance, there is no need to sacrifice or eat animals. Besides, he insisted, the gods consider the products of the soil to be the most beautiful and honorable gifts.

Diogenes Laertius recorded that Theophrastus wrote several books on animals. Theophrastus has been called the "father of ecology." He conducted the most extensive studies of plants in antiquity. More than any Greek philosopher, Theophrastus understood the difference between plants and animals, especially with regard to conscious awareness and suffering. He taught that piety and justice require us to refrain from harming others whenever we can. And animals can be harmed, whereas plants cannot. He observed that animals are capable of passion, perception and reason.

Humanism was gradually replacing mysticism. During the 1st century BC, Diodorus Siculus wrote his universal history of the world. Dismissing the idea of a golden age, he wrote that the first humans were vegetarians learning to cope with the elements. According to Siculus, humans in the beginning enjoyed neither peace nor bliss. They were brutish, undisciplined, and attacked by wild animals.

Plutarch (45-125 AD) was a Greek priest at Delphi. This gave him access to Greece's most ancient traditions. Plutarch was one of the few writers in the ancient world to advocate vegetarianism out of compassion for animals without referring to reincarnation. His essay "On Eating Flesh" is a thought-provoking literary classic:

"You ask me upon what grounds Pythagoras abstained from feeding on the flesh of animals," he began. "I, for my part, marvel of what sort of feeling, mind, or reason that man was possessed who was the first to pollute his mouth with gore and to allow his lips to touch the flesh of a murdered being; who spread his table with the mangled forms of dead bodies, and claimed as his daily food what were but now beings endowed with movement, with perception, and with voice.

"How could his eyes endure the spectacle of the flayed and dismembered limbs? How could his sense of smell endure the horrid stench? How, I ask, was his taste not sickened by contact with festering wounds, with the pollution of corrupted blood and juices?"

Plutarch challenged the flesh-eaters by insisting that if they felt nature had intended them to be predators, they should then kill for themselves what they wish to eat—with their bare hands, unaided by toolmaking or weapons. He also observed that the first man put to death in Athens was the most de-graded amongst knaves, but eventually the philosopher Polemarchus (what to speak of Socrates) was put to death as well.

He concluded that killing animals, whether human or otherwise, is a bloodthirsty and savage practice which only serves to incline the mind towards more brutality. His argument appears to link the needless slaughter of animals to capital punishment.

During the 3rd century AD, Porphyry made allusions to the golden age in *De Abstentia*. Porphyry was a disciple of Plotinus (205-270 AD), a neoplatonic philosopher who was renowned for his wisdom, asceticism, and deep spirituality. Plotinus acknowledged the reality of transmigration of souls and the equality of all living creatures. A celibate vegetarian, he would not consume even medicines which contained animal products.

Like his teacher Plotinus, Porphyry was vegetarian. He wrote *De Abstentia*, or *On Abstinence (From Eating Animal Food)* to another disciple, Firmus Castricius, who had abandoned both his spiritual life and his practice of vegetarianism. Porphyry gave every possible reason why Firmus should remain vegetarian. His work is divided into four separate books, each focusing on a different aspect of vegetarianism.

Porphyry wrote that before animal sacrifice began, the human race abstained from eating animals altogether. (*De Abstentia* 2:10) Humans originally sacrificed grass. When widespread famine occurred, animals were offered to placate the gods. This was unnecessary. Like the biblical story of Cain and Abel (Hebrews 11:4), the gods are more pleased with the faith of the worshippers than with the object of sacrifice.

Porphyry depicted humanity in a state of gradual decline since the golden age. All sacrifices in the golden age were "simple, pure, and bloodless." The degeneration of mankind began with the shedding of blood. However, even after men began to kill animals, they still protected animals which were domesti-cated and working cooperatively with humans. Porphyry wrote that the moral degeneration of man will continue to the point of cannibalism, but go no further. (2:31,53)

According to Porphyry, animals have rights. Animals are our brothers and sisters. Animals have been endowed with life, feelings, ideas, memory, and industry. The only thing animals may be said to lack which sets humans apart from them is the gift of speech. "If they had it," asked Porphyry, "should we dare to kill and eat them? Should we dare to commit these fratricides?"

Porphyry further observed that, in reality, animals do possess language, which the ancients were said to have understood. The birds and beasts communicate, but men no longer understand their language. Animals not only think, feel, and suffer, they learn to understand human language. Men may not understand foreigners, but that does not make them irrational brutes. Moreover, it is absurd to say animals lack reason when we admit that dogs, elephants, and many other animals can depart from reason—i.e., go mad.

In *De Abstentia*, Porphyry also dealt with Greek vegetarianism and its relationship to other ancient cultures. He wrote favorably of Egyptian priests, Persian Magi (Zoroastrians), the life of the Spartans as recorded by Lycurgus, the Jews, the Essenes, the *brahmana* priests of India, the Buddhists, and other traditions where religious vegetarianism has been observed. The Greeks called the holy teachers of India Gymnosophists. Porphyry described the fertile Ganges region as a paradise—as if the golden age still existed in other parts of the world.

chapter fourteen
Healthy, Wealthy, and Wise

The health advantages of a vegetarian diet are well-known in the American medical community, but are just beginning to gain acceptance in the popular culture. The ethical, nutritional and environmental arguments in favor of vegetarianism have been well documented by author John Robbins in his 1987 Pulitzer Prize nominated book, *Diet for a New America*, which makes ethical vegetarianism seem as mainstream as recycling.

It's healthier to be a vegetarian. During the period of October 1917 to October 1918, war rationing forced the Danish government to put its citizens on a vegetarian diet. This was a "mass experiment in vegetarianism," with over three million subjects. The results were astonishing. The mortality rate dropped by 34 percent. The very same phenomenon was observed in occupied Norway during the Second World War. After the war, heavy consumption of meat resumed, and the mortality rate shot back up.

The populations consuming the highest levels of animal flesh—the Eskimos, Laplanders, Greenlanders and Russian Kurgi tribes—also have the life expectancies, averaging about 30 years. Nor can such a short lifespan be attributed to harsh climate. The Russian Caucasians and Yucatan Indians, for example, live mostly on vegetarian foods and have life expectancies of 90 to 100 years.

The populations with the longest lifespans include the Vilacambans of Ecuador, the Abhikasians of the former USSR, and the Hunzas of Pakistan. The most remarkable feature of all these people is that they live almost entirely on plant foods. The Hunzas, for example, eat a diet that is 98.5 percent plant food.

Studies done at Yale University by Professor Irving Fisher demonstrated that flesh-eaters have less endurance than vegetarians. A similar study done by Dr. J. Ioteyko of the Academie de Medicine in Paris found that vegetarians have two to three times more stamina than flesh-eaters and they take only one-fifth the time to recover from exhaustion.

In recent years, there has been widespread concern about osteoporosis, which is epidemic in America, especially among older women. The popular myth has been to solve the problem by consuming more calcium. Yet this doesn't attack the root of the problem.

Osteoporosis is caused by excess consumption of protein. Americans overdose on protein, getting 1.5 to 2 times more protein than their bodies can handle. The body can't store excess protein, so the kidneys are forced to excrete it. In doing so, they must draw upon calcium from the bloodstream. This negative calcium balance in the blood is compensated for by calcium loss from the bones: osteoporosis. The calcium lost in the bones of flesh-eaters is 5 to 6 times greater than that lost in the bones of vegetarians.

Excessive protein intake also taxes the kidneys; in America, it is not uncommon to find many over 45 with kidney problems. A strong correlation between excessive protein intake and cancer of the breast, prostate, pancreas and colon has even been observed.

It must be pointed out that meat, fish, and eggs are the most acidic forming foods; heavy consumption of these foods will cause the body to draw upon calcium to restore its pH balance. The calcium lost from the bones gets into one's urine and often crystallizes into kidney stones, which are found in far greater frequency among flesh-eaters than among vegetarians. Studies have found that vegetarians in the United States have less than half the kidney stones of the general population.

The high consumption of saturated fat and cholesterol leads to artherosclerosis—more popularly known as "hardening of the arteries." Plant foods contain zero cholesterol and only palm oil, coconuts and chocolate contain saturated fat. Lowering the cholesterol and fat intake in one's diet lowers the risk of heart disease—America's biggest killer.

As far back as 1961, the *Journal of the American Medical Association* reported that "A vegetarian diet can prevent 97% of our coronary occlusions." Much has been said about the advantage of polyunsaturated fats as a means of lowering cholesterol in the blood. Unfortunately, this also has the adverse side effect of driving the cholesterol out of the blood and into the colon; contributing to colon cancer. The best way to prevent heart disease is to avoid foods high in fat and cholesterol.

Up to 50 percent of all cancers are caused by diet. Meat and fat intake are primarily responsible. The incidence of colon cancer is high in regions where meat consumption is high and low where meat consumption is minimal. A lack of fiber in the diet also contributes significantly to colon cancer.

It's important to remember that unprocessed plant foods are high in fiber and carbohydrates, while animal flesh has none. The highest incidence of breast cancer occurs among flesh-eating populations; meat eating women have a four times greater risk of developing breast cancer than do vegetarian women. There is also a greater risk of cervical, uterine, and ovarian cancer—all linked to diets high in fat. Men who consume large quantities of animal fat also have a 3.6 times greater risk of getting prostate cancer.

Diabetes is known to be treatable on a low fat, high fiber diet. Incidence of diabetes balloons among populations eating a rich, meat-based diet. Hypoglycemia is caused by the excessive consumption of meats, sugar and fat. Multiple Sclerosis is also treatable on a low-fat diet. MS is prevalent among populations where consumption of animal fats is high and is least common where such consumption is low. A brain tissue analysis of people with MS found a high saturated fat content.

Ulcers occur most frequently in diets which are acid forming, low in fiber and high in fats. Meat, fish, and eggs are the most acid forming of all foods, and animal flesh has no fiber and excess fat. Low fiber, high-fat diets are the principle cause of hemorrhoids and also diverticulosis—which affects 75 percent of Americans over the age of 75. Similarly, 35 percent of Americans are afflicted with some form of arthritis by the age of 35. Over 85 percent of all Americans over age 70 have arthritis, yet it is treatable on a fat free diet.

The United States Public Health Service estimates that some 60 million Americans are overweight. Exercise is helpful, but so is proper diet and nutrition. Foods high in fiber, low in fat and moderate in protein are most conducive to maintaining proper body weight.

Excess cholesterol forms gallstones. Gallstones, as well as gallbladder disease and gallbladder cancer are usually found in people with low-fiber, high cholesterol, high fat diets. Hypertension is virtually unknown in countries where the intake of salts, fat and cholesterol is low. At the University Hospital in Linkoping, Sweden, even severe asthma patients were found to be treatable on a vegetarian diet. Flesh foods in America are also contaminated with coliform bacteria and salmonella. Much healthier alternatives exist.

> "I have no doubt that it is part of the destiny of the human race in its gradual development to leave off the eating of animals, as surely as the savage tribes have left off eating each other when they came into contact with the more civilized."
>
> — *Henry David Thoreau*

Human beings differ completely from the naturally carnivorous species such as wolves or tigers. Carnivores have a very short digestive tract—three times the length of their bodies—to rapidly consume and excrete decaying flesh. Their urine is highly acidic and they possess hydrochloric stomach acid strong enough to dissolve muscle tissues and bones. Because they are night hunters who sleep during the day, carnivores don't sweat. They perspire through their tongue. Their jaws can only move up and down and their teeth are long and pointed, in order to cut through tendons and bones.

The carnivores are quadrupeds with keen eyesight and sense of smell. They possess not only the necessary speed to overtake their prey but also have sharp, retractable claws which enable them to pull their victims to the ground and hold them fast. The anatomy of natural omnivores, such as the bear or raccoon, is almost identical to that of the carnivores, except they possess a set of molars to chew the plant foods that they eat.

Herbivorous creatures such as sheep and cattle have a digestive tract 30 times the length of their bodies; they have several stomachs, which allows them to break down cellulose—something humans are unable to do. This is why we can't graze or live on grass. The urine and saliva of the herbivores are alkaline, and their saliva contains ptyalin for the predigestion of starches.

The *frugivores* (gorillas, chimpanzees and other primates) have intestinal tracts twelve times the length of the body, clawless hands and alkaline urine and saliva. Their diet is mostly vegetarian, occasionally supplemented with carrion, insects, etc.

Flesh-eating animals lap water with their tongues, whereas vegetarian animals imbibe liquids by a suction process. Humans are classified as primates and are thus frugivores possessing a set of completely herbivorous teeth. Proponents of the theory that humans should be classified as omnivores note that human beings do, in fact, possess a modified form of canine teeth. However, these so-called "canine teeth" are much more prominent in animals that traditionally never eat flesh, such as apes, camels, and the male musk deer.

It must also be noted that the shape, length and hardness of these so-called "canine teeth" can hardly be compared to those of true carnivorous animals. A principle factor in determining the hardness of teeth is the phosphate of magnesia content. Human teeth usually contain 1.5 percent phosphate of magnesia, whereas the teeth of carnivores are composed of nearly 5 percent phosphate of magnesia. It is for this reason they are able to break through the bones of their prey, and reach the nutritious marrow.

Linneaus, who introduced binomial nomenclature (naming plants and animals according to their physical structure) wrote: "Man's structure, external and internal, compared with that of other animals shows that fruit and succulent vegetables constitute his natural food." Dr. F.A. Pouchet, 19th century author of *The Universe*, wrote in his *Pluralite' de la Race Humaine*: "It has been truly said that Man is frugivorous. All the details of his intestinal canal, and above all his dentition, prove it in the most decided manner."

One of the most famous anatomists, Baron Cuvier, wrote: "The natural food of man, judging from his structure, appears to consist principally of the fruits, roots, and other succulent parts of vegetables. His hands afford every facility for gathering them; his short but moderately strong jaws on the other hand, and his canines being equal only in length to the other teeth, together with his tuberculated molars on the other, would scarcely permit him either to masticate herbage, or to devour flesh, were these condiments not previously prepared by cooking."

The poet Shelley, in his essay, "A Vindication of a Natural Diet," wrote:

"Comparative anatomy teaches us that man resembles the frugivorous animals in everything, the carnivorous in nothing...It is only by softening and disguising dead flesh by culinary preparation that it is rendered susceptible of mastication or digestion, and that the sight of its bloody juices and raw horror does not excite loathing and disgust...

"Man resembles no carnivorous animal. There is no exception, unless man be one, to the rule of herbivorous animals having cellulated colons. The orang-outang is the most anthropomorphous (man-like) of the ape tribe, all of whom are strictly frugivorous.

"There is no other species of animals which live on different foods in which this analogy exists...The structure of the human frame then, is that of one fitted to a pure vegetable diet in every essential particular."

Professor William Lawrence, FRS, in one of his lectures delivered at the Royal College of Surgeons in 1822, said:

"The teeth of man have not the slightest resemblance to those of the carnivorous animals, excepting that their enamel is confined to the external surface. He possesses, indeed, teeth called canine; but they do not exceed the level of others, and are obviously unsuited to the purposes which the corresponding teeth execute in carnivorous animals. Thus we find, whether we consider the teeth and jaws, or the immediate instruments of digestion, that the human structure closely resembles that of the apes, all of whom, in their natural state, are completely herbivorous (frugivorous)."

Professor Charles Bell, FRS, wrote in his 1829 work, *Anatomy, Physiology, and Diseases of the Teeth*: "It is, I think, not going too far to say that every fact connected with the human organisation goes to prove that man was originally formed a frugivorous animal. This opinion is derived principally from the formation of his teeth and digestive organs, as well as from the character of his skin and the general structure of his limbs."

Professor Richard Owen, FRS, in his elaborate 1845 work, *Odontography*, wrote: "The apes and monkeys, whom man nearly resembles in his dentition, derive their staple food from fruits, grain, the kernels of nuts, and other forms in which the most sapid and nutritious tissues of the vegetable kingdom are elaborated; and the close resemblance between the quadrumanous and the human dentition shows that man was, from the beginning, adapted to eat the fruit of the tree of the garden."

> "Behold! I have given you every plant-yielding seed which is upon the face of all the earth, and every tree with seed in its fruit; you shall have them for food."
>
> — *Genesis 1:29*

"Man, by nature, was never made to be a carnivorous animal," wrote John Ray, FRS, "nor is he armed for prey or rapine, with jagged and pointed teeth, and claws to rend and tear; but with gentle hands to gather fruit and vegetables, and with teeth to chew and eat them." According to Dr. Spenser Thompson, "No physiologist would dispute with those who maintain that men ought to have a vegetable diet." Dr. S.M. Whitaker, MRCS, LRCP, in *Man's Natural Food: An Enquiry*, concluded, "Comparative anatomy and physiology indicate fresh fruits and vegetables as the main food of man."

More recently, William S. Collens and Gerald B. Dobkens concluded: "Examination of the dental structure of modern man reveals that he possesses all the features of a strictly herbivorous animal. While designed to subsist on vegetarian foods, he has perverted his dietary habits to accept food of the carnivore. It is postulated that man cannot handle carnivorous foods like the carnivore. Herein may lie the basis for the high incidence of arteriosclerotic disease."

In *The Natural Diet of Man*, Dr. John Harvey Kellogg observes:

"Man is neither a hunter nor a killer. Carnivorous animals are provided with teeth and claws with which to seize, rend, and devour their prey. Man possesses no such instruments of destruction and is less well qualified for hunting than is a horse or a buffalo. When a man goes hunting, he must take a dog along to find the game for him, and must carry a gun with which to kill his victim after it has been found. Nature has not equipped him for hunting."

According to Dr. Kellogg, "The statement that man is omnivorous is made without an atom of scientific support. It is true the average hotel bill of fare and the menu found upon the table of the average citizen of this country have a decidedly omnivorous appearance. As a matter of fact, man is not naturally omnivorous, but belongs, as long ago pointed out by Cuvier, to the frugivorous class of animals along with the chimpanzee and other anthropoids.

"The hog is a truly omnivorous animal. Although he thrives best upon a diet of grass or clover, tender shoots, seeds, and succulent roots, he will eat animal flesh, raw or cooked, with avidity when hungry, and he does not hesitate to regale himself upon carrion, after his taste has been cultivated in this direction.

"Man is not omnivorous. He cannot subsist upon grass or raw grain. Taking his food from the hand of Nature, without the aid of cookery, he must confine his dietary to fruits, nuts, soft grains, tender shoots, and succulent roots...It is true he can acquire an appetite for meat, especially when cooked, but practically all animals can do the same. Hunters sometimes teach their horses to eat broiled venison and cows have been taught to eat fish with avidity. Du Chaillu found in the Island of Magero...that sheep and goats were fed daily on fish both raw and cooked."

Dr. Kellogg insists, however, that "cookery is no part of Nature's biologic scheme, and hence the fact that man is able to eat and digest cooked meat is no more evidence that he is carnivorous or omnivorous than the fact that he can eat and digest cooked corn is evidence that he is to be classified with graminivourous animals, like the horse, which are eaters of raw grains.

"The bill of fare which wise Nature provides for man in forest and meadow, orchard and garden, a rich and varied menu, comprises more than 600 edible fruits, 100 cereals, 200 nuts, and 300 vegetables—roots, stems, buds, leaves and flowers...Fruits and nuts, many vegetables—young shoots, succulent roots, and fresh green leaves...are furnished by Nature ready for man's use."

Dr. Kellogg further notes that "the human liver is incapable of converting uric acid into urea," and this is "an unanswerable argument against the use of flesh foods as part of the dietary of man. Uric acid is a highly active tissue poison...The livers of dogs, lions, and other carnivorous animals detoxicate uric acid by converting it into urea, a substance which is much less toxic and which is much more easily eliminated by the kidneys.

"Flesh foods are not the best nourishment for human beings and were not the food of our primitive ancestors," observes Dr. Kellogg. "There is nothing necessary or desirable for human nutrition to be found in meats or flesh foods which is not found in and derived from vegetable products."

Although writing in 1923, Dr. Kellogg's words confirm a recent statement by the American Dietetic Association, that, "most of mankind for most of human history has lived on vegetarian or near vegetarian diets."

"The human race in general has never really adopted flesh as a staple food," explains Dr. Kellogg. "The Anglo-Saxons and a few savage tribes are about the only flesh-eating people. The people of other nations use meat only as a luxury or an emergency diet. According to Mori, the Japanese peasant of the interior is almost an exclusive vegetarian. He eats fish once or twice a month and meat once or twice a year."

Dr. Kellogg writes that in 1899, the Emperor of Japan appointed a commission to determine whether it was necessary to add meat to the nation's diet to improve the people's strength and stature. The commission concluded that as far as meat was concerned, "the Japanese had always managed to do without it, and that their powers of endurance and their athletic prowess exceeded that of any of the Caucasian races. Japan's diet stands on a foundation of rice."

According to Dr. Kellogg, "the rice diet of the Japanese is supplemented by the free use of peanuts, soy beans, and greens, which...constitute a wholly sufficient bill of fare. Throughout the Island Empire, rice is largely used, together with buckwheat, barley, wheat, and millet. Turnips and radishes, yams and sweet potatos are frequently used, also cucumbers, pumpkins and squashes. The soy bean is held in high esteem and used largely in the form of *miso*, a puree prepared from the bean and fermented; also *to-fu*, a sort of cheese; and *cho-yu*, which is prepared by mixing the pulverized beans with wheat flour, salt, and water and fermenting from one and a half to five years.

"The Chinese peasant lives on essentially the same diet, as do also the Siamese, the Koreans, and most other Oriental peoples. Three-fourths of the world's population eat so little meat that it cannot be regarded as anything more than an incidental factor in their bill of fare. The countless millions of China," writes Dr. Kellogg, "are for the most part flesh-abstainers. In fact, at least two-thirds of the inhabitants of the world make so little use of flesh that it can hardly be considered an essential part of their dietary...The ancient vegetarian races of Mexico and Peru had attained to a high degree of civilization when discovered by Cortez, and were certainly far more gentle and amiable in character than were their flesh-eating conquerors, whose treachery and cold-blooded atrocities so nearly resulted in the complete extinction of a noble race."

Dr. Kellogg reports that the South American bark-gatherers live "almost wholly upon bananas and other equally simple vegetable food...Certain tribes of South American Indians who subsist wholly upon a non-flesh dietary, are remarkable for vigor and endurance...the natives of the great plateau of the Andes subsist almost wholly upon corn and potatos...the old Peruvians...were practically vegetarians." Dr. Kellogg quotes Charles Darwin as having described the laborers in the mines of Chile living "exclusively on vegetable food, including many seeds of leguminous plants."

Concerning Central Africa, Dr. Kellogg admits, "It is true that practically all the natives eat meat on occasion, but...the chief sustenance of the native is obtained from the products of the earth, which are most abundant in this fertile region. Maize, yuma, manioc, coconuts, palm cabbage, bananas, and a great number of fruits and nuts afford ample variety and sufficient nourishment without flesh foods."

Dr. Kellogg cites a Mr. Sarvis of the *Boston Transcript*, who wrote: "The Bantu race, who inhabit the great part of Central Africa, are almost entirely vegetarian... Generally, their food consists largely of a kind of millet, which is almost tasteless... Bananas and sweet potatos also form a very important part of the diet of the African races of the central parts...The natives also eat vegetables and salads of many kinds. In a few districts cattle are kept for the milk and butter, but the natives do not kill the animals for food...The Kavirondos wear no clothing whatever, and they are absolute vegetarians, the banana forming the base of their food."

The Ladrone Islands were discovered by the Spaniards around 1620. There were no animals on the islands except birds, which the natives did not eat. The natives had never seen fire, and they lived entirely on plant foods—fruits and roots in their natural state. They were found to be vigorous, active, and of good longevity.

Dr. Kellogg gives an account of the "Silesians, Roumanians, and many Oriental people," all of whom he says "are almost exclusively vegetarians, and enjoy a degree of vigor, vitality, and longevity not found among flesh-eating nations."

In his 1583 text, *Anatomy of Abuses*, Stubbes wrote that previous generations "fed upon graine, corne, roots, pulse, hearbes, weedes, and such other baggage; and yet lived longer than we, were healthfuller than we, of better complexion than we, and much stronger than we in every respect." A century later, Macauley noted that, "meat was so dear in price that hundreds of thousands of families scarcely knew the taste of it," while half the population of England, "ate it not at all or not more often than once a week."

Writing in the 1840s, Sylvester Graham observed: "The peasantry of Norway, Sweden, Denmark, Germany, Turkey, Greece, Italy, Switzerland, France, Spain, England, Scotland, Ireland, a considerable portion of Russia and other parts of Europe subsist mainly on non-flesh foods. The peasantry of modern Greece...subsist on coarse brown bread and fruits. The peasantry in many parts of Russia live on very coarse bread, with garlic and other vegetables; and like the same class in Greece, Italy, etc., they are obliged to be extremely frugal even in this kind of food. Yet they are (for the most part) healthy, vigorous, and active. Many of the inhabitants of Germany live mainly on rye and barley, in the form of coarse bread.

"The potato is the principle food of the Irish peasantry, and few portions of the human family are more healthy, athletic, and active...That portion of the peasantry of England and Scotland who subsist on their barley and oatmeal bread, porridge, potatos, and other vegetables, with temperate, cleanly habits (and surroundings) are able to endure more fatigue and exposure than any other class of people in the same countries. *Three-fourths of the whole human family*, in all periods of time...have subsisted on non-flesh foods; and when their supplies have been abundant and their habits in other respects correct, they have been well nourished."

Dr. Kellogg also found a vegetarian lifestyle to be the norm in much of Europe: "An official report shows that the diet of the Swiss peasant includes little or no meat. 'In the Schwyz canton, the people have long lived on plant food, without flesh. They are a fine set of independent mountaineers, and from this canton the freedom of the Swiss was born.' The peasants of northern Italy eat meat twice a year. They are remarkably robust and hearty.

"The hardy Scotch have never been great meat eaters. In the remote districts kailbrose, shredded greens and oatmeal over which hot water is poured, is eaten with or without milk...According to Douglas, writing in 1782, the diet of the Scotch of the East Coast was then oatmeal and milk with vegetables. He says: 'Flesh is never seen in the houses of the common farmers, except at a baptism, a wedding, Christmas, or Shrovetide.'"

Faced with the fact that apes can be trained to eat flesh foods, Sylvester Graham responded, "But if this proves that animal to be *omnivorous*, then the horse, cow, sheep, and others are all omnivorous, for everyone of them is easily trained to eat animal food. Horses have frequently been trained to eat animal food, and sheep have been so accustomed to it as to refuse grass.

"All carnivorous animals can be trained to a vegetable diet, and brought to subsist upon it, with less inconvenience and deterioration than herbivorous or frugivorous animals can be brought to live on animal food," acknowledged Graham. "Comparative anatomy proves that man is naturally a frugivorous animal, formed to subsist upon fruits, seeds, and farinaceous vegetable."

Dr. Gordon Latto notes that carnivorous and omnivorous animals can only move their jaws up and down, and that omnivores "have a blunt tooth, a sharp tooth, a blunt tooth, a sharp tooth—showing that they were destined to deal both with flesh foods from the animal kingdom and foods from the vegetable kingdom...

"Carnivorous mammals and omnivorous mammals cannot perspire except at the extremity of the limbs and the tip of the nose; man perspires all over the body. Finally, our instincts; the carnivorous mammal (which first of all has claws and canine teeth) is capable of tearing flesh asunder, whereas man only partakes of flesh foods after they have been camouflaged by cooking and by condiments.

"Man instinctively is not carnivorous," explains Dr. Latto. "...he takes the flesh food after somebody else has killed it, and after it has been cooked and camouflaged with certain condiments. Whereas to pick an apple off a tree or eat some grain or a carrot is a natural thing to do: people enjoy doing it; they don't feel disturbed by it. But to see these animals being slaughtered does affect people; it offends them. Even the toughest of people are affected by the sights in the slaughterhouse.

"I remember taking some medical students into a slaughterhouse. They were about as hardened people as you could meet. After seeing the animals slaughtered that day in the slaughterhouse, not one of them could eat the meat that evening."

Author R.H. Wheldon writes in *No Animal Food*:

"The gorge of a cat, for instance, will rise at the smell of a mouse or a piece of raw flesh, but not at the aroma of fruit. If a man can take delight in pouncing upon a bird, tear its still living body apart with his teeth, sucking the warm blood, one might infer that Nature had provided him with carnivorous instinct, but the very thought of doing such a thing makes him shudder. On the other hand, a bunch of luscious grapes makes his mouth water, and even in the absence of hunger, he will eat fruit to gratify taste."

Some argue that human intelligence has enabled man to transcend his physical limitations and function as a "natural" flesh-eater. If this is true, then we must also classify napalm, poison gas, and nuclear weapons as "natural," too, because they are also products of (misused!) human intelligence. Agriculture and cookery aren't found in nature, either. One might therefore argue if human technology is "natural," then human ethical behavior is equally natural.

"I am the very opposite of an anthropomorphizer," says writer Brigid Brophy. "I don't hold animals superior or even equal to humans. The whole case for behaving decently towards animals rests on the fact that we are the superior species. We are the species uniquely capable of rationality, imagination and moral choice, and that is precisely why we are under obligation to respect the rights of other creatures."

The myth that humans are naturally a predator species remains popular: "The beast of prey is the highest form of active life," wrote Nazi philosopher Oswald Spengler in 1931. "It represents a mode of living which requires the extreme degree of the necessity of fighting, conquering, annihilating, self-assertion. The human race ranks highly because it belongs to the class of beasts of prey. Therefore we find in man the tactics of life proper to a bold, cunning beast of prey. He lives engaged in aggression, killing, annihilation. He wants to be master in as much as he exists."

The fact that predators exist in the wild does not imply man must automatically imitate them. Cannibalism and rape also occur in nature. Robert Louis Stevenson, in his book, *In the South Seas*, wrote that there was little difference between the "civilized" Europeans and the "savages" of the Cannibal Islands: "We consume the carcasses of creatures with like appetites, passions, and organs as our own. We feed on babes, though not our own, and fill the slaughter-houses daily with screams of pain and fear."

Moreover, the popular argument that it is 'natural' for us to utilize murdered animals as a source of food does not (ecologically) justify factory farming and raising livestock as we know it today. It justifies *hunting*. The Native Americans, the Eskimo and other hunter-gatherer tribes have traditionally lived more in harmony with their environment than does modern man in urban civilization.

Half the water consumed in the United States, for example, goes to irrigate land growing feed and fodder for livestock. Huge amounts of water are also used to wash away their excrement. In fact, U.S. livestock produce twenty times as much excrement as does the entire human population; creating sewage which is ten to several hundred times more concentrated than raw domestic sewage. Animal wastes cause ten times more water pollution than does the U.S. human population; the meat industry causes three times as much harmful organic water pollution than the rest of the nation's industries combined. Meat producers are the number one industrial polluters in our nation, contributing to half the water pollution in the United States.

The water that goes into a thousand-pound steer could float a destroyer. It takes 25 gallons of water to produce a pound of wheat, but 2,500 gallons to produce a pound of meat. If these costs weren't subsidized by the American taxpayers, the cheapest hamburger meat would be $35 per pound!

The burden of subsidizing the California meat industry costs taxpayers $24 billion annually. Livestock producers are California's biggest consumers of water. Every tax dollar that the state doles out to livestock producers costs taxpayers over seven dollars in lost wages, higher living costs and reduced business income. Seventeen western states have enough water supplies to support economies and populations twice as large as the present.

Overgrazing of cattle leads to topsoil erosion; turning once-arable land into desert. We lose four million acres of topsoil every year, and 85 percent of this is directly caused by raising livestock. To replace the soil we've lost, we're chopping down our forests. Since 1967, the rate of deforestization in the U.S. has been one acre every five seconds. For each acre cleared in urbanization, seven are cleared for grazing or growing livestock feed. One-third of all raw materials in the U.S. are consumed by the livestock industry, and it takes three times as much fossil fuel energy to produce meat than it does to produce plant foods.

Ecological arguments in favor of vegetarianism can be found in the Bible; arguments supporting vegetarianism are as old as mankind. The Bible contains numerous cases of conflicts directly caused by the practice of raising livestock. These include contested water rights, competition for grazing areas, and tension between agriculturalists and nomadic herdsmen.

The settled agricultural communities resented the intrusion of nomadic tribes with their large herds of cattle, sheep, and goats. The animals were considered a menace. Besides the threat to the crops themselves, huge herds of livestock caused damage to the land through overgrazing.

For this reason, the Philistines (whose primary agricultural pursuits were corn and orchards), discouraged nomadic herdsmen from using their territory by filling in many of the wells in the surrounding area. One of the earliest accounts of conflict among the herdsmen themselves in found in the story of Lot and Abram:

"And Lot also, which went with Abram, had flocks, and herds, and tents. And the land was not able to bear them, that they might dwell together; for their substance was great, so that they could not dwell together. And there was a strife between the herdmen of Abram's cattle and the herdmen of Lot's cattle." (Genesis 13:5-7)

Abram moved westward to the region known as Canaan, while Lot journeyed to the east; settling in Sodom. Peaceful resolutions, however, were not always possible. There are several references in the Bible to clashes between the Israelites and Midianites. The Midianites were wealthy traders who owned large numbers of livestock, as did the Israelites, who brought their herds with them when they left Egypt. Livestock require vast areas of land for grazing. They also need water, which has never been abundant in that part of the world. The strain placed on the land's resources is mentioned in Judges 6:4: "And they encamped against them, and destroyed the increase of the earth."

The depletion of resources created by the people and their livestock moving into this territory is described in Judges 6:5 with this analogy: "For they came up with their cattle and their tents, and they came as grasshoppers." Another passage states that after a vicious battle with the Midanites the Israelites increased their herds with the livestock of their slain captives. This included 675,000 sheep and more than 72,000 beehives.

Vegetarianism is relevant to both our modern world and its religious teachings. The livestock population of the United States today consume enough grain and soybeans to feed over five times the entire human population. American cows, pigs, chicken, sheep, etc. eat up 90 percent of our wheat, 80 percent of our corn, and 95 percent of our oats. Less than half of the harvested agricultural acreage in the United States is used to grow food for human consumption. Most of it is used to grow livestock feed.

In *The Wealth of Nations*, economist Adam Smith noted the advantages of a vegetarian diet: "It may indeed be doubted whether butcher's meat is anywhere a necessary of life. Grain and other vegetables, with the help of milk, cheese, and butter, or oil, where butter is not to be had, afford the most plentiful, the most wholesome, the most nourishing, and the most invigorating diet. Decency nowhere requires that any man should eat butcher's meat."

Ronald J. Sider, in his 1977 book, *Rich Christians in an Age of Hunger* pointed out that 220 million Americans were eating enough food (largely because of the high consumption of grain fed to livestock) to feed over one billion people in the poorer countries.

The realization that meat is an unnecessary luxury, resulting in inequities in the world food supply, has prompted religious leaders in different denominations to call on their members to abstain from meat. Paul Moore, Jr., the Episcopal bishop of the Diocese of New York, made such an appeal in a November 1974 pastoral letter calling for the observance of "meatless Wednesdays."

A similar appeal had previously been issued by Cardinal Cooke, the Roman Catholic archbishop of New York. The Reverend Eugene Carson Blake, former head of the World Council of Churches and founder of Bread for the World, has encouraged everyone in his anti-hunger organization to abstain from eating meat on Mondays, Wednesdays, and Fridays.

> "Is this not the fast I have chosen? To loosen the chains of wickedness, to undo the bonds of oppression, and to let the oppressed go free? Is it not to share thy bread with the hungry, sheltering the oppressed and the homeless? Clothing the naked when you see them, and not turning your back on your own?"

> — *Isaiah 58:6-8*

What does the future hold? If the world population triples in the next century, then meat production would have to triple as well. Instead of 3.7 billion acres of cropland and 7.5 billion acres of grazing land, we would require 11.1 billion acres of cropland and 22.5 billion acres of grazing land. But this is slightly more than the total land mass of the six inhabited continents! We are already desperately short of groundwater, topsoil, forests and energy.

Even if we were to resort to extreme methods of population control—abortion, infanticide, genocide, etc.—modest increases in the world population during the next century would make it impossible to maintain current levels of meat consumption. On a vegetarian diet, however, the world could support a population several times its present size. The world's cattle alone consume enough to feed 8.7 billion humans. Father Thomas Berry, a Catholic priest, author, and founder of the Riverdale Center for Religious Research in New York, wrote in 1987 that "vegetarianism is a way of life that we should all move toward for economic survival, physical well-being, and spiritual integrity."

Would it be unusual for a Christian teacher to teach compassion towards animals to the point of vegetarianism? Abstinence from meat as nonviolence and as asceticism has its place in the Christian tradition. Some of the most distinguished figures in the history of Christianity have been vegetarian.

The early Christian fathers followed a meatless regimen. Until the 1960s, the Roman Catholic Church had ruled that Catholics observe certain fast days and abstain from eating meat on Fridays in remembrance of the death of Christ. After 1966, the rule was relaxed, so that Catholics need only abstain from meat on the Fridays of Lent.

There is nothing, therefore, in Scripture or the Christian tradition that would prohibit Christian denominations from admitting that the concession to kill animals granted by God in Genesis 9:3 along with the prohibition against consuming animal blood which is repeated again in Acts 15 does not represent His highest hopes for humanity (Genesis 1:29; Isaiah 11:6-9); recognizing God's love and goodness towards the animals; citing the lives of the saints and religious leaders in Christianity who taught compassion for all living beings; and recognizing the virtues of vegetarianism.

In his book, *Animal Rights: A Christian Assessment of Man's Treatment of Animals*, the Reverend Dr. Andrew Linzey writes with regret: "It has, I think, to be sadly recognized that Christians, Catholic or otherwise, have failed to construct a satisfactory moral theology of animal treatment."

Vegetarianism is ethical, healthier, "environmentally correct," and economical. It's been said that if everyone had to kill animals every day for his or her own meat, most of us would choose vegetarianism. The vegetarian way of life is consistent not only with human anatomy, the Bible, and Christian tradition and theology, but with Western spirituality in general.

Bibliography

"Adams, Carol J., *The Sexual Politics of Meat* (New York, NY, Continuum Publishing Company, 1990)

Akers, Keith, *A Vegetarian Sourcebook* (Arlington, VA, Vegetarian Press, 1986)

The Animal Kingdom and the Kingdom of God (Edinburgh, UK, Centre for Theology and Public Issues Press, 1991)

Arnetta, Frances, *What the Bible Says About Vegetarianism* (Selden, NY, Christians Helping Animals and People, 1991)

Arnetta, Frances, *Animal Rights: A Biblical View* (Selden, NY, Christians Helping Animals and People, 1991)

Barber, Dr. Theodore, *The Human Nature of Birds* (New York, NY, St. Martin's Press, 1993)

Barclay, William, *The Gospel of Matthew, Vol. 1* (Philadelphia, PA, Westminster Press, 1975)

Barkas, Janet, *The Vegetable Passion* (New York, NY, Charles Scribner and Sons, 1975)

Bartlett, Kim, "An Interview with Reverend Andrew Linzey," *Animals Agenda*, 1989

Berg, Rabbi Phillip S., *Wheels of a Soul* (New York, NY, Research Centre of Kabbalah, 1984)

Berman, Louis, *Vegetarianism and the Jewish Tradition* (New York, NY, KTAV Publishing House, Inc., 1982)

Berry, Jr., Rynn, *The Vegetarians* (Brookline, MA, Autumn Press, Inc., 1979)

Boswell III, James O., *Slavery, Segregation and Scripture* (Grand Rapids, MI, William B. Erdmans Publishing Co., 1964)

Boyd, B.R., *The New Abolitionists: Animal Rights and Human Liberation* (San Francisco, CA, Taterhill Press, 1987)

Braunstein, Mark Matthew, *Radical Vegetarianism* (Los Angeles, CA, Panjandrum Books, 1981)

Brennan, William, *The Abortion Holocaust* (St. Louis, MO, Landmark Press, 1983)

Buber, Martin, *Moses: The Revelation and the Covenant* (New York, NY, Harper & Row, 1958)

Burke, Abbott George, *Spiritual Vegetarianism* (Geneva, NE, St. George Press, 1991)

Burwash, Peter, *A Vegetarian Primer* (New York, NY, Athenium, 1983)

Chandler, Russell, "Churches Asked to Consider the Feelings of Animals," *Los Angeles Times*, November 23, 1985

Cohn-Sherbot, Dan, ed., *Using the Bible Today* (London, Bellew Publishing, 1991)

Cox, Peter, *Why You Don't Need Meat* (London, Thorsons, 1987)

Dasa, Chaitanya (Brother Aelred), *Encounter: Christ and Krishna* (Armidale, Australia, 1990)

Dasa, Satyaraja, *You Mean That's in the Bible?* (Brooklyn, NY, Satya Series, 1984)

Dasa, Satyaraja, *East West Dialogues* (Brooklyn, NY, FOLK Books, 1989)

Dasa, Satyaraja, *Om Shalom* (Brooklyn, NY, FOLK Books, 1990)

Dionne Jr., E.J., "Gov. Ventura Shoots From the Lips Again," *San Francisco Chronicle*, October 6, 1999

Dombrowski, Daniel A., *The Philosophy of Vegetarianism* (Amherst, MA, University of Massachusetts Press, 1984)

Dunkerly, Rick, "Re-examining the Christian Scriptures," *The Animals' Voice Magazine*, Vol. 2, No. 4 (North Hollywood, CA, 1989)

Dunkerly, Rick, "Hunting: What Scripture Says," *Inroads*, Number 14 (North Wales, PA, INRA, 1992)

The Edenite Creed for Life (Imlaystown, NJ, The Edenite Society, 1979)

Evans, Rose, *Friends of All Creatures* (San Francisco, CA, Sea Fog Press, 1984)

Evans, Rose, "Book Review," *Harmony: Voices for a Just Future*, Vol. 4, No. 6 (San Francisco, CA, Sea Fog Press, 1994)

Ewing, Dr. Upton Clary, *The Essene Christ* (New York, NY, Philosophical Library, 1961)

Ewing, Dr. Upton Clary, *The Prophet of the Dead Sea Scrolls* (New York, NY, Philosophical Library, 1963)

Ferrier, Reverend J. Todd, *On Behalf of the Creatures* (London, Order of the Cross, 1903)

Four Essays on Vegetarianism (Washington, MS, Old South Vedic Society, 1987)

Fox, Michael W., *St. Francis, Animals and Nature* (Washington, DC, Humane Society of the United States, 1989)

Free, Ann Cottrell, ed., *Animals, Nature and Albert Schweitzer* (Washington, DC, Flying Fox Press, 1982)

Giehl, Dudley, *Vegetarianism: A Way of Life* (New York, NY, Harper & Row, 1979)

Golding, Rabbi Shmuel, *A Guide to the Misled* (Jerusalem, Israel)

Grassi, Joseph A., *Underground Christians in the Earliest Church* (Santa Clara, CA, Diakonia Press, 1975)

Gregory, Dick, *Dick Gregory's Natural Diet for Folks Who Eat* (New York, NY, Harper & Row, 1973)

Hill, William Bancroft, *The Apostolic Age* (New York, NY, Fleming H. Revell Co., 1972)

The Higher Taste (Los Angeles, CA, Bhaktivedanta Book Trust, 1983)

Hoffman, Daniel P., *An American Sarvodaya Pilgrimage* (Thanjavur, India, Sarvodaya Prachuralaya, 1966)

Jesus was a Vegetarian: Why Aren't You? (Imlaystown, NY, The Edenite Society, 1976)

Kaiser, Larry, "Benjamin Franklin's Vegetarian Views," *Vegetarian Journal*, Vol. XI, No. 6 (Baltimore, MD, Vegetarian Resource Group, 1992)

Kellogg, Dr. John Harvey, *The Natural Diet of Man* (Battle Creek, MI, Modern Medicine Publishing Company, 1923)

Kersten, Holger, *Jesus Lived in India* (Shaftsbury, UK, Element Books Ltd., 1986)

Kowalski, Gary A., *The Souls of Animals* (Walpole, NH, Stillpoint Publishing, 1991)

Larson, Dr. Martin A., *The Story of Christian Origins* (Joseph J. Binns/ New Republic Books) 1977

Lavine, Dr. T.Z., *From Socrates to Sartre: The Philosophic Quest* (New York, NY, Bantam, 1984)

Linzey, Reverend Andrew, *The Status of Animals in the Christian Tradition* (Birmingham, UK, Woodbrooke College, 1985)

Linzey, Reverend Andrew, *Christianity and the Rights of Animals* (New York, NY, Crossroad Publishing Company, 1987)

Linzey, Reverend Andrew and Regan, Dr. Tom, ed., *Animals and Christianity* (New York, NY, Crossroad Publishing Company, 1988)

Linzey, Reverend Andrew, and Regan, Dr. Tom, ed., *Love the Animals* (New York, NY, Crossroad Publishing Company, 1989)

Linzey, Reverend Andrew, "Blessed Are the Meek," *The Animals' Voice Magazine*, Vol. 5, No. 2 (North Hollywood, CA, 1992)

McDaniel, Jay, "The Liberation of All Life," *The Animals' Voice Magazine*, Vol. 2, No. 4 (North Hollywood, CA, 1989)

McDougall, John A., and Mary, *The McDougall Plan* (Piscataway, NJ, New Century Publishers, Inc., 1983)

Moll, Lucy, "Christian Vegetarians: Answering the Call," *Vegetarian Times*, Issue 125 (Stanford, CT, Cowles Magazines, Inc., 1988)

Moorhouse, Reverend Norman, "Here is Something Very Beautiful and Lovely," *Back to Godhead*, Vol. 14, No. 4 (Los Angeles, CA, Bhaktivedanta Book Trust, 1979)

Newman, Albert Henry, *A Manual of Church History* (Valley Forge, PA, Judson Press, 1964)

Regan, Dr. Tom, *The Case for Animal Rights* (Berkeley, CA, University of California Press, 1983)

Regan, Dr. Tom, "Religion and Animal Rights," *The Animals' Voice Magazine*, Vol. 2, No. 4 (North Hollywood, CA, 1989)

Regenstein, Lewis G., *Replenish the Earth* (New York, NY, The Crossroad Publishing Company, 1991)

Robbins, John, *Diet for a New America* (Walpole, NH, Stillpoint Publishing, 1987)

Rose, Kenneth, "The Lion Shall Eat Straw Like the Ox," *Back to Godhead*, Vol. 19, No. 11 (Los Angeles, CA, Bhaktivedanta Book Trust, 1984)

Rosen, Steven, *Food for the Spirit* (New York, NY, Bala Books, 1987)

Schwartz, Dr. Richard H., *Judaism and Vegetarianism* (Smithtown, NY, Exposition Press, 1982)

Should Real Christians be Vegetarian? (ISKCON pamphlet)

Siegel, Richard, and Rheins, Carl, ed., *The Jewish Almanac* (New York, NY, Bantam, 1980)

Silver, Abba Hillel, *Moses and the Original Torah* (New York, NY, MacMillan Co., 1961)

Singer, Peter, *Animal Liberation* (New York, NY, Avon Books, 1975)

Smith, Dr. Houston, *The Religions of Man* (New York, NY, Harper & Row, 1958)

Spiegel, Marjorie, *The Dreaded Comparison* (New York, NY, Mirror Books, 1989)

Stump, Keith W., "Seeing the World Through Islamic Eyes," *The Plain Truth*, Vol. 48, No. 6 (Pasadena, CA, 1983)

Sussman, Vic, *The Vegetarian Alternative* (Emmaus, PA, Rodale Press, 1978)

Tatum, W. Barnes, *In Quest of Jesus* (Atlanta, GA, John Knox Press, 1982)

Taylor, Thomas, trans., *Porphyry on Abstinence from Animal Food* (New York, NY, Barnes & Noble, 1965)

Teasdale, Wayne, "A Commentary on the Universal Declaration of Nonviolence: part 2," *Harmony: Voices for a Just Future*, Vol. 5, No. 1 (San Francisco, CA, Sea Fog Press, 1995)

Teasdale, Wayne, "The Primacy of Nonviolence as a Virtue," *Embracing Earth: Catholic Approaches to Ecology* (Maryknoll, NY, Orbis Books) 1994

Vaclavik, Dr. Charles P., *The Vegetarianism of Jesus Christ* (Three Rivers, CA, Kaweah Publishing Company, 1986)

Vernes, Geza, *Jesus the Jew* (London, Collins & Sons, 1973)

Wallechinsky, David and Wallace, Irving, ed., *The Peoples' Almanac* (Garden City, NY, Doubleday & Co., Inc., 1975)

Wessels, Reverend Dr. Marc A., "Voices Within the Church: Christians and God's Other Creatures," *Inroads*, Number 19 (North Wales, PA, INRA, 1992)

Wessels, Reverend Dr. Marc A., *The Spiritual Link Between Humans and Animals* (North Wales, PA, INRA, 1990)

Index

About the Author

Writer and activist Vasu Murti was born and raised in Southern California in a family of South Indian brahmins. He holds degrees in Physics and Applied Mathematics from the University of California. He has written articles on a number of different topics, including secularism, science versus religion, animal rights, nuclear power, handgun control, Buddhism, abortion, illegal immigration, and drug legalization. He is a regular contributor to *Harmony: Voices for a Just Future*, a "consistent ethic" publication on the religious left. Vasu is a "card-carrying" member of the ACLU, Feminists For Life, Amnesty International, and People for the Ethical Treatment of Animals.

Printed in the United States
29469LVS00002B/89-124

9 780971 667617